THE BRIGHT SIDE

THE BRIGHT SIDE

JACK RIEWOLDT

WITH ADAM McNICOL

**SIMON &
SCHUSTER**

London · New York · Sydney · Toronto · New Delhi

THE BRIGHT SIDE
First published in Australia in 2023 by
Simon & Schuster (Australia) Pty Limited
Suite 19A, Level 1, Building C, 450 Miller Street, Cammeray, NSW 2062

10 9 8 7 6 5 4 3 2 1

Sydney New York London Toronto New Delhi
Visit our website at www.simonandschuster.com.au

A catalogue record for this
book is available from the
National Library of Australia

ISBN: 9781761102202
Limited collector's edition ISBN: 9781761424908

Cover design by Meng Koach
Image of Jack with trophy: © Ryan Pierse/AFL Photos
Image of Jack with Poppy: © Michael Willson/AFL Photos
Limited collector's edition print of Jack kicking: © Daniel Carson/AFL Photos
Limited collector's edition print of Jack headshot: © Dylan Burns/AFL Photos
Limited collector's edition print of Jack running: © Will Russell/AFL Photos
Cover photography by Yianni Aspradakis
Typeset by Midland Typesetters, Australia
Printed and bound in Australia by Griffin Press

MIX
Paper | Supporting
responsible forestry
FSC® C018684
www.fsc.org

The paper this book is printed on is certified against the
Forest Stewardship Council® Standards. Griffin Press holds
chain of custody certification SCS-COC-001185. FSC®
promotes environmentally responsible, socially beneficial
and economically viable management of the world's forests.

For every kid from an island that has a dream

CONTENTS

FOREWORD

By Gerard Whateley

For a while, Jack Riewoldt looked destined to become footy's clown prince. That will read harsher than it's intended to sound; that figure of fun and foolery is among the most loved in the game's history. The brash talent with the showy edge. The jester with the cheeky smile, big personality and penchant for trouble.

The lineage tends to dictate they are key forwards whose highs are giddy, and lows lean towards the bizarre. The combination conjuring a pantomime edge – hero to the faithful, villain to the rest, but eminently and captivatingly watchable.

Young Jack had that market cornered. The cocky kid with the blond tips who was going to win the crowd through his goalkicking feats. Are you not entertained?

He'd flip the bird to rival fans. Invent phantom defenders who pushed him to con the umpires. He'd crawl up the stairs to the interchange bench, whispering for his coach like a child trying to wake a sleeping parent in the middle of the night – except in front of 40,000 spectators and millions watching on television.

He could accidentally divulge club secrets, earning the wrath of the coach and a foot up the arse. And he would run from trouble, seeking refuge on a train, having not thought for a moment where it might lead him. It was a reasonable metaphor for his early journey.

All the while, he was kicking goals by the bucketload and taking hangers for fun, earning acclaim and fame in equal portions.

Such incidents drew scorn. But, also, a grudging affection. It was largely innocent and harmless. He was anointed the ultimate rascal. It might very well have won him a place in footy folklore, making him the centrepiece of folly long into retirement. Where there was a laugh to be found or mischief to be made, you'd find old Jack. The Hall of Fame has a Peter Pan in every corner.

But that's not really who Jack was. Or, at least, not entirely. It was a curious and unfortunate set of events.

He was far more vulnerable and trusting than he might have let on. The proverbial kid from Tasmania on the adventure of a lifetime in the big smoke. Chasing the shadow of an older cousin he idolised. Playing the game he'd learned from his local-legend father.

Once he dropped the façade, let people see him as he truly was and shared his soul, he became a leader and a spokesman. This was as true inside the walls at Punt Road as it was outside.

He had the Copernican Revolution that success revolved around the team rather than himself. The glory was to be shared, not coveted. A goal given as satisfying as a goal kicked. A ball brought to ground as important as a towering mark secured.

He was an emblematic figure in the transformation of Richmond from selfish to selfless. The premierships of the era will be revered for the moral contained within as much as the joy they prompted.

Jack shared his story each week with us on *AFL 360* through bitter failure and ultimate success. He had a generous touch that would make fellow players immediately comfortable across the desk. He risked breaking the cliches and spoke from the heart even when it came at a personal cost.

No player shared the abrupt Covid displacement and shock of hub life with such rawness as Jack. At a time of uncertainty, he couldn't rationalise why he had abandoned a young family in Melbourne lockdown to play footy in Brisbane. His critics said he'd weigh the team down with such an attitude. Instead, he drove the Tigers to the hardest flag ever won.

The guise of the elder statesman suited Jack even better than the brash youngster. He had a deep appreciation of his legacy at Tigerland and his place with Kevin Bartlett, Jack Titus and Matthew Richardson. He possessed the understanding to swap guernseys with a longtime rival at their final meeting and the self-deprecating humour to celebrate leading Rampage to the only AFLX title.

In his final season, you didn't have to search too hard to hear a story of Jack coaching an opposition defender during a match while pitted against him, leaving an aspiring footballer better than he found him a couple of hours earlier.

Jack's reach stretched beyond the field he loved and into the hearts of those on the outside. On the day his retirement was announced, talkback radio flooded with tributes from the Tiger faithful who had first donned his No. 8 as kids and had remained loyal through their journey to adulthood. They hadn't known footy without Jack as their hero and talisman.

Broader still were the tributes of those who had enjoyed chance encounters with Jack up the street, in a café or at a footy clinic. Such contact left an impression. To meet him was to like him. Your friendly neighbourhood superstar.

In our house, there's the fondest recall of Grand Final night 2016. Jack ended up at our ABC end of season celebration. He wanted to sit at the family table. After dinner, he ventured upstairs with the kids to watch *Mrs Doubtfire*. He won the crowd one dining table, one loungeroom, at a time. All became fiercely devoted to him.

As a story arc, Jack Riewoldt grew up better than any player in recent football memory.

Through it all, he continued to kick goals by the bucket-load, finger raised after putting his kick through the big sticks, earning adulation and repute. He took marks that would snatch your breath away for their fearlessness and flair.

And though he matured and refined, he never lost his showman flair. He's ruined premiership celebrations for every future generation – none will ever eclipse Jack on stage with The Killers belting out 'Mr Brightside' at the MCG.

1

BELLERIVE BLUFF

I have lived in Melbourne for more than fifteen years, and might well live in Victoria for the rest of my life, but I'll always call Tasmania home. Hobart is, simply, where my heart lies and my soul belongs. The house I grew up in – a two-storey weatherboard with a white picket fence where my parents, Chris and Lesley, still live – sits on King Street, a little road that runs diagonally across a rising ridge called Bellerive Bluff.

Our place sits at nearly the highest point on that hill, perched up there for the view of the waterfront and the sprawl of our small capital city below. Follow the road down to its either end – northwest or southeast – and you'll reach a geographic end point and landmark, the banks of the meandering Derwent River, hemming in our quiet little patch from both sides.

For most of the time I lived in that house, my life revolved around things rarely more than a few kilometres away. My schools mostly weren't far by bike, nor was the Little Athletics club to the north in Kangaroo Bay, or the soccer club next door to it in Montagu Bay. My favourite sporting venue, Bellerive Oval, the home ground of the Tasmanian cricket team and of our local footy club, Clarence, was all of 600 metres from our front door.

My dad's parents, Helga (Oma) and Heinz (Opa), came to Australia from Germany in the early 1950s, and lived just down the road from us, closer to the shoreline. When the school bell rang and my parents were still working, my brothers and I used to ride our bikes there. Traffic was never an issue. It was almost like growing up in a country town, which, I suppose, is not surprising. Hobart was home to perhaps 120,000 people when I was kid, whereas my kids will grow up in a growing metropolis – soon to be Australia's biggest city – of five million people or more. But what you give up in peacefulness, you make up in opportunity.

We didn't always stay within our sleepy corner of the world either. Often, we went to Oma and Opa's shack. For the mainlanders reading, that's just what people in Tassie call their holiday homes, whether tin shed or mansion. Theirs was closer to the former but to us that tiny white fibro shack was Shangri-La. It's where the wider Riewoldt clan – uncles and aunties and cousins – would gather for hot stretches in summer, for afternoons broken up and frittered away in the best possible way, playing beach cricket and darts. We did drag netting, too, and I was the tallest, so I had to walk into the water the farthest, wading out at dusk, hoping to catch the odd mullet and avoid stepping on a stingray or being eaten by a shark. Dad took us out in the family tinny, too, towing kids behind on a surfboard and catching flathead for dinner. I'll never forget the sand at nearby Dodges Ferry, where we could slide down the dunes on our boogie boards into the water. Those sandy hillocks are almost gone now, eroded by weather and time.

A few times a year we went north to Devonport to see Mum's parents – Nairn (Granny) and Ivan (Grandad) – never missing the annual pilgrimage there for lunch on Christmas Day. Granny used to make the Christmas pudding, filled with apples and nutmeg and raisins, then topped with brandy and set on fire. My brothers and I didn't like the flavour much – I haven't come across many kids who do – but we'd stomach that old-fashioned dessert anyway, knowing that Granny had baked it special with a threepenny bit hidden inside. If you got the prized threepence in your piece of pudding, you could trade it for 50 cents, and with that buy a trove of mixed lollies – ghost drops and sherbet bombs and big boss cigars.

I cherished those trips to Devonport most for the time I spent with Grandad, who passed away when I was thirteen. Ivan Eade had been a teacher for many years and seemed like the most intellectual person in my orbit. When I looked up at his towering bookshelves, I couldn't comprehend how many million words were inside, and how many of them he had read. He loved cricket and treasured his huge collection of the *Wisden Cricketers' Almanack*, a big block of bright-yellow spines stacked together on a shelf. I loved that he had written a book, too – *Life's Little Pieces of Magic* – a collection of short stories about his experiences in the world. Maybe memoir runs in the family. Don't they say that telling your stories is how you come to know them?

I was clearly brought up with an appetite for exploration, something my family fostered by bestowing great freedom. From a young age we were allowed to roll around our suburban area, along the arterials and streets by the water's edge. I used to marvel at the mighty Tasman Bridge, the scene of one of Australia's worst maritime disasters. I remember being told how, in 1975, a ship had collided with several pylons in the structure, causing a section to collapse onto the boat below. Four cars plummeted forty-five metres after driving off the break in the carriageway. My life was too untroubled to fathom that kind of tragedy.

I used to head to school early on icy winter mornings, so my mates and I could play on the frozen wooden edging around the playground, sliding on our sneakers along the layer of white frost on top of the timber into chilly mud puddles. We would be cold and covered in filth by the time the bell rang. I had boundless energy then, and sometimes still do. Mum jokes that I was annoying, always asking questions, needing constant entertainment, forever preoccupied with what we were doing next. Sometimes I still am.

I shared a room with my brothers – a huge one up on the second floor. We each had a corner where our beds and drawers were, and the carpet between us was our field of dreams. It was basically an indoor sports centre, a site for make-believe Test matches and one-dayers, grand finals and grand slams. One side of the room has a wide window through which you can see the Derwent River and the peak of Mount Wellington beyond. I accidentally hit a tennis ball clean through it one day, and watched the massive, fractured pane of glass fall in long, jagged shards to the ground below. Oops.

Soccer was our sport, so the walls were covered in posters of Leeds United and Harry Kewell. They weren't purely decorative either, but in fact strategically pinned there to hide the holes we had made in the plaster. Charlie, my youngest brother, had that big room all to himself in the end, and after he moved out Mum and Dad decided to clean up. That's when the posters came down, our crimes were uncovered, and the plasterer was finally called.

We had a cubby behind the house – and a healthy backyard. It was there you'd find our cricket pitch, where we played with real cricket balls, which of course led to many more broken windows. The pitch ran downhill, too, with the batsman at the bottom, meaning a charging fast bowler could build up a frightening amount of pace. We played infamous and hard-fought Boxing Day Tests in that yard, which we mowed and manicured and nicknamed the 'Riewoldt Dome'. Those games started as a family affair but later became an annual reunion for my mates, too, especially after so many of us moved away to the mainland.

As the eldest, I was the boss. That kind of sibling hierarchy is natural, but it's only now that I recognise it as the origin of my interest in leadership. People have a simplistic view of me sometimes, as someone who started life as a rascal, then matured into someone worth following – as if I could lead the way for others only after learning tough life lessons from a series of public gaffes, messy mistakes and sad events. But I've always thought that characterisation was reductive, and lazy. I've been in charge of myself and others – the first brother to try most things, and then bring two little brothers along with me – all my life. Leadership wasn't just some switch that got flicked in a few crucible moments.

We went through so many phases and fads and trends together – soccer and cricket, music and footy, art and lacrosse – and I always took charge. I came to almost everything with the confidence of an eldest child, but also knowing I had gifts, from anticipation to hand–eye coordination. I played nine holes of golf once with my dad in a town called Swansea, and shot a 54. I'd never played before, and I beat my dad. I was six.

Three decades later and I'm falling for hobbies and pastimes with the same vigour. My wife has a nickname for me – 'one-hit wonder' – because of my ever-expanding list of interests, each one picked up swiftly and later dropped. Surfing and fishing, cycling and building, gardening and books. I buy all the gear, immerse myself in the minutiae, and persist to the point where I'm experiencing maybe not mastery but certainly competence and flow, before moving on to something else. When I did something well, I wanted to do it to an extreme.

As kids we became obsessed with skateboarding, for instance, and when Tony Hawk's *Pro Skater* came out on PlayStation, we built ramps at home out of two-by-fours and plywood. I waxed up the gutter on the street outside our house, rubbing candles on the concrete kerb for frictionless rail slides. When we wanted to test ourselves, Mum and Dad let us catch the bus 20 minutes down to the Lauderdale

Skatepark. We weren't much good – I could do a kickflip, and an ollie, and probably a frontside fakie – but we thought we were unreal.

I wasn't a faultless leader, and Charlie, the youngest of our little gang, copped the worst of my miscalculations. The first time he broke a bone on my watch was at Bellerive Oval, while Dad was coaching the Clarence reserves and we were kicking the footy playing 'markers up'. We used to make Charlie stand at the front, so we could jump on his back, but I decided he needed a turn at the fun stuff, too, and came up with a way for him to take a screamer. The plan was for Harry to kick the ball above my head, and when Charlie leapt onto my back to catch the footy, I would rise up, vaulting the little guy into the air – as he yelled Capper! – for the mark of the century. Unfortunately, I pushed upwards early, he lost balance and fell backwards. He dropped quickly with one arm outstretched. It was meant to break his fall, but it broke instead. He fractured the same arm during a friendly game of soccer much later, when I made him be goalkeeper and kicked a flat basketball at him. It was a solid strike, and the deflated heavy ball was all it took to crack the same limb.

Unfortunately, injuries became the constant in Charlie's sporting life, cruelling what might have been a fine career. He was certainly the most athletically gifted among us. Despite being four years younger than me, and two years younger than Harry, Charlie could find a way to best us at most ball games. He was well on his way to being drafted as an AFL player. He played senior footy for Clarence as a teenager, and kicked five goals for Tasmania in an under-16 championships game against New South Wales, but a couple of months later, he ruptured the anterior cruciate ligament in his knee. By the time he was twenty-one, he'd undergone four knee reconstructions. He must have got that vulnerability from Mum, who tore her ACL more than once, too. I'm sad Charlie never got the opportunity to play AFL. I always believed he was good enough, but luck wasn't on his side.

Harry, meanwhile, is the smart one. Is that because he applied himself more in class, or did he apply himself more in class because study came naturally? Either way, he's the one who became a chemical engineer, doing work I can scarcely understand. He's the one who loves witty British television shows like *QI* and *Taskmaster* and *8 Out of 10 Cats Does Countdown*. He's the one who seems the most likely product of a marriage between two teachers.

For most of their working lives, Mum and Dad were sports teachers, meaning exercise and teamwork were as valued as learning and analysis. I did well enough at school, but often played the class clown, too. The teachers never let me go too far, however. Threatening to ban me from physical education was all they ever needed to bring me back into line. As the firstborn son of a pair of educators, I knew what was expected of me. We're an expressive family. Come to know us, and you'll know where we stand.

Dad was always renowned as being tough on the footy field but a gentle giant off it, and quiet at home. His confidence was subdued, but it was there. And Mum? She's always been ebullient and creative, and nudged us to be the same. One school holidays, with her encouragement, we all dyed our hair orange. The next school holidays we dyed it blue. We weren't afraid to go out in public looking that way either. I wore an orange jacket and purple hair to my Grade 6 dinner. I guess that's what they taught us: life can be so much fun, if you treat it that way.

2

BOWLERS
AND BANNERS

Our talent for sport is as much nature as nurture. It is for everyone, I suppose.

Mum, Lesley, played representative basketball for Tasmania as a teenager, and was an All Star when playing in senior basketball for Devonport and Launceston. A point guard and old-fashioned forward, her strength in hoops was assists and rebounds, more so than shooting. In essence, she's a team player, what the cultural leaders at Richmond these days might call a 'connector'. She's also the first cousin of Rodney 'Rocket' Eade, the former Hawthorn player and Sydney Swans, Western Bulldogs and Gold Coast coach. Athletic ability is in her blood.

Our old man, Chris, meanwhile, played 297 games for Clarence in the Tasmanian Football League, where everyone still knows him as 'Cabbage'. Dad is humble, retiring, and not one for talking up his exploits, but his resume speaks for itself. He won three premierships with Clarence (1979, 1981 and 1984) and was among the best players in each of those grand finals. He won the club best and fairest twice, and the award is now named in his honour. He represented Tasmania eighteen times in state games, was selected in Clarence's *Best Team 1947-2001,* and is a member of the AFL Tasmania Hall of Fame. I wasn't around to see him play at his peak, but there are a few grainy video clips online. No. 7 looks to me like a great mark with a solid kick, a strong centre half-forward and ruck, with the frame to fill out any guernsey.

The veterans and legends of footy in Tasmania tell me that the most famous match of my old man's career was the 1979 TFL Grand Final between Clarence and Glenorchy, the Kangaroos and the Magpies. There was no love lost between the teams. Inside the four walls at Clarence, Glenorchy were known as the 'Savages' (who played at 'Savagelands'). It was one of the most passionate rivalries in Tasmanian football. It was widely expected that Glenorchy, which had former Hawthorn superstar Peter Hudson at full-forward, would win easily, and indeed, almost 25,000 people crammed into North Hobart Oval to watch Hudson kick six goals in what would be the last game of his career. The match was going entirely to script until the dying minutes, when half-back flanker Tony 'Bumpy' Triffitt kicked a sodden ball into attack for Clarence. The waterlogged Sherrin slipped through the legs of a Glenorchy defender, allowing wingman Tony Chadwick to kick a goal and put the 'Roos in front. Clarence hung on by three points, delivering Glenorchy's fourth grand final loss in a row. They lost the following year, too.

Dad's three brothers – my uncles Joe, Ray and Peter – also played for Clarence, a generation of talented players born to a family with no connection to the game. Their parents had emigrated to Australia from Germany after the Second World War and knew nothing of this strange sport. Indeed, the eldest, Joe, was born in Germany. Joe has told me that he was a fantastic player, but others have said that might be fanciful, or fabricated, though I won't name names. There was definite talent, however, in his son, my first cousin, Nick Riewoldt, the number one pick in the 2000 AFL draft, who played 336 games for St Kilda, ten seasons as captain, won six best-and-fairest awards, and five selections in the All-Australian team, in a career deemed worthy of the AFL Hall of Fame.

While I don't remember seeing much of Dad on the field, I was at quite a few of the games when he was the playing-coach of a local footy club in a little town called Richmond, twenty-five kilometres northeast of Hobart. The Blues play in a competition known as the Old Scholars Football Association, and while I could have stood by the fence there and watched Dad lead them, I was much more taken with exploring the big cypress hedge not far from the oval.

Dad later coached the reserves at Clarence, and by then I was thrilled to tag along, particularly to the away games in Launceston and Burnie, sitting on a bus with sixty big blokes and a few kids, heading to the other end of the state on a foot-balling mission. When we play interstate games in the AFL, the guys all like to say that those trips to Perth or Adelaide or Brisbane or Sydney give everyone a chance to connect. They're right, and I feel like I've been doing that all my life.

One weekend I went with Dad to an away game against Burnie at West Park. The league was sponsored by Chickenfeed (Tasmania's answer to The 2 Dollar Shop), so every club had the Chickenfeed logo on the front of their jumpers, and they had a competition at half-time where kids tried to kick a footy into a bucket. I stepped up and booted one straight in, winning a $50 Chickenfeed voucher in the process. I went on a spree in that shop, buying a money tin with a picture of a $100 note on it, too many lollies to stomach in one sitting, and too many trinkets to count. While it was only a $50 Chickenfeed voucher, it felt like a million bucks.

Another afternoon at Bellerive Oval, I went to jump the picket fence on the outer side of the ground and slipped. I fell onto one of the metal posts that held up the pickets and tore a twelve-centimetre gash in my leg. The club trainer and Dad laid me down on the counter of the canteen, so the club doctor could assess the wound. I thought they were about to stitch me up right there, surrounded by my favourite kiosk snacks, but they took me into Royal Hobart Hospital, where I was left with a well-tended wound and a permanent reminder to climb carefully.

Despite my proximity to the game, and where I ended up, I didn't play a lot of Aussie rules as a child. I spent two seasons with the Bellerive Bombers (the club later merged with the nearby Howrah Roos to form the Clarence Junior Football Club) but I can't recall much – if anything – from those games. Soccer was always my sport. I lived for the beautiful game, the world game, the round-ball game, and played for the Montagu Bay Junior Soccer Club. I was a striker, of course, always up front, always trying to find the back of the net. I played well enough to make the state trials a couple of times, too, occasionally travelling around Tasmania to play in tournaments against kids from every corner of the island.

When the 1998 FIFA World Cup was on, my brothers and I learned the colours, national flag and capital city of each of the competing thirty-two nations, and in between we were consumed by English Premier League (EPL) matches. Mum and Dad would let us stay up that little bit later than normal on Monday nights, to watch the one-hour SBS highlights show hosted by Les Murray. Grandad and my uncles Richard and Geoff were fervent West Ham supporters, but when Socceroos star Harry Kewell joined Leeds United in 1996, that was all we needed to swear allegiance to the Peacocks. And by the time the mercurial Mark Viduka came on board in 2000, the Whites were well and truly our team. (I'll never forget the headline following one of the big Aussie striker's first games for the club: 'Viduka 4 – Liverpool 3'.)

If soccer was winter, then indoor cricket and Little Athletics were summer. The Clarence Little Athletics Centre was close, and I started there in 1999, when I was eleven. You used to get little felt badges based on how many events you competed in, with one badge for twenty-five events, and another for fifty events, seventy-five and 100, too. I wanted as many as possible, but my knack was for shot put. I made it as far as the state championships a couple of times, and in 2002 I made it onto the under-13 state team, travelling to Adelaide to compete in the Australian Championships. I even won a bronze medal. Fifteen years later – a lifetime later, really – I was nominated for inclusion on the Little Athletics Australia Roll of Excellence. And I was touched.

Athletics wasn't always an organised affair for us. When I was ten I put together a triathlon at home, with a run and a ride and some other physical challenge. Coming into the last leg, Harry and Charlie were hot on my heels, and, as the eldest, that simply wouldn't do. My competitive nature kicked in, and so I jumped on my bike without wasting any precious seconds putting on my helmet. I took off down our street on my BMX, pedalling like a lunatic, and as I hit top speed, I passed a police car. I saw its lights, heard its siren, and rode home as fast as I could, before sprinting into the house and hiding under my bed. I heard the police knock at the door, then nodded solemnly as they told me off, kneeling down to reprimand me while I remained hidden under the bed. I didn't like being caught, but I don't like losing either.

The indoor cricket centre was barely 500 metres from home, and I spent so many afternoons and nights there. My favourite ritual after each game was a bag of hot chips with far too much sauce and an unhealthy amount of chicken salt. The end-of-season meal plan was heading next door to Pizza Hut, for all-you-could-eat slices of Supreme and Hawaiian and Meatlovers.

In the summer months, cricket was our passion and pastime, almost a vocation. We could walk to Bellerive by ourselves, using our own membership cards to get us in through the gates, with money for food and idle hours to spare. After each drinks break, all the kids would queue up near the fence to wait for the drinks cart to return, staking out the best spot in the hope that the 12th man would give you a leftover Powerade or toss you a free packet of Wrigley's Extra. In 2021 I hosted a radio show with former Australian captain and wicket-keeper Tim Paine, and we interviewed the great Ricky Ponting. 'Punter' vividly remembered all the kids of Hobart jostling to get near that drinks cart, and laughed out loud when I told him that one of them was me.

We didn't get to see a lot of our local hero in person, given he played only the odd game back home for Tasmania when on a break from international duties. Instead, we found figures to revere from the Tassie Tigers team – names you likely wouldn't know, such as Mark Atkinson, the wicket-keeper, or Dan Marsh, the captain, or Shaun Young, an all-rounder who played one Test match plus a few one-dayers for Australia, and my favourite of all, Mark Ridgway, a big, fast outswing bowler who was said to use the strong breezes from the Derwent River to move the ball through the air. He seemed gargantuan to me then, yet when I finally met him at a charity golf day a few years ago, he was average height – short, in fact. Memory is funny like that, always coloured by our enthusiasms, susceptible to sentiment.

But the city did come alive on those rare days when international cricket came to town. Mum helped us make a banner – by painting on bedsheets – and we always got to the ground early to find just the right spot, sometimes in the hope of winning a banner competition but mostly just hoping that whatever silly thing we had written would get a few seconds of attention on the broadcast. One year I won a competition to toss the coin before a one-day game between South Africa and New Zealand and was given a South African team shirt. I wore that thing down to its final fraying thread.

I did follow AFL, too, though not as much as other sports, and definitely not as religiously as so many others do. I barracked for the Sydney Swans, actually, because of Mum's connection to Rodney Eade, their coach at the time. One year during Rocket's stint at Sydney, Dad and I went to Waverley Park to watch them play Hawthorn. He got us tickets in the Swans family area, and I sat next to Troy Cook, an emergency for the game. The crowd was raucous that day, and after the final siren an old Hawthorn supporter was taunting those near him, as some fans do, and I started crying. Troy put his arm around me and smiled: 'Don't worry, mate.' I loved Michael O'Loughlin and Adam Goodes, Paul Kelly and Stuart Maxfield, but from that point on, Troy Cook was my favourite player.

In truth, however, most of the football heroes of my youth were the Clarence players that I saw in action at Bellerive, like midfielder Gavin Cooney, who was drafted by West Coast in 1990 but returned home after only one week in Western Australia and became a superstar in the Tassie league, playing 314 games and winning five premiership. I ended up playing alongside him when I was fifteen. Long before that home ground received its modern makeover and became Blundstone Arena, I watched these guys destroy opponents from all over the state, and I practically lived amid the wooden bench seats of the beach stand, chasing after every errant ball kicked out of play, or, when my Dad was playing, running down into the changerooms to pinch a bottle of Sustagen.

I spent so many freezing winter days in and on and around that ground. Life was simple and good, and my interests were numerous and varied. Footy was just another element within a broad young life, lived in constant motion – just one thing among many, no more or less important than anything else. But that was about to change.

3

PEROXIDE TIPS

My cousin Nick, six years older than me, was my idol as a kid. His family had moved north to the Gold Coast when I was only two, and I sometimes wonder if that distance served to magnify his importance to me – as that bigger, older, faraway athletic relative. Living in the heat and light of the Sunshine State, his exploits just seemed to burn a little brighter. Our family briefly followed his to Queensland, Dad taking a chance to coach the Coolangatta Blues in what was then known as the Gold Coast Australian Football League. Both my parents took a break from teaching, too, Dad working as a concreter and Mum trying her hand as a florist, but I was only three and our stint there didn't last more than a year. Tasmania has that kind of lure on its locals sometimes, like true south on a compass, dragging and drawing you back from where you came.

I followed Nick's progress instead from afar, including his cricketing exploits. Nick kicks with his right foot, but had that odd ambidextrous quality that made him a left-arm pace bowler. He was a big, blond quick and played in representative teams as a teenager – even development squads with Mitchell Johnson and Shane Watson. He reckons he could have been a Sheffield Shield cricketer, and he's probably right. Maybe that's why he always gets annoyed when the media run those lists of AFL players who might have had careers at the crease – Jonathan Brown and Brett Deledio, for instance, or Luke Hodge and Luke Ball – and make the grievous mistake of somehow leaving out his name. But, in truth, cricket was never a real consideration.

The adrenaline rush that comes with playing footy in front of a crowd, plus the camaraderie that comes from a physically bruising battle with your mates, and the mere fact that the game itself made use of his greatest asset – *that heart and those lungs heaving and pumping like pistons as he strode up and down the field, again and again* – how could cricket compete with that? When Nick was sixteen he played in a reserves footy premiership with Southport in the QAFL, and that was it. He was a one-sport boy forever.

I knew he was talented, too. We would get reports about his teenage performances in national championships, his membership of various state squads, and the chance he was given to play a few reserves games for the Brisbane Lions. He came down and trained at Clarence at one point, and a few of the club heavyweights tried – and failed – to lure him south, away from the AFL, and to suit up instead for the 'Roos. But it wasn't until he was drafted in 2000 by St Kilda – with the very first pick – and I saw footage of him standing on stage wearing his Saints polo shirt, that I became infatuated with following in his footsteps.

Until then I had dreams – albeit muted dreams that I didn't share far and wide – of playing in the English Premier League. I had cried in 1998 when Iran kicked those late goals at the MCG, after Australia had led 2–0. I'd been livid when the Socceroos were so badly mistreated on their 2002 trip to Uruguay. And in 2006, when John Aloisi kicked the goal that finally sent Australia to a World Cup, I went bananas with my brothers in the big room at home (and probably put a hole or two more in those walls). Even now I sometimes daydream about what might have been if I had stuck with soccer. Would I have fought my way into an A-League side, and toiled in relative obscurity? Or could I have emulated Viduka and become a striker in the most famous league in the world, my dad one day cutting out a newspaper clipping with the headline 'Riewoldt 4 – Tottenham 3'? (Mum has a theory. She reckons I would have become Cristiano Ronaldo. Mums are good like that.)

Instead, I found myself gravitating to our indigenous game, and Nick wasn't the only reason either. Junior high school played a part. A quick explainer here for non-Tasmanians: in the Tassie school system, you go to a primary school, then a high school for Years 7–10, then a college for Years 11 and 12. My secondary schooling began at a Catholic boys' junior high called St Virgil's, which had a strong sports program – and an ethos that bordered on tribal, with football at its core. Still headstrong but also impressionable, I wanted to make friends, and team sport served that function. How many mates do you meet in life because of the games you play together, or the teams you blindly follow? Sport is a source of community in this country – probably in all countries. All of us who play games or watch them end up bound together in the most unconditional, bizarre and beautiful way – by mascots and colours and creeds.

In my first year of high school, I was picked to play for my first representative squad – a team called Southern Swans, made up of the best players from the Hobart area. I might have made that squad because of my surname, but I didn't care. I remember playing in a round-robin competition against the Northern Bushrangers, made up of kids from Launceston and the towns of the north-east (like Sam Lonergan, who played for Essendon and is now an assistant coach at Richmond) and the North-West Sharks with kids from Devonport and Burnie (like Grant Birchall, who would go on to play in four AFL premierships with Hawthorn). The best performers in the round-robin competition were picked to join the development squad that trains and sorts and feeds young players into what would ultimately become the Tasmanian team for the national under-16 championships. I could scarcely believe I was one of them.

Back at school, there were so many sports on offer, and we prided ourselves on competing hard in every instance. I found myself competing at athletics carnivals, and joining the water polo team. But I also sensed this growing need to carve out time for football, and football alone. It seemed like the only way to reach that upper echelon of success. There's a theory that bucks this idea, of course, in a book called *Range*, which describes what happens to two anonymous child athletes

24

trained in completely different ways. One child devotes himself daily to a singular sport, refining every aspect of his regimen until he is without peer, and rises to the top of the world. The other child experiments and plays all games on offer, favouring none, until forced to choose one late in his teenage years, and yet he too rises to the top of the world. The narrow-focus athlete was Tiger Woods. The athlete with range was Roger Federer. Is one method healthier than the other? Does one produce a better athlete – or person – than the other? Who knows? I had focus. But I also had range. Like most things in life, you meet yourself somewhere in the middle.

When I was fourteen I was picked in Tasmania's initial thirty-player squad for the 2003 national under-16 championships, but when the squad was reduced to twenty-five, I was cut. I was heartbroken by that. For so long I stewed on my disappointment – perhaps the first blow to shake my confidence – but I also let it motivate my work ethic. I took advantage of being included in a pathway program – a talent conveyor belt. As one of the younger players, I could have fallen through the cracks, but I made it my business to develop in tandem with the older boys. I knew I needed fitness, for instance, so I became a boundary umpire at one point, to stay close to footy in my spare time, earn pocket change, and build my engine. I made the squad the following year.

I made tough choices, too. At the start of 2004, my final year at St Virgil's, I had to align myself with a local footy club. The school – including my coaches and my mates – all expected me to join Hobart. It was just what St Virgil's boys did. But my family history is with Clarence – I was never going

25

to run out for anyone but the 'Roos. I felt guilty delivering that news, and devastated to be separating myself from the friends and mentors I knew, but playing senior football in the red and the white, just as Dad and his brothers had done, was a given. It wasn't even an expectation within the family, so much an expectation within myself.

I started in the under-19s in 2004, but quickly played reserves, and seniors, too. My first game in the seconds was a match against New Norfolk. I lined up on the wing, kicked a handful of early goals, and took a flying mark in front of the grandstand. A few wild men of the Eagles were none too pleased by this. When I went to full-forward for a rest, one of them came up and belted me. Left with blood on his hand, he wiped it off on my jumper. I was terrified, but it hadn't gone unnoticed. Dad was the Clarence runner that day and came steaming out onto the field. He was only a few steps from me, and still sprinting, when I stepped aside like a matador with a cloak, dodging an enraged bull. Dad ran clean through that New Norfolk player, flattening him outside the goal square. That hit earned a six-week suspension from the league – and loving gratitude from his son.

Sometimes it was just as bad in the under-19s, where some of the wild units were scarier than adults. We played New Norfolk in one under-19s grand final, for instance, and I came across one real rugged operator. Early in the game I took a hanger over him and kicked a goal, so he jogged past – 'Good luck doing that again' – and told me he was going to smack me all game long. He did, too, yet I never took a backward step. I suppose I was lucky – I had protection. When you play community football, and the people within your club have watched you grow up – seen you chasing balls in grandstands as a kid or sidling into the rooms to hear half-time speeches – you know those same figures are going to have your back. I was never alone out there.

I got belted often as a kid playing open-age footy. Most of the time it was grown men deciding to target the youngest player on the field – not exactly tough – but, to be fair, I sometimes brought that punishment upon myself. I never went out of my way to sledge opponents, but perhaps I was cheeky. Or perhaps everything just looks cheeky when you're tall and skinny and far younger than anyone else on the field, and you have long blond hair and play the way I played, jumping on people's heads and kicking goals and running around celebrating. I was a bouncing, grinning kid with a fundamental and abiding belief in myself and my footy. It honestly didn't matter if I was verbal or not, because that kind of play and that kind of self-confidence positions you as the cocky young rooster regardless.

It was thrilling, though. In my first senior game, I slotted a goal from the boundary line – a drop punt from the Bellerive Beach end of our home ground – and a clip of the kick ended up being featured on the 'Almost Football Legends' segment of *The Footy Show*. I was getting match payments for the first time, too. These days, AFL match payments are $5,000 a game. I was getting $50 a game, more than enough for me to promptly tell my parents that my days of doing chores for pocket money were over.

In the mid-2000s, St Kilda started playing a couple of home games each season in Launceston. That was great for our family, as we were able to go and watch Nick play without having to fly to Melbourne. Nick always got us into the rooms after the games, too, which to me was like Christmas. One time at York Park, we went to the post-game function and Nick introduced me to St Kilda's senior coach, Grant Thomas, who gave me one piece of advice: 'Be as good a kick on your left foot as you are on your right'. To achieve that, he said, I needed to kick the ball 500 times a day. It was probably a passing comment – that singular nugget he gives to every kid who asks his advice – but I took it on as gospel. At training I used to kick next to a guy with a palindromic name – Leon Noel – and he was the gun in the year above me, an under-16s All Australian, who had the sweetest, neatest left foot ever. Every training session I tried to mirror him – copying his ball drop, the way his toe pointed forward, the way he held his opposite arm out for balance. And for the next two years whenever I was on the way to school, I had a pattern for chipping the Sherrin up to myself as I walked: *three steps, kick off the left, three steps, kick off the right, three steps, kick off the left, three steps, kick off the right*. I still do it even now, when my goal kicking is a bit off, or if I feel like I need to sharpen something up. It orients me – *three steps, kick off the left, three steps, kick off the right* – and centres me somehow.

When my four years at St Virgil's had come to an end, I moved to Rosny College, a public school, for Years 11 and 12. My parents were on another stint away from teaching. They had set up a café and florist business called Cabbage's – one of very few cafés on the eastern shore. I was on my own adventure, doing weights of a morning at North Hobart Oval, with more than a dozen hotshot junior players – training almost as a squad but then playing for different teams against one another on weekends. I'd get to that gym in the darkness of 6am, and pick up those old weights that didn't match. The heavy metal was teal green and a little rusty, and all locked up behind a garage roller door. It was an archaic space that was clearly never meant to be a weights room, but had been requisitioned and repurposed anyway, and made into this place where masculinity and testosterone mixed with competition and dreams. Then I'd go to the café on the way to school, and Dad would make me a vanilla milkshake with raw eggs for added protein, like I was Rocky Balboa. I ate lunch there as well – my standing order was potato wedges with sour cream and sweet chilli sauce. Because the café was near Bellerive Oval, Tassie cricketers went there often, so I got to know Damien Wright and Tim Paine. I felt myself becoming a kind of little brother in a wider regional sporting fraternity.

During my two years at Rosny College, I was consumed by the ambition to play in the AFL, and it took me into so many sides. I made my senior debut for Clarence in 2004, when I was just fifteen, but people looked out for me because I was Chris Riewoldt's son, a local, one of them – a Clarence boy from a famous Clarence family. My chief chaperone was a key forward and club legend named Brad Dutton, whose father had played with my dad. Brad was skilful and tough, but also a bit of a peacock. He was a showman, with flair and a head wobble – the Tasmanian equivalent of Dermott Brereton. I would kick a goal, and he would walk up to my opponent – 'Mate, he's only fifteen, and he's giving you a bath!' – and goad

29

them on my behalf. I probably took some of that attitude from him, and walked taller when I knew he was near. These were my idols.

I began playing well, and I remember sitting at the dinner table one night when Dad piped up. 'Well,' he said, 'I think you might have me covered as a player.' That was Dad's style, whether he was delivering praise or a reprimand – never over-bearing, never demanding, never feeling the need to push me onto the path he once walked, never trying to relive his own exploits through mine. He let me learn things my own way, with one simple piece of advice: 'Go out there and have fun.' Mum was the same. Her support was fierce and unwavering, but never proscriptive. She would take you to the starting line and set you free – 'See you at the finish' – sharing nothing but her unshakeable faith that you were going to be okay along the way.

I played only one game of school footy for Rosny College. It was in 2006, against Guildford Young College, in a match that was more of a social kick-around than a contest. Rosny's jumpers were bright yellow, so our nickname was 'The Bananas'. We made a banner for ourselves to run through and raised money for a shield to hand to the winning team. We called it the 'Justin Sherman Shield' in honour of, yes, Justin Sherman, who'd played for Rosny in the previous year's game before being drafted by the Brisbane Lions. We adopted the track *Hollaback Girl* by Gwen Stefani as our team song because of one lyric: 'This shit is bananas . . . B-A-N-A-N-A-S.' Our team included Mitch Thorp (who was selected by Hawthorn with pick six in that year's AFL Draft). Tom Collier

30

(who was drafted by the Brisbane Lions in 2007) played for Guildford Young. I think we won by a couple of goals.

But the most important thing about that school was the girl I met there. Carly Ziegler was my age, sixteen, and we were in the same Year 11 English and health studies classes. We were strangers in a sense, having never met, but she had heard all about me through the local high school network, having gone to the other Catholic school on the opposite side of the city. I had played footy with her friends, and so my name came up occasionally, yet we hadn't crossed paths. That's actually strange, given how small the pool of teenagers is within the eastern shore of Hobart – and how intertwined your circles become by a certain age. It's like we were living lives in parallel, our tiny worlds powering along without colliding, until now.

With Carly and I attending the same school, our connections overlapped and grew. We hung out in the common room together, a space she always says was made cacophonous mainly by me, playing kick-to-kick in the hall, laughing and guffawing at full volume, forever with a ball or bat in hand. Carly was quiet, at least compared to me, and couldn't stand me at first. She likes to say that on those rare days I missed school – for footy, or illness – the place seemed silent by comparison, tranquil without a Sherrin constantly hitting the roof, serene without the cry of 'heads up' ringing throughout the room.

But she also thinks she misunderstood me in those early days. What some might have mistaken for arrogance, she began to understand was probably something else – something closer to a defence mechanism. And maybe it was. Most of the kids at Rosny College had been together for four years prior, making me something of a newcomer or interloper. Being loud and chirpy and (possibly, painfully) cheerful and in your face was my way of introducing myself to a new group.

I don't know that she fell for me quickly, but she at least started to see who I was. We were still at a stage of life where it's not really cool to answer the teacher's questions, or be seen engaging with the course content, but I did. If I was there, I reasoned, I might as well be fully there. In class, I was always happy to speak up, and speak my mind. Carly likes to say I was unapologetically myself, in that I said what I meant and I meant what I said. Maybe that sometimes came with a side serving of cheek, but again, everything goes back to an over-riding but implicit family philosophy: life is for living.

I think that's what won her over in the end. Carly was so serious, and so studious, and in some ways so afraid of making the wrong move or saying the wrong thing. Grades were important to her. Punctuality was important to her. Saying the right thing in the right moment was important to her. I would start an essay two days before it was due, or study overnight for an exam the next day, but such things were unthinkable to her. Unfathomable, really. In many ways we're opposites, and you know what they say about opposites . . .

She liked that I was creative, too. At one point I stumbled onto the process of screen printing T-shirts and gave it a try. I created my own brand: Feng Shui. I'd come up with abstract designs, or funny phrases, in interesting fonts. I was copying what I liked from skater apparel. I remember a brand called Sodium sold in stores, with a T-shirt that read '1986 World

Shopping Cart Racing Championships'. I loved that, so I plagiarised the design. I was basically a fashion designer for a couple of months, and then I wasn't. With me it's almost always about what's next. I got a new phone for my birthday, and it was so advanced it had a video function. Naturally I started making fake music videos, singing Paul Kelly's 'To Her Door' into the pixelated camera of a first generation flip phone. I was a director and a performer, until – once more – I wasn't.

Dating in a sleepy city like Hobart was limited. We were teenagers, so we went to the mall – Eastlands – to get a milkshake from the food court and walk around. Or we would go to my house and play Crash Bandicoot – Carly was far better than me – on the PlayStation. And on weekends she would come and watch me play footy with a circle of friends. In most ways it was a typical teen romance.

In the 2006 pre-season I was invited to train with the Tassie Devils VFL team. If I had come through the system a few years earlier, I would have played for the Tassie Mariners in the Victoria-based TAC Cup (now the NAB League), and in an elite under-18 competition against kids my own age. But Tasmanian teenagers were robbed of that opportunity after the Mariners withdrew from the TAC Cup following the 2002 season. Instead, we had to toughen up and play against men in the VFL, while we waited for the national under-18 championships to come around in the middle of the year.

Still, steel sharpens steel. Nothing accelerated my development so dramatically or organically as training with a VFL program. It made you compete against people who were all bigger and all stronger and all faster, but also all fundamentally more mature, and they could give you an insight into playing and training at that higher level. It was like serving an apprenticeship. I was like a young tradie, learning in the best possible way – on the job, by diving in and doing what was needed.

I was growing up, and rapidly. I had my driver's licence and drove my grannie's grey Nissan Pulsar (before it got stolen), then their red Mitsubishi station wagon, before later owning my own purple Combi van. I brought that thing to Melbourne, too. I had a part-time job at a Sportsco store as well, and spent most of the money I earned there on shoes and footy boots. Mum used to call me Imelda Marcos. I was constantly clothed in sports gear, and dropping money on more. I visited Nick once in Melbourne and all I wanted was to see the nearby Nike store. When I got my first game with the Tassie Devils, I celebrated by purchasing a pair of silver Nike Tiempo footy boots. And yet, I wasn't just consumed with material goods. I had a spiritual side that found its way into my everyday life, and it did so even with those Tiempos.

I decided I wanted to have my grandad, Ivan Eade, on the field with me in my VFL debut. As I mentioned, Grandad had passed away when I was 13. He'd been afflicted by mouth and throat cancer, but at that age I hadn't realised how sick he was until he died. His funeral was the first I had ever been to – and my first experience of death. More than 600 people came to celebrate his life in Devonport, and they spoke and wept and shared stories and made toasts. I wanted a tribute of my own, so I photocopied a picture of him from inside his book, the one he wrote with that whimsical title I loved – *Life's Little Pieces of Magic* – and I stuck it to the inner sole of one of my boots, so

I would look at him before I put them on that day to play, and have him with me out there on the field.

We played Port Melbourne, and I played up forward on Toby Pinwill, who would go on to become a Borough legend, winning the VFL best and fairest twice and playing in two premiership teams. I got a couple of kicks, but the real excitement came later, staying in Melbourne for the weekend, following my adult teammates out on the town, letting loose in the big smoke, sinking beers at Q-Bar in Chapel Street at 4am. I was seventeen.

During the second half of the season, I played another seven games for the Devils, running around with ex-AFL talent like Ben Beams, Nathan Street and Justin Plapp. There were current AFL players who joined us, too, like Josh Gibson and Troy Makepeace, also Jade Rawlings, a gun footballer being let down by his body who later coached at Richmond, and showed me the ropes early, acting as my guardian in the clinches.

I was slowly being pulled into the orbit of the AFL – the industry and its identities. Amid my season of playing for different teams in different places, Nick teed up some work experience for me at St Kilda. I spent two weeks there, doing barely anything but buzzing around the edges, the proverbial fly on the wall. I remember a one-on-one training session with Saints assistant coach Terry Daniher, and I had no idea who he was. No idea he was captain of two Essendon premiership teams in the mid-1980s. No idea he was a bona fide AFL legend. That probably says as much about Terry's down-to-earth demeanour as it does about me. I stayed with Nick and his teammate Justin Koschitzke. St Kilda had a deal with Sanitarium at the time, meaning their house was filled with boxes of Weet-Bix, which I thought was incredibly cool.

The year you get drafted moves swiftly, week after week, game after game, drawing you inexorably towards your destiny, or just a new destination. Another football highlight came with playing for Tasmania in the 2006 national under-18s championships in Melbourne. The previous year I had played a minor role as a defender, but this time around I played up forward and was able to raise the eyebrow of one or two recruiters. Not long after that, I played in a game for an Allies team against a combined Victorian metro-country side. Our coach, three-time Brisbane Lions premiership player Craig 'Fly' McRae, gave me the honour of captaining our team. Fly was just starting out in coaching, but the traits he later showed as an assistant coach at Richmond – and which the wider world now sees in his work at Collingwood – were already on show. His is a highly analytical mind, married with extraordinary emotional intelligence, making him clever but creative, disciplined but fun.

The best moment, though, happened at home, when I lined up with Clarence in the Southern Football League finals. I'd broken my collarbone that year, and sat on the bench nursing that fracture through a few games, just so I could qualify to play. Now we had made it through to our second straight Grand Final, and were desperate to make amends for falling at the final hurdle the year before. I wore No. 7 – the number worn by my old man – and kicked four goals and six behinds in a thirty-seven-point victory. It was a pinnacle moment in so many ways – not just the exclamation mark on my junior career, and not just the end of another season, but the end of a phase of life. You might call it the day I came of age, or the day when I truly convinced myself that I could make it to the AFL. That match was confirmation of something I had begun to feel throughout that season: a sense of belonging.

After the game, I was interviewed by a local media crew. You can find the clip on YouTube. There I am in the change rooms, peroxide tips in my hair, smiling widely. (I was in those rooms again only recently, for a full-circle moment, at the long-awaited announcement of an AFL team for Tasmania. Little had changed, but of course everything had changed, too.) Twice when asked how I felt about winning the flag, I replied in my best Tassie drawl that it was 'unbelieeevable'. And then they asked how it felt to play my final game for Clarence before heading to the big league next year. The draft was still weeks away, so I shrugged my shoulders: 'If it happens, it happens,' I told them. 'I'm quite happy to stay here at Clarence for the rest of my life, because I love it here!'

That was true up to a point. But I was also hellbent on making my way to the AFL. I wasn't nervous about the prospect, nor was I worried about the faint possibility of not getting drafted. I was living completely in the moment. Every weekend it felt like there was something incredibly important to do – there was never a pause or a lull where I might have sat still and dwelled or fretted on what was coming next, or tried to forecast where each of my decisions would take me. I never worried about putting all my eggs into the football basket, and pushing everything else to the side, because everything was real and unreal, and speeding forward in real time. My mind simply never wandered too far from what I was doing – and, in truth, it rarely does. That's always been helpful in tough times. Internalised belief is a great gift. It stops your stumbles from turning into falls, and bestows this happy knack for knowing not just what you *want* to be, but what you *will* be, too.

4

WIGGY AND PUP

One minute I was running around with my mates at Clarence, overindulging in premiership celebrations and generally running amok in my city, and the next minute I was in the uber professional confines of the Australian Institute of Sport in Canberra. This was the AFL Draft Camp, held the week after West Coast defeated Sydney by one point in their second successive down-to-the-wire Grand Final.

It was hard to know where you sat during the evaluations they devised for us. The drills that tested kicking, marking and handballing skills gave me the chance to play to my strengths. By contrast, I struggled with the three-kilometre time-trial (twelve minutes) and beep test (Level 13). And I had no idea what they would make of my personality.

The setting felt like one long, active job interview, but I didn't try to be anyone other than myself. The players at these camps are mostly kids, and mostly painfully shy, too. They barely know themselves or one another. They speak when spoken to, leaping and sprinting and kicking and catching on command. They file into mess halls to eat lunch quietly, chewing in silence. I was the opposite. I was loud, and confident, and carried on as always.

I talked to everyone, and over everyone. Having played with senior footballers, I fell into a natural footy-club banter and asked questions of all the coaches. Compared to the kids around me – conspicuously keeping their heads down and eyes forward – I was practically bellowing the fact that I belonged. My longtime Richmond teammate Shane Edwards was at the camp as well and reminds me often how annoying and obnoxious he found me then. He told me once that when his dad picked him up at Adelaide Airport afterwards, Shane got into the car and his first words to his father were about me, this Tasmanian extrovert with a chainsaw voice: 'Thank God I'll never have to see Jack Riewoldt again,' he said, 'because that bloke was *painful*.'

The whole event could not have been more pivotal to my future, and yet I treated it casually. The only interviews I had with AFL clubs prior to the draft were at that draft camp, yet I remember only one of them, with Port Adelaide. The man asking most of the questions was Power coach Mark 'Choco' Williams, an identity renowned for left-field thoughts and oddball queries.

'So,' he asked, 'how many games are you going to play?'

I smiled – 'I'll play 300' – and he looked at me dismissively.

'You know that only two per cent of players play 300 games?'

I regretted my comment afterwards – the flippancy or ignorance of it – and hoped it wouldn't count against me. But surely a healthy dose of self-confidence is worth something in a league that batters and bruises the fragile egos of so many young men every week. Lance Franklin was asked on his draft camp what his weak points were as a player. He said he couldn't name any.

In the lead-up to the draft itself, I soaked up what were likely to be my final few weeks living at home. I kept my Year 12 studies on track, turned eighteen, celebrated adulthood, and then Friday November 24 arrived. In 2006, the AFL Draft wasn't held over two days like it is now, and it wasn't shown on TV. It started at around 10.30am and was conducted entirely online. I followed the selections while sitting in front of a desktop computer at home. I only had a couple of mates over to watch it with me, worried by what might happen if I wasn't picked. I'd been to a draft party the year before, hosted by a mate named Sam Iles, whose name was never called. (Thankfully, Sam was later invited to train with Collingwood, and the Magpies selected him with the second pick in the pre-season draft. He played seven games for the Pies and twenty-six for Gold Coast.)

I had almost no idea what to expect. The media had linked me to Collingwood, which had picks eight and ten, but the depth of analysis then was scant compared to what it is now. There were very few 'phantom drafts' to study, and whatever intelligence the recruiters had gleaned was held largely within their list-management teams. There were sketchy message boards and internet forums you could find – I was partial to scanning Big Footy for the odd mention of my name – but precious little official commentary on where the scouts really thought I was about to end up. The local papers and radio stations and TV news networks seemed certain I was going to be picked in the first round, but it was hard to trust such a parochial press. Hobart's media was always going to inflate the importance of any Tasmanian with a shot at the AFL, talking you up as a star and predicting some prodigious future. I couldn't rely on that – not with so much emotion at stake.

The number one pick in the draft was Bryce Gibbs, selected by Carlton. Scott Gumbleton went to Essendon at number two, before North Melbourne took Lachie Hansen. Matthew Leuenberger (Brisbane Lions) and Travis Boak (Port Adelaide) were selections four and five. My Rosny College teammate Mitch Thorp was taken by Hawthorn with selection six. This would turn out to be a controversial choice, because of the next player selected. Joel Selwood would play more than 300 games, win three premierships and captain the Cats for the better part of a decade. Mitch, chosen one pick before him, played only two AFL games before heading home.

When Collingwood's first-round selections arrived, they ignored me and instead selected Ben Reid with pick eight (he would go on to become a premiership player and All Australian) and Nathan Brown with pick ten (he would also play in the 2010 premiership). St Kilda took David Armitage with pick nine and the Western Bulldogs selected Andrejs Everitt with pick eleven. I thought I was a chance to go to Melbourne at pick twelve, only for the Demons to choose James Frawley instead. Pondering what might happen from there, I was nervous. Richmond had selection thirteen, and the Adelaide Crows held pick fourteen. I wanted to go to a Victorian club.

I crossed my fingers and hoped the Tigers were interested. I refreshed the AFL website. Refreshed it again. And again. It finally updated and there was my name. I was going to Tigerland. My mates and I erupted – with joy, yes, but relief as much as anything. Within minutes my phone was ringing. My new coach, Terry Wallace, wanted to congratulate me, welcome me, and remind me that he would see me at Punt Road Oval in two days. It was really happening. And happening fast.

Looking back, the 2006 draft was a turning point for Richmond. In the previous two drafts combined, the Tigers had seven selections inside the top twenty-five. Of the players chosen with those picks, only Brett Deledio played more than 150 games in yellow and black. Some of them, like Danny Meyer (seventeen games), Jarrad Oakley-Nicholls (thirteen) and Cleve Hughes (sixteen) hardly played at all. Maybe they were drafted too early. Maybe they buckled under the burden of that pressure to perform. Maybe they struggled because the club had such poor development programs when they arrived. Or maybe they just didn't quite have that lucky edge – that winning combination of gifts and spark and timing and work ethic that creates a career. Either way, the contrast with the class of 2006 is stark. I was taken first, and Shane Edwards second, the two of us combining for more than 600 games and six flags.

In the days immediately after I was drafted, before I had to pack my bags and fly across Bass Strait, I had enough time to squeeze in a party and say thank you to the many people who had helped me. David Charlesworth, the father of my best mate James Charlesworth, a legend of Tassie footy, had supported me and given me the constructive feedback I needed. Hamish Ogilvie is now the national recruiting manager for the Adelaide Crows, but back then he was the AFL's state development manager in Tasmania – a policeman from Melbourne who went down to Tassie, joined Clarence, lived just down the road from me, and gave me a chance by picking me for all those development squads. These people were hard on me, and comforting to me, and most of all believed in me. Now I had to believe in myself. Leaving was emotional. I felt like a country kid saying goodbye to the comfort and familiarity of a small town for the hustle, bustle and bright lights of the big smoke. It sounds like a cliche. It's also true.

On Monday, November 27, I arrived at Punt Road Oval for my first official day as a Richmond player, along with my fellow draftees Shane Edwards, Daniel Connors and Andrew Collins. There was Carl Peterson, too, who was raised in Kununurra. I remember seeing his highlights and being wowed by the most unbelievable leap. In person, he was always smiling, teeth gleaming. He finished with us in a year, eventually went to Hawthorn, and ultimately became a bush artist. We brought in rookies, too. Tasman Clingan, from Lake Bolac, was a cracking kid who also only lasted a year. Rookies were paid a pittance then, perhaps $30,000 a year, and most never made it off that list. The last arrival was Jake 'The Push Up' King. Kingy was different – he had played at Coburg the year before, and so he had a few Richmond connections already. Some people seem tough but it's just bravado; he was tough. Yet also kind and caring, qualities he developed at the Tigers.

We were given a tour of the facilities and, to my immense excitement, kitted out with a bag full of Richmond gear. New shorts, socks, footy jumpers and training tops. A little backpack and a large duffle bag, both with number 8 embossed on the outside, the former for bringing my things to training and the latter for hauling my gear on interstate trips. Motorola sponsored the club, and we were given free Motorola phones. As a cohort of draftees, you end up spending so much time together during your first pre-season – a natural tendency that was amplified in us by the fact that we weren't from Melbourne. I was from Tassie, Shane was from Adelaide, and Dan and Andy were from country Victoria. We hung out at Victoria Gardens Shopping Centre, and often ate dinner together for comfort and security, becoming like a nervous little wolf pack among the big dogs. We were as tight knit a group as you could imagine.

When the time came for introductions to the playing group, I was starting from scratch. I didn't really know anyone – not by name or face or reputation. I had been so focused on playing footy the past two years that I had barely watched any AFL, and when I did it was only to see Nick playing for the Saints. I knew of Matthew Richardson – a superstar forward from Tasmania. I knew of Brett Deledio, the silky number-one pick in the 2004 draft. I knew of Nathan Brown and Joel Bowden, but that was about it. In the early training sessions, I was constantly mucking up names when calling for the ball. It helped that I had my own nickname. Travis Ronaldson was the captain of Coburg, and I played with him at Tassie Devils, where I'd been called 'Roo Pup', as in, a younger version of my cousin Nick 'Roo' Riewoldt. In time, that simply became Pup, and it stuck. At one point Chris Newman and Brett Deledio called me 'Wig', and later 'Wiggy', because I would sit at the back of the meeting room surveying everything, like a big wig. Nicknames are like that. My old man is called 'Cabbage' because when he got to Clarence they said he had a head like a cabbage. It stuck, to the point where my parents later named their café and florist shop Cabbages. (And to our children, he's not grandpa, he's 'Cabpa'.)

Fortunately, there were also people in leadership positions who made me feel at home. Another old Tassie Devils teammate, Jade Rawlings, was now an assistant AFL coach with Richmond and head coach of the Coburg Tigers, which at that stage was Richmond's affiliate team in the VFL and the place I would most likely start my career. One more familiar face was my old under-18s Allies coach Craig McRae, who had only recently taken on a development role at Punt Road. It was nice to have them both near.

Meeting the senior coach was daunting. I was in awe of Terry Wallace, assuming he knew everything there was to know about footy. I learned his history – how he was a tremendously decorated player, winning three premierships with the Hawks and two best-and-fairest awards, along with another two best-and-fairest awards during his playing stint with the Western Bulldogs, when he led them to two preliminary finals. 'Plough' had presence – and self-confidence. He went out of his way to make the draftees feel welcome. One weekend he invited us to his house to watch a boxing bout on pay-per-view. I hate boxing but figured you don't turn down an invitation from the boss. By that stage, we had been worded up by the older players that Terry loved to work on his tan, so while we were at his place our main aim was to find his tanning bed. And we did. Footy clubs are like that – held together at times by jokes and yarns and characters.

Pre-season training was tough, but I was living my dream. Not even the most exhausting running session could wipe the smile from my face. When you first get to an AFL club, you're so determined to adapt and belong that you assume everything unfolding in front of you is best practice. When someone comes up to you and says, 'Don't you dare eat butter on your bread', you comply without question, assuming this is just the way things are done.

But I can see now that Richmond was shaky at the time, almost patched together in some ways, lacking methodology and culture and resources. It was an array of little things, mostly. Wheelie bins for ice baths. Outdated audiovisual equipment. Tables with mismatching chairs. Walls that were bare and scuffed – not branded and bold as they are now. Each little thing adds up, and you begin to feel as though you're not part of an elite sporting organisation so much as some kind of suburban club on steroids.

There were big things, too. The oval was an odd shape, very small, and one pocket flooded with every downpour. The Richmond Cricket Club was still based there, so the middle in summer was a rock-hard wicket block, which in winter turned into a sticky, black quagmire. (We weren't allowed to train on it during cricket season either, and instead had to drive an hour to Craigieburn.) The club was also mired in debt, and understaffed across the board. A couple of torpedo punts away, across Olympic Boulevard, Collingwood's players were enjoying a state-of-the-art training and rehabilitation centre at Olympic Park, with an army of coaches and trainers and physios.

The old place was not without its charms, though. The change rooms may have been substandard, but you could sense the history behind each old locker, and they made a great noise when you slammed them shut. The old Richmond social club was still there, too – a two-storey structure with a bar downstairs. The carpets were green, and the brick exterior was marked with people's names in recognition of their fundraising. It was also where the club held its important press conferences, and where we had lunch after training every Thursday. The menu was always the same: lasagna, white bread rolls and a lettuce salad.

In my first month at the club, I lived with Nathan Brown, a gifted forward and competition star – a man about town who lived on Acland Street, St Kilda, opposite Mink, a bar and nightclub that specialised in vodka. Travelling around town with 'Browny' in his BMW X5 (which had a TV inside) felt like hanging out backstage with a rock star. He was the man.

You started to sense the possibilities that football might afford – and the opportunities that were ours. That's how me and some of the other younger players were talked into putting money into a drink called MonaVie, made with glucosamine and Brazilian acai berries. Our captain, Kane Johnson, and vice-captain, Troy Simmonds, were trying to set up a business in Australia, but it turned out to be a pyramid scheme and went bankrupt. I can't remember how much money I put in, but it wasn't the only cash I lost through hasty investment. At one stage the playing list chipped in to buy a racehorse called Tiger Time, and gathered in the Graeme Richmond Room to watch its first race. Tiger Time staggered across the finish line, and, from what I'm told, was 'sent to a good home'.

I also enjoyed an important stroke of luck, being placed with a host family – the Daltons – who proved to be some of the most generous, kind and interesting people I have come across in my life. Rob and Lisa welcomed me into their Brighton home with open arms, as did their three sons – Sam, Jack and Max. Rob was on the Richmond board at the time. He later became acting CEO of Sport Australia, and was a partner at Ernst & Young, the multi-national consulting firm. They looked after me like I was one of their sons, and their home was a virtual palace, with a tennis court and swimming pool.

I heard horror stories from other players about their living arrangements, either with families who lived more than an hour's drive from training, or share house situations with other young players – pairs or trios of innocents fending for themselves, without basic cooking or cleaning skills. Many jumped from place to place, too – four weeks here, six months there, never quite settling down. Meanwhile, I would come home, crash from physical exertion at 4pm, and wake up to a hot dinner on the table and every creature comfort I could desire. Even when I caused chaos, like the time I accidentally put my Nissan X-Trail in the wrong gear and drove through their garage door, the Daltons were kind and supportive. They remain friends – more than friends, actually – who spoke at our wedding and are like an extra set of grandparents to our kids.

Probably the most stressful part of moving away was the thought of being separated from Carly. We had broken up in October, before the draft, and yet it still felt strange and sad moving on to something else, somewhere else, without her. She had been part of the dream. We had made a trip to Melbourne to visit universities where she might want to study, going to open days at Monash and La Trobe, thinking about a potential life up there. She was utterly devastated when I broke things off.

But there was a view then, within clubland, that you bring a fair bit of baggage if you bring a girlfriend with you at the start of the journey. You felt like you were meant to read between the lines and let such things go. *You've got one chance, kid. It's make or break time. No distractions.* It's not something that's spelled out to you explicitly, but you get this clear sense of suddenly being something other than a boy. You're now an asset.

That's since shifted. New draftees arrive all the time now with partners in tow. Jack Graham. Jayden Short. Shai Bolton. I think of someone like Seth Campbell, a Tassie boy whose girlfriend's parents took him in when he was fourteen. If Seth came north to play in Melbourne but had to lose his closest relationship, and a big part of his life, it could only make him a worse footballer.

The other big shift is in the number of women working within clubs, and not just in administration and marketing and merchandise, but on our side of the building. When I arrived, I think there was one woman in the football department –

a player development manager named Lauren Cooper. Now there's admin executive Sam Smith, club psychologist Dr Sam McLeod, mindfulness coach Emma Murray, wellbeing manager Nadine Haidar, Indigenous liaison Angela Burt, not to mention the women in remedial massage and communications and the AFLW team. Young players especially often yearn for that female role model in their life, someone to offer a different kind of advice, or support, or lesson. I wouldn't even say the place is more female-friendly, so much as finally well-rounded.

Carly, meanwhile, was contending with her own plan. When I was drafted everyone went into town, and even though it was hard, she came and celebrated and congratulated me. I think in a way she was almost thankful I wasn't going to be in the state anymore, because my name was everywhere. She didn't lose sight of her dreams, either, knuckling down to finish Year 12. She decided on a gap year, to save money for a move up to Melbourne alone. She worked in government, squirreling away everything, saving so well that years later, the war chest she had accumulated became the deposit on our first home.

In the end, we were broken up for all of four months, which was pre-season training for me, and something else entirely for her. In that time, her mum had a baby and her dad had a heart attack. She became the grown-up person in her household, going off to work while her father was on bedrest and her mother was nursing. She would walk around Eastlands sometimes pushing her baby brother, Owen, in a pram, imagining the thoughts and whispers from others: 'Did Jack and

51

Carly get secretly pregnant, and now she's here while he's off playing footy?'

It was a trying time, and, in a way, those tough circumstances became my opening for communicating – my reason to reach out. Because I still loved her, and I wanted her back. I started texting a little at first, then came home for Christmas.

'Can I come visit?' I messaged.

'Why?' she replied.

Carly had gotten used to life without me – 'If someone doesn't want to be with me, then I don't want to be with them' – and she told me as much, point blank: 'I've got my own life. How can I make sure you're 100 per cent on this? On me?'

I told her how much I missed her, how I had made a mistake, how I was homesick, missing not just the place but all the familiar people in my life.

She forgave me, and looked at me, and told me what I would need to do: 'If this is going to happen, you're going to have to go speak to my parents about it, and right some wrongs.' I appeared on her doorstep in Hobart one day, and could read what her mum and dad were thinking from the expression on their faces: *Oh my god – the footballer's back. Is he going to break her heart all over again?* I apologised to them as best I could – as best as any contrite eighteen-year-old boy could, owning up to doing the wrong thing. 'I'm sorry I put her through this,' I told them. 'I made a mistake. And, selfishly, I've realised I need her more than ever.' (Funnily enough, the next time I went to the house to have a serious conversation, I was letting her dad, Gary, know I was going to propose.)

It was difficult to plead my case, but we settled on brief visits at first. Once a month she would come over for a long weekend. The Daltons were taken aback at first, mainly by me just announcing that Carly was going to visit. I don't think I ever really asked, and I'm not sure they were ready for two teenagers hanging out together in their house, getting up to mischief. But they loved Carly – everyone does – and so she got into a cycle of saving up money and annual leave, and flying over on a Thursday night then back on a Sunday night. She did that for the entirety of my first year in football. In fact, it's where our love of The Killers was born.

You might remember I made a cameo during one of their performances? I'll tell you that story later. For now, just know that every time I picked Carly up at the airport, we were filled with excitement, and we would listen to that band the whole drive home – albums like *Sam's Town* and *Hot Fuss* – while talking about what we were going to do and see. Her favourite song was *Read My Mind*. You should give it a listen. It's about a breakup, of sorts – about moving on and leaving a two-horse town for the promised land, about taking the green light and following your restless heart, about a teenage queen and a chosen one, about faith and signs and stars. It could almost be our song, really.

5

PARTY TIME

I was delighted to be given the No. 8 guernsey at Punt Road. In the late 1970s and through the 1980s, another forward from Tassie – Michael 'Disco' Roach – had worn the number for 200 games, kicking more than 600 goals, and becoming a famed member of Richmond's 1980 premiership. The club hadn't won a flag since that day, so the players from that side were held in reverence. I desperately wanted to emulate Disco's feats and continue that tradition of Tassie boys kicking goals in yellow and black. But first, I needed to get a game.

I was lucky enough to be picked in the team to play in one of our early practice matches, which was held at Carlton's home ground, Princes Park. And that first game left me with an injury that I carry to this day. Someone stood on the pinky finger on my right hand, breaking bone and damaging ligaments. I had surgery but the finger never really came good. It annoyed me so much at times that in the latter part of my career, I had the knuckle fused. I've got very limited movement in that finger now, but the pain has largely gone.

Still, I was okay to rejoin training within a week. That's one of those revelations that comes to you quickly playing AFL: how the body can overcome the most violent little traumas, and – with the right surgery and rehab and management – bounce back quicker than you would have imagined was possible. Most people might be bedridden by busted limbs and bone bruising, but players – aided by the finest medical care and an imperative to push through discomfort – find a way to play. Being an over-confident young man, I hit the ground running, pushing and panting on the track, hoping to impress and believing myself a chance to play in our season opener against Carlton. But I don't think the coaching staff ever had me in their selection calculations. When it came to putting together a forward line, Matthew Richardson, Jay Schulz and Kayne Pettifer were well ahead of me in the pecking order and were given the nod. They kicked nine goals between them in a seventeen-point defeat, and a few days later I played my first game for our VFL team, the Coburg Tigers.

A lot of the boys hated going out to Coburg, where the facilities were even more rustic than Punt Road's, but I loved it. Playing out there under the guidance of three-time Hawthorn premiership player Andy Collins was my idea of fun. The club was filled with friendly and down-to-earth people. We would train on a Friday night, under lights, and have pasta with the team before heading home, and then drive back to the northern suburbs for the game that weekend. Richmond fields its own VFL side today, so they train in the same facilities as the AFL squad, never leaving our little base at Tigerland, but we spent hours every week motoring along the Tullamarine Freeway and along Bell Street to get to the ground we called 'the burger ring'.

I loved the sights and smells there, the liniment and mud and canteen chips, and the way it reminded me of playing for the Tassie Devils and Clarence. The captain, Travis Ronaldson, had played in Tasmania and took me under his wing, giving me the confidence to be myself. Craig McRae was important, too – integral, actually – in creating this bond between the first-year players, encouraging stupid but spirited competitions between us. We would come in and do weights on our days off, for instance, because we were racing to see who could bench 100 kilograms first. (Shane Edwards was as thin as a whippet then, yet somehow managed to press that bar up before anyone else.) We were a winning side, too, at a time when the AFL side were not. Winning always helps.

I also enjoyed playing alongside Alastair Neville and Paul Shelton, talented players and big accumulators of the footy, who became leaders to us despite having no affiliation with Richmond. Alastair was unlucky never to make it onto an AFL list, while Paul was rookie-listed by Hawthorn and the Brisbane Lions but didn't play an AFL game. I suppose Alastair was probably too small. I guess Paul was probably too slow. There are so many stories like that, of gifted footballers who could have been anything if they'd been given one extra trait, and a little opportunity.

I played pretty good footy early on in the VFL, kicking goals and celebrating by playing up to the hardy Coburg supporters sitting in the small grandstand on the wing. I concentrated on the hard stuff, too, knowing the coaches would want to see tackles and pressure and not just flamboyance and flair. After all, did I want to impress the crowd, or the coaching staff?

I wasn't backward in coming forward when it came to finding out if any of my work was being noticed. I made a habit of walking into Terry Wallace's office and asking him whether I was doing enough. Plough's office was the first one in the corner when you walked through the front door of the club, and I'd go in and ask for five minutes, sitting down to talk to him about how I could get a game. Young players don't do that much anymore. I don't know whether they just haven't got the conversation skills or the courage to go in and ask, but I encourage them to. People think of the VFL as a kind of proving ground, where you can hone your skills and under-standing of the game, until you're ready. But I think if you stay in the VFL too long, all you ever get ready for is playing good VFL footy. I don't want to see that happen to the likes of Sam Banks and Thomson Dow and Tyler Sonsie, so I nudge them to nudge the coach. I didn't so much nudge as elbow. 'What have I got to do? Why am I not playing? How do I fix this? What do I need to improve?' You can learn something from the answers to those questions, and even if you don't, you're at least developing a relationship with the most important figure at the club. You're letting him know that you want it, and you're ready for it, even if you're not.

Perhaps because of those chats with Plough, I was named as an emergency for several AFL games during the first part of the season. Each week I'd eagerly await news of who was in the team, assuming my turn was just around the corner. But it turned out that Shane Edwards, willowy and quiet, was the first draftee to debut, called up for our round-four game against the Western Bulldogs. I can clearly remember the team meeting when we found out he was playing. We cheered and hollered and high-fived, his selection giving us all permission to believe in ourselves that little bit more. We all went along to the MCG to watch Shane play, too. He looked so skinny against grown men, but he also showed flashes of what was to come – that ability to handle the pace of the game, to compute what was needed and deliver at the highest level. I wanted that, badly.

Over the next fortnight I went from thinking I was next to playing in the VFL reserves, which was as low as you could go. I hadn't done anything wrong, but the senior VFL side had a bye, and all draftees needed fitness, so we suited up for the twos. More than a few AFL-listed players were in that group, meaning we slaughtered this poor bunch of boys from Frankston. We must have won by 250 points. But that's not the main reason I remember that day.

In the evening, Richmond played Geelong at Docklands, and the Cats were under the pump. They had started the season as one of the premiership favourites, but had suffered some bad losses and their coach, Mark 'Bomber' Thompson, was on the verge of being sacked. Before the game, plenty of pundits tipped Richmond to win, but I arrived at the stadium during the first quarter, and the Tigers were already trailing by five goals. By the time I wandered into a supporters' function to do a quick Q&A with some of our members at half-time, we had conceded twenty goals and were down by 107 points. I didn't know what to say. Those early public appearances were hard enough as it was. They were often poorly run and understaffed, and we did them frequently. They could be fun, or they could be tedious, but we were an unsuccessful club – and in that position you need to raise funds, and access to players is one of the simplest routes. You begin to experience fame and recognition. You say something about the game plan and the supporters lean in as if you're sharing some profound truth. Crack a mildly funny joke and a room of 100 fans collectively piss themselves laughing. They really love you, or maybe they don't really love you, because would they love you the same, would they love you at all, if you didn't play for Richmond?

Geelong ended up winning by 157 points, a result that left Richmond winless after six rounds. The final score was 35.12 (222) to 9.11 (65). If not for our four-goal last quarter, we would have lost by the greatest margin in VFL/AFL history. The stat that summed up the game for me was Andrew Mackie's four goals . . . *from a half-back flank*. Not only did the Cats play a brilliant brand of attacking footy, they were also ruthless in defence. Cameron Ling held Brett Deledio to three disposals, and was still terrorising him in the dying seconds of the last quarter. After a period of showing promise without really delivering – not consistently, anyway – it all came together for the Cats that night. Several Cats players have admitted in recent years that if the club had sacked the beloved and admired Bomber, the success they enjoyed wouldn't have happened. Geelong wouldn't have won a premiership, they say, let alone three in five years. In hindsight, it seems a pure sliding-doors moment.

By contrast, we remained a yo-yo team throughout 2007 and 2008. On our day we could beat anyone, but if we were a fraction off we could lose by twenty goals. These dramatic fluctuations in form summed up the Terry Wallace era. Plough could coach you to beat a top-four side one day, engineering some specific game plan to counter their best, but the following week his best laid traps for the opposition were left unsprung. These days, you have your fundamentals and style and stick to them no matter who you're facing.

Some small part of me does miss the idea of the chop-and-change tactician, though. The legend of some of the greatest AFL coaches is built on their left-field moves and wily psychological operations (PSYOP). Think of Kevin Sheedy. Or Malcolm Blight. Think of Ron Barassi deciding in the middle of a game – the middle of the 1970 Grand Final, no less, in front of 121,866 people – to change tactics completely and implore his Blues to eschew long kicks and instead handball at all costs, then reeling in a forty-four-point deficit to win what was later called 'the most consequential match in history' and 'the birth of modern football'. This idea of a mastermind seeing some glitch in the matrix and exploiting it on field, bamboozling an opponent with a positional or tactical switch, is part of the romance of football. But it's also not sustainable. And for every brilliant light bulb set play, there's more than a few experiments that explode in the lab. I remember playing against Collingwood one day, and Dimma put myself and Alex Rance – the full-forward and full-back – into the midfield alongside Trent

Cotchin and Ivan Maric, while young Todd Elton stood Travis Cloke. That midfield unit must have looked like an island of misfit toys, and I'm sure some people looked on in wonder, curious and excited to see what would happen next. What happened next was Cloke kicked the first five goals, and from that moment on, I stayed up forward and Alex stayed down back. Moments of coaching genius are rare.

While our AFL team was having a horror start to the season (a loss to Port Adelaide in round seven took the team's record to 0–7), I kept thrusting my name up for selection by playing well in the VFL. I was confident that Andy Collins was pushing my case after he told *The Age* in early May that I had been in 'terrific form' and had 'become a significant leader in a young group'. He added: 'His work rate, courage and team play has been of the highest class and he has really settled and is a popular member of Coburg.' Sometimes players say they don't pay any attention to media, but it's not always true.

Accidents happen sometimes, don't they, and occasionally they have an incidental impact. So it was with my AFL debut. I had played good footy, but what truly opened the door was an unintentional kick to the head of Matthew Richardson, delivered by teammate Andrew Krakouer in a match against Adelaide. The friendly fire of Krakouer's errant leg fractured Richo's eye-socket, a nasty hit that looked as though it would sideline Richo for a few games. Straight away, on the Monday morning in the lead-up to the Dreamtime game against Essendon, I marched into Plough's office and told him I was ready. I had more front than Myer, as they say, but a couple of days later I was called back into that very room and told I was in the team. I was buzzing, and giddy.

In the middle of the week the club announced my impending debut, and I was asked to be part of the Dreamtime press conference with Plough and 'Sheeds'. It was the twenty-seventh and last season for the Bombers coach, and he remained a consummate shit stirrer. One of the journos went to ask me a question and Sheeds butted in.

'It's a scary game, Jack,' he said with a grin. 'There'll be 70,000 there. You'll be sweating before you even get to the ground.' I chuckled and waited for another question, which soon came: 'What's the largest crowd you've played in front of?' I explained that there had been a few thousand in the stands when I played in grand finals for Clarence, but that I had only ever watched one game at the MCG, a Carlton versus Collingwood clash before I was even drafted. Sheeds sensed another opening: 'Are you feeling nervous yet?'

When our team to play the Bombers was announced, Plough joked during the press conference that I had been annoying him flat out about getting a game: 'He knocks on the door four times a day and asks whether it's this week, and has even offered himself up as a ruckman to help us out there.' Yet the big surprise was not my inclusion, but that Richo would play and Jay Shulz was dropped. Richo hadn't trained at all that week. I assumed he would be a late withdrawal.

The day before the game we had a light training session, which these days is known across the AFL as the Captain's Run. After that, I was presented with my club tie. At that time, we still wore our club suits to games, not the tracksuits

63

we now wear, so getting your tie was a big deal. Down the bottom it was embroidered with the number 1072. I was going to be the 1072nd player to run out in a VFL or AFL game for the Tigers.

I spoke to my cousin Nick a few times that week. He was great at making me feel at ease, advising me to approach the game like I was a kid about to line up for the under-10s in Tassie. Nick's key piece of advice: 'Go out there and be yourself.' Pundits had already started comparing us to one another, so it was a good reminder: we're very different players, and people would understand that once they saw me in action.

On the day of the game, I was so nervous. My parents, my brothers and Carly had flown over, but I wasn't in a mood for socialising. I spent half the day watching the clock, and when the time to go to the MCG finally arrived, my heart was racing as I put on my suit and did up my tie. I must have expended so much nervous energy that afternoon, and as I walked into the rooms, one of the first players I saw was Richo. I could tell he was going to play, just by his body language. Richo was a warrior. It would take more than a fractured eye socket to keep him off the park.

'What are you going to bring?' Plough asked.

'I'm going to kick a goal,' I said, smiling, 'and get the crowd going.'

In the first minutes of the game, everything seemed to happen at light speed. People always talk about the pace of the game at the top level, and in your first taste it flashes by your eyes. I struggled to feel the tempo, get near the ball, let alone get it in my hands. I did not kick my promised goal.

I did not get the crowd going. My opponent, Richard Cole, didn't need to do much to curb my influence. Some guys find themselves so overawed that they start hoping the ball won't come to them. Thankfully I wasn't like that. In fact, I tried to take a screamer over Richo and almost held it. My confidence never really waned.

Only a small margin separated us and the Bombers all game. We trailed by seven points at quarter-time, then led by three points at half-time. At the final change, we were thirteen points up and the feeling in the huddle was strong. After eight straight losses, we were in the box seat to break our drought. And then it happened.

During the final quarter, with the game in the balance, Cameron Howat marked the ball on the wing and kicked it towards Richo and his opponent, Mal Michael, who were just outside the 50-metre arc. Michael was in the front position but misjudged the flight of the ball and ran under it. Richo put one hand in his back and one in his side, to hold him out. The ball floated over the top and Richo marked it. As he turned and ran towards our goal, the umpire blew his whistle and paid a free kick against Richo – *hands in the back* – but Richo didn't hear the whistle. He kept running, slotted a brilliant goal from near the boundary line, and punched the air as the Richmond supporters rose. The umpire stood still, and not only reaffirmed his decision to pay the free kick, but also waved for a 50-metre penalty. Richo went berserk, while I sat helpless on the bench, head in my hands.

The umpire made the right call, based on a rule change from the start of the 2007 season, but he had applied the strictest interpretation in this instance – not at all in keeping with the spirit of the game. It was cruel. Essendon managed to scramble their way to a two-point margin at the final siren, after which Matthew Lloyd kicked a goal and they won by eight.

In the rooms, the mood was desolate. The players were giving their all every week, without any positive reinforcement from the scoreboard. Getting that breakthrough win had become the be-all and end-all for the group. It's funny how differently I look at losses like that now, in a more level-headed club. We still get disappointed when we lose, but we ride these ups and downs. We know we can't win every week, and we also know that there are things to learn from any and every loss. Back in 2007, the whole atmosphere within the club would fluctuate according to how we went each week on the field. When we won, the place would be abuzz. When we lost, which was often, it was like the sky had fallen. In hindsight, I don't think the key leaders within the club focused enough on the big picture questions, like how do we build a game plan to bring sustainable, long-term success? Everything was about the short term, the sugar fix, the next win.

When I look at our team from that first game, I can't help but think it was actually a pretty good side, and that maybe those guys were victims of culture and outlook and system. Chris Newman, Joel Bowden and Nathan Foley come to mind as footballers who were failed by method and mood. They were great players and great people, and they deserved more success. Greg Tivendale is another. A speedy winger and back flank, he could kick the ball so far on this sweet left foot. I can't help but think how well he would have slotted into the 'fight forward' chaos game plan that won us our premierships in 2017, 2019 and 2020. Then, of course, there's Matthew Richardson, who played in just one winning final in his 282-game career.

Richo was an astonishing athlete. I don't know whether people outside the club ever fully understood his aerobic abilities. He was a monster on the track, and a beast in the gym. Watching him do bench presses was a spectator sport, and trying to keep up with him on a lap of the tan track was utter folly. And he tried, and tried, again and again, pouring every last bit of himself into each contest. They say he wore his heart on his sleeve, and his exasperation on his face. All I could see was effort and care. Devotion, really.

He was marked hard for that expressiveness though, just as I was later. Emotion is rarely graceful, and frustration is difficult to disguise, and both open you up to criticism. But they boil up sometimes and bubble over once in a while, and all you can hope is that people will slowly come to see where that depth of feeling springs from, and why and how you care. There was a time when the football public was split on Richo, but they love him now. His and my journeys are similar like that, benefiting from longevity and the greater understanding that brings.

I finished the game with only two kicks, two marks and three handballs, yet if we'd beaten Essendon I think I might have been given another week to prove myself. Instead we lost, and I was dropped back to the VFL. I returned there keen to impress and get promoted, and I played with confidence. It was also a stint marred by a bout of what you might call over-enthusiasm.

We played Carlton's VFL side, the Northern Bullants, at Preston City Oval, and in the first half I kicked five goals on big Irish firebrand Setanta Ó hAilpín, and we entered the main break more than ten goals up. As we walked to our rooms I said to a few boys, 'It's party time', not realising I had said it loud enough for the coaches to hear. That mightn't have been a problem if we had kept playing well in the second half, but instead we collapsed, and lost. In the rooms afterwards, Jade Rawlings started ripping into us, and pointed squarely at me: 'We've got blokes saying it's party time!!! *Well, is it party time now?!* IS IT?!!' It was the biggest spray of my whole career. I felt small. And I deserved it.

Thanks to Shane Edwards, the 'party time' story became part of club folklore. Every year, Shane would tell the draftees the same tired tale, and then often when we were leading games at half-time, he would walk past with a smile: 'Is it party time?' Then I would mutter, with hopefully a straight face: 'It is definitely *not* party time.'

I was in and out of the side that first year, finishing with eight games and seven goals to my name. But it was a stepping stone, a small dose of what was to come. I also had the good fortune to play in the 2007 VFL Grand Final with Coburg, taking on Geelong. The Cats were at their peak as a club (the AFL side would break its forty-four-year premiership drought with a record-breaking 119-point win over Port Adelaide the following week), and we were no match for them in our big game either. Tom Hawkins was there, and played well. Tom Lonergan kicked six goals and won the best-on-ground medal just a year after losing a kidney due to a collision in an AFL game. They tore us apart. We lost by seventy-four points.

I was ready to let my hair down, but any glimpse of a regular 'party time' was cut short by a major health scare. I had what's called a tricolour mole in the middle of my back. Dad and Carly were onto me about getting it checked out, and at the end of the season I showed it to our club doctor, Greg Hickey. He examined it – 'I don't like the look of that' – and sent me off to a dermatologist. They did a biopsy and it was cancerous. Funnily enough, I don't remember being that nervous, just expecting to wander in and have it cut out and move on. Everything did happen quickly, too. Almost immediately, I was at the Peter MacCallum Cancer Centre getting a large chunk of my back removed. I can remember all of it happening. They gave me a local anaesthetic, and as I lay face down I could feel the surgeons hacking away at my back, even though I couldn't feel any pain.

I was told later that the mole was 0.9 millimetres thick. The dermatologist explained that once they get to one millimetre thick you're in trouble. That's when they look at taking your lymph nodes out. Things get drastic fast. When you take all that into account, I dodged a reasonably big bullet. It wasn't due to sunburn either. (I've always been diligent about sunscreen, having fair skin.) I just got unlucky to have hereditary skin cancer, then lucky to discover it in time. Not that I comprehended my good fortune. Despite needing a skin graft to repair the wound where the melanoma was excised (there were twenty-odd stitches in my back, and there's a decent scar there to this day), I went to the races and got drunk with my mates a week after the surgery. I suppose at that age you think you're bullet-proof. These days, however, I get regular tests and check-ups, and get jumpy whenever I see any strange mark on my kids.

The end of 2007 was a big moment for Carly, too. She had worked and saved and applied for university, and being offered spots at La Trobe and Monash was to her like being drafted. And choosing one – Monash University, a Bachelor of Arts, then later a Masters in Organisational Leadership – was like her own grand final. Not many of her family had studied before, so she was understandably excited and justifiably proud. A world of newness and foreign cultures and like-minded explorers was opening up to her. It was thrilling.

She had missed the deadline for applying to live on campus though, and that had been the dream. She was devastated to miss out on that quintessential Halls-of-Residence experience and began considering her options. I asked the Daltons if she could stay with them, with me, for just a few months until she got settled. They had my interests at heart and immediately said yes, but before long we were looking for our own place to live.

I bought my first piece of real estate in early 2008 – a two-storey, two-bedroom modern townhouse in Glenhuntly Road, Caulfield South – and we moved in together, a pair of 19-year-old Tassie kids now in a big mainland city, one of us in the grand halls of higher learning and the other in the cathedral of professional sport. We muddled our way through, equal parts daunted and exhilarated by this new life.

I owe her so much from that time, too. Carly had always been more mature than me, and to be honest, probably still is. She had worked in the real world, and seen that side of things, and knew how to keep me organised. Footy can be all-consuming, especially when you're young and trying to make it in the game. At times it can make you act with extreme selfishness, whether you're going out of your way to be selfish or not. Without her, I would have gotten carried away being a hot-shot AFL player, which would not have been good for me or my football.

People speak about having mentors – these guiding figures they seek out for clarity and wisdom. They're usually older, maybe former bosses or one-time coaches, boasting age and experience and war stories. But in a balanced relationship, your partner is your greatest mentor. That's what it was like for me, anyway. Whenever I got ahead of myself, Carly would pull me back. Whenever I felt like shit, she would pick me up. We were a great team back then. We're an even greater team now.

6

STRAWBERRIES
AND CREAM

At the start of the 2008 pre-season, all Richmond players had to write a note about what we wanted to achieve in our time in the AFL. On a scrap of lined paper, torn from a notebook, I wrote this . . .

> *I, Jack Riewoldt, have the desire to captain the Richmond Football Club in the future, but I will only achieve this if I work hard and continue to respect the position I am in. Hard work, passion, want, and love of the fight – these things will get me there.*

I signed my note and dated it: 26.11.2007.

Not long after, we each had to fill out a form titled 'Becoming an Elite Player'. The form had two columns: one listed your strengths and weaknesses, and the second column was headed 'Becoming Elite in these areas'. Among the strengths I listed for myself were spirit/enthusiasm, goalkicking, lifestyle, training habits and competitiveness. My weaknesses, at least as I saw them back then, were fitness, strength/power, leading, ground balls and marking. Then finally, at the bottom of the form, I completed a section titled, 'How do you want to be remembered?'

> *I want to be remembered as the most passionate player Richmond has ever seen towards the club and his teammates, and to be remembered as a great captain.*

That summed up my approach. I was all in. The summer slog seemed to fly by and soon it was time for the pre-season competition, known then as the NAB Cup. I find it amusing to look back on how we approached our pre-season games in that era. The coaching staff took them so seriously. I suppose at that stage Richmond always seemed under pressure or under-performing or just plain underwhelming, so the theory was that any win – even a win in the middle of February – would keep the public and press off our backs for a while.

Terry Wallace was so keen to see players push their own case to play in those NAB Cup games that he awarded points for certain behaviours or feats during training. You might get points for a personal best in the three-kilometre time trial, or points for maximum effort during sprint drills. He called it 'the NAB 18', and it meant the players with the most points would be selected in our first NAB Cup game. Of course, the coaches could manipulate the whole process if they wanted to, and I'm fairly certain they did that for Brett Deledio. Lids was only twenty and already one of our best players, but he was also way off the pace only a couple of weeks before our NAB Cup opener against St Kilda at Docklands. No matter – a special week of training suddenly worth 'double points' fixed that problem. Lids ran around like a superstar, racked up a heap of points, and was picked to play. Not that it helped. The Saints rested half of their best players and still beat us by forty points.

I shake my head at that kind of approach to the pre-season games. What were we thinking? Once we became a successful club, we approached those matches like glorified training drills, used to address very specific needs. A player returning from injury can run around for a quarter one week, then two quarters the next week, building volume and load into his legs. A full-time full-back like Noah Balta can be played at full-forward, to get a taste for the role in case he's needed there during the regular season. By 2023, the practical and pragmatic approach to pre-season games was taken to its logical endpoint by the entire AFL, with opposing teams even agreeing to play out the final minutes of various quarters as if one team were ahead by a goal and the other team behind by a goal, and then the reverse, so that each club gets a chance to practise what they might do in a tight finish, first holding a lead, then chasing a lead. As you age you also learn the wisdom of pacing yourself for the long season ahead, and how getting all fired up for a bit of organised circle work is a waste of energy.

I spent the first three rounds of that year in the VFL, before I was called up for our round-four game against Fremantle at Subiaco. I loved playing on the wide expanses of Subi and managed to gather seventeen disposals and seven marks in a sixty-four-point win. The following week I kicked three goals against the Western Bulldogs, and from then on, I became a regular part of the Richmond side. My arrival as a bona fide player came later that season, again at Subiaco, against the West Coast Eagles. On a classic Sunday afternoon in Perth, we put on a clinic, kicking twelve goals in each half and winning by seventy-seven points. I made the most of some brilliant lace-out delivery to finish with five goals. I still looked like a schoolboy playing against men, but my nous and guile were starting to shine through. Defenders began putting a lot more time into me after that game.

I could be my own worst enemy in those early years, too, including holding on to a set of bizarre superstitions. When I was playing for the Tassie Devils, for instance, one of my team-mates, Brett Geappen, swore by his habit of eating a whole bag of Strawberries and Cream lollies the night before a game. I did it once and played well, so that was that. I simply had to do it every week – in exactly the same way. For example, if I found out someone else had eaten one of the lollies from the bag, I couldn't handle it, so I would have to go and buy another bag and start again. That was all there was to it. I couldn't – and wouldn't – tempt fate when it came to the footy gods.

Other superstitions came and went. I might have had lasagne before a game and then played well, so I'd suddenly want to have that same meal before every game. One time a drink became my superstition *du jour*. Josh Gibson played with me at the Tassie Devils when he was on North Melbourne's list, before he moved to Hawthorn, became a superstar and played in three premierships. And he told me once that he would drink half-a-dozen bottles of Gatorade the night before a game. That became my gospel. I had to do the same thing, because clearly that's what it would take to make it in the AFL. But the first time I sucked down that much sugar in an evening I wound up wired and jittery, and never did it again.

I had other habits that took up more time and mental energy than they should have. I hated wearing long socks – didn't like wearing them pulled up to the knee, nor pushing them down into a scrunched bundle above my ankle – so I used to cut my socks down. I wasn't the only one. The AFL took notice and started fining players for doing so. Nathan Brown was one of the first caught and penalised. But I was smarter than him. I took my socks to a seamstress and got her to remove a few of the yellow and black hoops from the middle of each sock. Once the remaining pieces were sewn back together, the top part of the sock – carrying that all-important AFL logo – looked untouched, and I escaped any sanction.

As a team, we seemed to be turning a corner, too. Matthew Richardson was playing amazing football on a wing, and we won eight of our last eleven games, including a twenty-nine-point win over Hawthorn, the team that would go on and win the premiership. We beat Melbourne in the last round by eighty points, but it wasn't enough to elevate us into the finals. For the umpteenth time in Richmond's recent history, we finished ninth on the ladder, only half a win behind eighth-placed Collingwood. Richo's run of form was so good that he almost won the Brownlow Medal, finishing equal-third with Geelong superstar Gary Ablett on twenty-two votes, just two behind Western Bulldogs midfielder Adam Cooney. Richo was thirty-three at the time, and pretty much the entire football world wanted him to win. His career is one that any player would dream of having, and yet it's sad that he didn't play more football roaming higher up the ground, wreaking havoc with his unparalleled mix of size and strength, speed and stamina, and skill. He's one of the great key forwards, but it's frightening to imagine what he could have done if he'd been set free to run where he pleased. There was a dark period during that upswing in the season, too. It was late June when Graham Polak – a regular in our AFL team who'd finished in the top ten in our best and fairest the year before – went out for some drinks with a few of the boys. He started to cross Dandenong Road to catch a taxi and was struck by a tram. He spent time in an induced coma and was very lucky not only to survive but to escape serious brain injury. The incident was a wake-up call. None of us was bulletproof. Graham made a remarkable recovery and managed to play five more AFL games, but he was never the same dynamic player. Life takes cruel turns sometimes.

Considering that moment now, fifteen years later, it's interesting how much the world has changed. We went to recovery the next day, and I remember sitting in the physio room at Punt Road with a group of the younger players. We'd all heard that a Richmond player had been hit by a tram, but we didn't know who, or if they were okay or in critical danger. We were trying to piece it all together by texting one another and through a process of elimination. Today, the club would communicate with us swiftly, but even without that everyone would know – WhatsApp would solve the equation. There are so many different Richmond Football Club groups through WhatsApp, from 'Thailand 2022' to 'NBA Sweep' to

'The Richmond Major' (for organising our players' golf tournament). There are groups for various lines, and the football department as a whole, and the leadership group and a players-only group, and one for every premiership reunion. Right now, I'm in fifteen different WhatsApp conversations – if someone at the club were hurt overnight, I'd know about it almost immediately.

Amid all the good and bad swings, little could have prepared me for the way the club became the centre of the footballing universe during the 2009 pre-season. What am I referring to? The one and only Ben Cousins. Ben had endured a torrid time since playing in West Coast's 2006 premiership. He'd battled substance-abuse problems and spent time in rehab in the USA. The Eagles had eventually terminated his contract, before the AFL suspended him for twelve months for bringing the game into disrepute. AFL chief executive at the time, Andrew Demetriou, said it would be very difficult for Ben to return to the game's highest level. By late 2008, however, his suspension was finished and the pre-season draft was around the corner. Stories emerged with whispers about the handful of clubs considering taking a punt on him. Richmond kept coming up, as did Collingwood, St Kilda and the Brisbane Lions.

The day before the pre-season draft, Plough got the whole group together and told us that despite the media frenzy surrounding Cousins, we would *not* be selecting him. Twelve hours later, however, we did exactly that. I still don't know what changed, but it wasn't a particularly divisive issue. I'm sure some players thought selecting him was a bad idea, assuming Ben was a bad egg who could harm the club's culture and violate any unspoken 'no dickheads' policy. A few of the staff probably had similar thoughts. I'm sure the media department was nervous.

Broadly speaking, on Ben, the players were divided along age lines. The younger guys were just happy being in the AFL system and weren't thinking too deeply about the art and alchemy of list management. Some of the older guys no doubt pushed hard to grab Ben, thinking the leaders could set him on the straight and narrow, so he could help us play finals for the first time since 2001. Our flurry of wins had created an off-season of fanciful belief in anything, perhaps a top-four spot, and with Ben at his best, maybe even a flag.

Football teams invariably contain the full spectrum of personalities. You get the wildest of men – and those suited to accounting. You get loners and rogues, carers and bullies, sinners and saints. Ben was largely an enigma. We knew him from afar as one of the great midfielders – a Brownlow medallist, captain and premiership star – who'd suffered a drug-addled downfall – and that entire circus came with him to town. With that kind of profile, you might imagine someone sidling into a new space with his tail between his legs, embodying caution, even trepidation. But while Ben was certainly private, he would just as readily throw himself into the group. He was funny and bubbly and charming, and so accepting of all. He was giving of himself, too, particularly for the sake of the younger players. There were no airs or graces, and no instances where ego took over. It was easy to see why he'd been regarded as such a talismanic and charismatic leader. You could see why people were attracted to him.

Thousands of people turned up to see Ben's first training run with the team. He and Richo ran laps together and the crowd went crazy. I didn't yet know what pre-finals training sessions were like, but when I look back now, this was almost as big as some of our pre-grand-final sessions in 2017, 2019 and 2020. The TV stations had their choppers hovering above Punt Road Oval getting vision of the whole spectacle. The phones were ringing off the hook, too, our membership rising from 30,000 to 37,000 seemingly overnight.

All that excitement and expectation continued to build right up to our Thursday night season opener against Carlton on March 26. In the Terry Wallace era, there was always such a huge and unhealthy build-up to the start of the season. Inside the club, the mantra was that we needed to start well. There was just so much – too much – emphasis placed on one game against one team.

The fans were so excited that almost 90,000 people turned up to see Ben's first home-and-away game in yellow and black, and his first match at the MCG since the 2006 Grand Final, in which he helped the Eagles defeat the Swans. Just twelve seconds into the game, Ben had his hands on the ball, the crowd roaring as he dished off a handball to Daniel Jackson at half-back. A few seconds later, Andrew Raines booted a long drop punt inside our forward line and Richo, who'd started on the wing, steamed past me and my Carlton opponent, Bret Thornton, and took a chest mark. The noise was deafening. Richo's shot, from about forty metres out on a forty-five-degree angle, hit the post. The Tiger fans in the crowd let out a huge sigh, and as strange as it sounds, our season completely went to shit in that moment. By quarter-time, we were five goals down. By three-quarter-time, we were ten goals down. Ben tore his hamstring in the last quarter, and by the time the final siren sounded the margin was eighty-three points.

We ended up losing our first four games, then in round six Matthew Richardson tore his hamstring off the bone – not long after kicking what would prove to be the 800th and last goal of his brilliant career. It was a sad end. Richo would officially retire in November, having played 282 games. Only three of those games were finals and of those finals, the Tigers won just one of them.

Richo didn't get a retirement speech. There had been talk, right up to the very end, about him potentially playing on, even into the new season, and then that talk was suddenly over, and he was suddenly gone. Out. Finished. That happens sometimes. Darren Gaspar was dropped a month or so into my first season and, feeling insulted, was annoyed or angry with Plough. He didn't want to go back to Coburg, and so he was done. *Thanks, but no thanks.* And no speech either, just as there were no long, tearful and taped goodbyes for Joel Bowden or Nathan Brown.

We do those partings better now – making sure those players who've given so much of themselves receive a fitting send-off. Maybe we do that these days only because so many of these guys – Shaun Grigg, Dave Astbury, Shane Edwards, Jason Castagna – have played in flags. I hope that's not the only reason. A person who's handed all their effort and heart to the club deserves a farewell, whether they held a premiership cup or not. But a combination of timing and circumstance can mean there's often no right moment to celebrate the end. Ivan Maric did as much to change the culture at Richmond as any player, but his last game for the club was a losing VFL Grand Final at Marvel Stadium. He was trying to play senior football right up until the end, which came for him in the change rooms there, sitting in a concrete basement with a doctor threading stitches into his eyebrow. Not everybody gets the happy ending they deserve.

Still, Ivan has an important development role at the club now, scaffolding our young players and training our rucks. He remains firmly stitched into the fabric he helped weave. And while Richo's departure left a void on-field, he too has stayed in the fold, working in club media. His identity is rightly hand-cuffed to Richmond. The footage of him crying when we won the flag in 2017, and the audio as well when they crossed to him over the boundary line, sobbing with happiness, showed how he's still the heart and soul of Richmond.

He wasn't the only person in the footy department to finish up that year. Our win–loss record slumped to 1–8, and it was clear within the playing group that Terry Wallace wasn't going to survive as coach. We staggered past Fremantle by three points at Subiaco Oval, but it was too little too late to save his job. Plough's resignation was announced on June 1, and he coached us for the last time that Friday night, against his old side, the Western Bulldogs. We lost by sixty-eight points.

Despite what I said about the shortcomings of his coaching – our lack of any brand or style, and that tendency to play a reactive game – I was sad to see him lose his job. As a young player who had never been through something like that before, I felt as though everyone involved in the club had failed, and that we were all being judged. Terry was a great salesman. In the lead-up to every season he was able to convince us that we were close to being a top side. He gave us – the young players, in particular – belief that if we just tidied up a few things in the way we played, we'd be fine. But the key issues were never addressed. Our preparation wasn't methodical. Our opposition scouting was amateurish. We became accustomed to losing, to going on holiday in September. They used to have the AFL Live site on Punt Road Oval, so we'd be finishing up for the season just as they began laying out the plastic flooring for events to celebrate the pinnacle of the sport, and you just got used to that. It's such a hard cycle to break. With the benefit of hindsight, I can see that the change most definitely needed to happen, and I'm not left wondering why or how but rather how he lasted that long.

After Terry departed, Jade Rawlings took over as caretaker coach, and that freshened up the place. I liked playing under Jade, and had a great relationship with him, going back to those days in Tasmania. I don't think it's right to describe a caretaker coach as having a free swing, but that's often how the commentariat sees things. There's always pressure on AFL coaches, even if they expect to be in the role for only a few weeks, because those weeks can have a huge influence on where their career goes next – or whether it goes anywhere at all.

To Jade's credit, he coached in an unselfish way, trying players in different positions, giving the younger boys a chance in the seniors. He wasn't sacrificing our future to win games and lift his prospects of a senior coaching appointment, but instead uncovering potential gems for the next coach to polish. One of those young players was Tyrone Vickery, who would play alongside me in the forward line for years to come. Ty debuted in Jade's first game, which was against West Coast on a Saturday night at Docklands. He kicked a goal and we won by fifteen points. (Mitch Morton, the ultimate footballing journeyman, kicked five goals, and later ended up at the Sydney Swans, playing in their 2012 premiership.)

Jade was the first person to introduce us to the idea of professional football clubs as social spaces for people other than players. When Plough was in charge, I remember that Carly felt as though she'd never been inside the club, except for occasional, fleeting access to the changerooms on gameday. Jade was more modern in his approach, providing that pastoral care and bringing families into the fold. One of the first things he did in charge of the group was a mystery tour, in which players and partners came to Punt Road, then jumped on a bus that took us around Melbourne on a little pub tour, with a hypnotist in tow for entertainment. It was a little thing but made a big difference.

The low point of Jade's coaching tenure was the match against Collingwood in round twenty, which was marred by an ugly brawl that was started by some of our players. We lost the game by ninety-three points, but we won the fight. Jake King belted Alan Didak into next week. Joel Bowden tried to grab the ball and play on while everyone else was throwing punches. In hindsight, it was a little embarrassing. In our last four games of that season, we were beaten by an average of eleven goals and finished second-last on the ladder. The form of Brett Deledio was one of the few high points. He copped a bake halfway through the season for running around and doing his own thing. But he played some scintillating football in the second half of the season and won our best and fairest for the second successive year – an amazing effort given he was only twenty-two.

A final ray of sunshine was seeing Ben Cousins recover from his hamstring injury. The excitement around his arrival had well and truly dissipated by the time he returned for our round-seven game against the Brisbane Lions at the MCG. But he had twenty-two disposals and kicked a goal that afternoon, and he continued playing good footy thereafter. People forget, but the top five in our best and fairest that season were Deledio, Dan Jackson, Chris Newman, Richard Tambling . . . and Ben Cousins.

Ben stayed on for the 2010 season as well, for a total of thirty-two games in yellow and black, and still stays in touch with some of the boys who were at the club at the time. I got a call from him after he was released from jail in 2018. He wanted to say hi and tell me he was enjoying the way I was playing the game, and how the team was going. It's nice when someone reaches out, nice to know you made a sufficient impression to be contacted out of the blue.

Ultimately, I'm glad Ben was brought to the club. I think it showed that footy has a compassionate side – that the game is prepared to give people a second chance – even if society isn't always so generous. Life is complicated, and people are, too. Looking at someone like Ben helps you understand those complications, and maybe avoid them yourself. He wasn't a teacher, but I learned from him all the same.

7

JEKYLL AND HYDE

No one knew it at the time, but before the 2010 season had even begun, the building blocks of a long-term club revival had been laid.

The first key appointment was that of Brendon 'Benny' Gale as chief executive in August 2009. He and I bonded immediately over our state of origin. Tasmanians are automatically attracted to fellow Tasmanians, which sounds ridiculous – even mildly incestuous – but when you meet someone else from the least-populous state in the country (an entire island mass with only slightly more people than Canberra), there's a kind of recognition, rather like that nod you give to someone you know when you cross paths in the hallway. It's a tip of the hat – a sense of seeing someone for more than who they are but where they're from, and what made them. And Benny wasn't a complete stranger, either. I knew him through his previous role at the AFL Players' Association, and the wider football world knew him as an erudite operator – clever and measured.

He's tall, too, and that stood out. Sometimes tall people just convey a presence, as if they understand the world that little bit better, because they can see it all from their high vantage point. He's a big man, the Chief, and he had a big vision.

The second key appointment, which came three weeks later, was that of Damien Hardwick as our new senior coach. In winning the position he'd beaten a field of candidates that included Ken Hinkley, Alan Richardson, Mark Neeld and Kevin Sheedy. None of the players knew much about 'Dimma' before he arrived. I certainly didn't. I knew that he'd won a couple of premierships as a player and I had some memory of those Grand Finals for Essendon and Port Adelaide. I knew his style on the field was aggressive, even antagonistic, that body-on-body was his metier. But the way a footballer plays so often doesn't reflect their personality off the park. He had worked in banks, or maybe as an accountant. Would he bring sober, numeric precision to his work – or white line fever? Maybe both? Our first meeting was in the old Graeme Richmond Room at the club, and his harder edge was there from the start.

There was one other crucial piece of recruiting done in late 2009, of course. Thanks to our terrible season we had pick three in the national draft, and our list managers used this to select Dustin Martin. Although Dustin had been a star with the Bendigo Pioneers in the TAC Cup in 2009 and had been named in the All-Australian team after playing for Vic Country in the national under-18 championships, he was still seen as a somewhat risky choice. He wasn't the finest endurance athlete, but more strikingly he was far, far removed from the usual private-school scholarship boys that clubs love taking at the pointy end of the draft – the ones with polish and poise. Dusty was polite, but his hair was spiky and defiant, almost punk. He was quiet, too, almost inscrutable, and gave outsiders a kind of 'Don't argue' with his eyes – that trademark flat stare into the middle distance was already perfected.

It was also obvious he would require support and scaffolding. Dustin did an early photo shoot at Punt Road, for instance, and the media were trying on whatever they could with the brash young recruit, asking him to lift his shirt so they could take pictures of the 'Live free, Die free' tattoo on his midriff. Our media manager at the time – a former high-powered lobbyist and now AFL executive, Jude Donnelly – was having none of it, tearing out onto the oval to give the snappers with their cameras a vicious spray. We knew immediately that Dusty would be the kind of player to draw outsized attention just from his aura and presence, but when we first saw him moving on the track – composed and skilful, balanced and powerful – the nature of his inevitable celebrity was clear: he was going to be a star.

When we started our first pre-season under Damien, I'm pretty sure I wasn't the only player fearing the new coach was going to smash us. I used to worry a lot about pre-season. The running. The heat. The sun. The sweat. And my greatest fear was that he would put us through a brutal pre-season as a way of showing us who was boss. Dimma had spent the previous couple of years working as an assistant coach at Hawthorn and we had no doubt he had learned a lot from Hawks boss Alastair Clarkson. Clarkson was a very aggressive player who became a very aggressive coach, and we knew Dimma was cut from the same cloth.

Having taken on a playing group that really didn't stand for anything, Dimma took charge straight away. He was a bit like a drill sergeant and had an instant impact. There was suddenly a lot more urgency about the way we trained, but he wasn't out to train us into the ground as part of some kind of ego trip. He simply wanted us to start developing the elite habits and mentality that he had seen in the great teams he had played for and coached. There were no surprises – he had outlined his approach in his first press conference.

'Every club I've gone to has had a great "team-first" culture, and that's something I believe very strongly in,' he said. 'I know it's easy to say, but it's not easy to deliver. I think I can deliver a blueprint for success that's going to take the Richmond Football Club to their eleventh premiership in the not-too-distant future.'

He made his intentions clearer at a club function.

'I look back with envy at the Hafey era, the period between 1967 and '74, and the four premierships that go with it – the most successful era of this club. Ruthless, relentless and, most importantly, uncompromising. These are the words used to describe those great teams. The sooner these words become associated with our current group, the closer we will be to that elusive eleventh premiership.'

His competitive fire was obvious, and he won me over immediately. I also liked that his door was always open, and I was more than happy to walk through it every couple of days to chat about how we were going to play as a team, as well as how he wanted me to play. He seemed to enjoy the chats, and we developed a great working relationship right away. The things he would eventually become famous for – dad jokes and elaborate storytelling – came out quickly, too.

We did a pre-season camp competition in the style of *The Amazing Race* down at Wye River in early 2010, and Dimma was in his element. He had us competing in all sorts of challenges – groups riding mountain bikes in the hills, splashing out into a dangerous ocean swell on paddleboards, assembling IKEA tables, and finishing at the pub in Lorne where twenty beers would be lined up for each team to skol. Dimma likes testing people, throwing them into uncomfortable situations, but always returning everyone to the fold, like family. On the last night of camp we had a big party, and this young side with a young coach and young assistants all tied one on together. It's not so common to get carried away like that today, but it was necessary and right for this group to connect at the outset. And Dimma was in the centre of it all, laughing and telling jokes. He was clearly a coach we could all fall in behind.

Something similar was unfolding in club administration, where Brendon Gale was embarking on his own revolution. In early March, on the eve of the home-and-away season, the players, coaches, staff and board members gathered in our gym to be presented with Brendon's ten-year plan. It was titled 'Winning Together', and it was extraordinarily bold. In the first five years we were aiming to make the finals three times, clear the club's multi-million-dollar debt and sign up 75,000 members. In the following five years, the aim was to win three premierships and boost our membership to 100,000.

'Together, our entire club is motivated by the vision of our future in 2020,' he told the dozens of players and staff gathered in the auditorium. 'It's a vision of greatness and leadership that we describe as THE POWER and THE GLORY. By 2020, we aspire to have won our thirteenth premiership; consistently provide the most exciting and powerful match-day experience in the competition; once again have the strongest support base in the nation; and enjoy the strongest emotional connection with our members and fans.'

Many people, particularly those in the media, openly mocked Brendon's plan. After all, a club that hadn't made the finals for the best part of a decade was aiming to win three premierships in the next ten years. When he went on *Footy Classified* on Channel 9 to sell his ambition, Garry Lyon and Caroline Wilson were dismissive, but he remained resolute. With the modern-day marvel of social media, I've seen that clip pop up again and again, and it's fair to say it puts a smile on my face every time.

'It starts with a vision,' he said. 'We're not here just to compete. We have a vision to compete and to be the best – the best on the field, the best off the field. If we're not – *if we're not locked into that* – then we may as well pack up and go home.'

We certainly weren't going to be competing for a premiership in 2010, but I was confident that we could be competitive. It didn't feel as though we were starting from scratch, yet it soon became clear that we were doing exactly that. We had lost so much experience from our list in 2009, with Nathan Brown, Matthew Richardson and Joel Bowden all departing. Dimma's brief was to play the kids, so that's what he did, and as a result we lost our first nine games under him, thrashed in most of them.

Guys like Brett Deledio, Troy Simmonds and Chris Newman, who had been our captain since the start of the 2009 season, had to carry so much of the load, and it was tough on them. We were not unlike Gold Coast or Greater Western Sydney in their early years – a handful of high-end draft picks, a smattering of experience, and a bunch of kids in between – lining up against hardened sides like Geelong, St Kilda and the Sydney Swans. A Facebook group was started called 'I hate it when I'm kicking the footy around and Richmond try to recruit me', which quickly gained more than 50,000 members. Halfway through the season, some smart-arse bookies began paying out on bets that Richmond would finish with the wooden spoon. We were – everyone said – the worst team since the dying days of Fitzroy.

But in round eight, we'd gone within a whisker of beating Hawthorn. The Hawks had crashed back to earth since their 2008 premiership, missing the finals in 2009 and now sitting near the bottom of the ladder with a 1–6 win–loss record. Their president, Jeff Kennett, was on the verge of sacking their coach, Alastair Clarkson. Little separated us all afternoon, but when Cyril Rioli kicked a goal for Hawthorn twenty-three minutes into the last quarter, handing the Hawks a fifteen-point lead, it looked like we were dead and buried. Matt White kicked a goal for us to make things interesting, then I kicked one. With about a minute remaining, we were only three points down.

We rushed the ball forward, then the Hawks repelled our attack with a long kick towards the wing. Hawthorn midfielder

Sam Mitchell looked set to take the mark, only to have the ball punched away by my gutsy teammate, the late Shane Tuck. The ball hit the deck, then bounced up into Tucky's arms. He grabbed it and ran inside the 50-metre arc, with Mitchell in pursuit. As Tucky shaped to kick, Mitchell dived forward and dragged him to the ground, winning a free kick for holding the ball. As Dwayne Russell described it on the broadcast, it was a game-saving tackle. A number of Hawthorn people have since clarified that it was a coach-saving tackle. Clarkson survived, the Hawks turned their form around and made the finals, and in the coming years Clarkson led them to another three premierships.

Two weeks later, we finally broke our drought when we defeated Port Adelaide in torrential rain in Adelaide. Only 16,000 fans were there to see it, but it was a win I'll remember for the rest of my life. Ben Griffiths was making his AFL debut and Richmond legend Kevin Bartlett came to Adelaide to present Griffo with his jumper. We had to cut our warm-up in half because 'KB' went on and on and on. And the whole long story – about how he had met and talked with Ben's family – was completely fabricated. It poured rain throughout the game, and we loved every minute. The spirit and camaraderie that Dimma had been working so hard to create was finally on show. We worked for one another, and saw reward for that effort, winning by forty-seven points and holding the Power to just three goals on their home ground.

We were sodden and smiling as we entered the rooms, and we sang the song so bloody loud, with so many players in the centre of the circle for the first win. I started a little tradition of my own that day, too. As the sound of 'Oh we're from Tigerland' echoed around the room, we got to a point in the song where there's a little pause – immediately after 'We never weaken 'til the final siren's gone' – and I got carried away. I punched my fist in the air and screamed 'Go you Tigers!', and I must have liked the way that sounded – like a personal exclamation mark – because I did it every time we won from that game onwards until 2017. I can't say exactly why I stopped when I did. I read something on social media once – an accusation that it was selfish, somehow making a celebration of team success all about me – but ultimately it just felt right to let it go and for me to recede into the group.

From there, we were consistently competitive as a team, even winning four games in succession between rounds twelve and fifteen. I found myself in the middle of a hot streak of form – so hot that I ended up winning the Coleman Medal for the AFL's leading goalkicker. How do you do that in a team that wins just six games? I think it was a perfect storm. I started believing in myself a lot more. I had played enough footy at the highest level to start feeling comfortable (I played my fiftieth game in round four). It was sad to see Matthew Richardson retire, but his departure gave me a lot more opportunity in the forward line. People looked for me more often – and they found me waiting. Half-a-dozen times that year I kicked the first goal of the game, which always gives you confidence. That habit started in pre-season intra-club scratch matches in Craigieburn, when I did it three times.

It's hard to explain why that's such an advantage for a key forward. The commentators will simplify it by spouting some cliche like 'it gets you up and about' and gives you confidence in your kicking, but a better way to think about it is in terms of direct competition. Most players walk onto the field and have an opponent they're trying to defeat or overcome. As the full-forward, the moment you kick that first goal, it puts the full-back you're standing next to on his back foot. Suddenly you're in front and he's behind, and because he knows this, you're almost playing with house money. If you're young, and up against someone who's older and better, it can make them doubt themselves, too, even just that little bit. And there's almost no equivalent for them, either. If they outpoint you in the next contest with a spoil or mark, it doesn't have the same impact. They're *still* behind you. Intercepts are valuable, but nowhere near as valuable as goals. It's also good for the team, because when you kick a goal as the centrepiece of the offence, everyone feels as though they have something to aim for, as if the game plan is working as it should. I love that feeling. I'm lucky enough to have enjoyed it often, too. I've actually kicked the first goal of the game more often than any other player in AFL history. To be honest, it's probably just luck.

One of the most enjoyable examples came on a Sunday afternoon at the MCG, in our round-twelve match against West Coast. More than 30,000 people turned up to the early match, even though we'd recorded only one win for the season so far. The sun was shining, and I was skipping on air, kicking the opening four goals of the game. It was like a dream. The boys kept kicking the ball my way and I kept marking it. They weren't all lace-out passes that allowed me to take the ball in the clear. There were a few occasions where my opponent, which for most of the game was Will Schofield, was right there with me. But I kept thrusting my hands at the ball and it just kept sticking in my fingers, again and again.

I went into the last quarter with seven goals to my name, and the ball continued coming my way. I crumbed off a pack and dribbled one through at the ten-minute mark, then got a free kick close to goal at the twenty-minute mark. With only a couple of minutes left in the game, Shane Tuck launched a long bomb into our forward line. I found myself in a wrestle with Schofield, pushed off him at the last moment and marked on my chest while tumbling backwards. I was in the right forward pocket – the wrong side for a right footer – but crept out a little to open up the angle. The Sherrin hit my boot perfectly, and the drop punt sailed straight through for goal number ten. It was incredible.

As the umpire prepared to bounce the ball back in the middle of the ground, our runner came out to me. 'Dimma doesn't want you doing any interviews post-game,' he said. 'It's got to be all about the team.'

I was stunned, and a little frustrated, too, but when the siren sounded and a microphone was put in front of me, I told them I didn't want to talk (on coach's orders). I still struggle to believe that happened. I had played the game of my life. It was the first time in a long time that anyone had kicked ten goals in a game. In what had been mostly a dark season, it felt petty not to celebrate something so rare and positive. But I came to understand Dimma's reasoning in that instance, too. He wanted to protect me – from fame and adulation and the kind of attention the spotlight can bring. He was also starting out

as a senior coach, and for a competitive beast like him everything – simply *everything* – had to be about the team.

I finished the season with seventy-eight goals and thirty-
nine behinds in a team that won six games and lost sixteen. The
next-best goalkicker at Richmond that year was Andy Collins
with fifteen. Funnily enough, I never kicked that many goals in
a season again. And that was a good thing. No successful teams
in modern football are overly reliant on a lone key forward.
Still, I received plaudits for my efforts in 2010, and those things
count, too. People will tell you that they don't play the game
for individual awards but rather for premierships, and that's
certainly true. But to imply that it doesn't matter when you
win your first AFL best and fairest (as I did that year) or that
you shouldn't be proud of being named at full-forward in the
All-Australian team for the first time (as I was then) would be
foolish and wrong. We play the game to play it well – *to be our
best, or the very best* – and to enjoy it when we do.

Change is the one constant within football clubs. We might
think of teams as largely homogenous groups, but their
make-up and structure are so different year on year. More
than a handful of players are delisted or traded or retired each
off-season, so teams are then topped up with new recruits and
draftees and rookies. It happens again and again, and again
and again, to the point that a few seasons go by and the list
becomes largely unrecognisable.

In Damien's second season in charge, Andy Collins
departed, traded to Carlton. It was sad to see him go. He was

one of the guys to whom I was closest in those early years. I'll never forget the day he was flattened by Lewis Roberts-Thomson late in a 2010 game against the Swans; his response was to dust himself off, kick two late goals and get us over the line by four points. I still hear from Andy every now and then. He went back to his family farm near Bridgewater after leaving Carlton and coached his local club to a few flags.

I was great mates with Andy, but I also became great mates with the man we brought in as part of that trade: Shaun Grigg. It would take a few years for his potential as a player and a leader to be realised, but Shaun was one of the main reasons we became so successful later. As was another player we brought into the club during that period – Bachar Houli, who we were lucky enough to lure from the Bombers and pick up in the pre-season draft. I had gone to Dockland in 2008 to watch him debut against North Melbourne, and been thrilled to watch him run and dominate on his left foot from the beginning. It was great to have his run and carry and skill on our side.

I was added to the Richmond leadership group during that off-season, too, standing alongside our captain, Chris Newman, as well as Nathan Foley, Daniel Jackson and Brett Deledio. Trent Cotchin and I – at twenty and twenty-two respectively – were the youngest members of the group. We were voted in by our peers, and yet I still don't know that we had the best process for determining our leaders. I suspect, for instance, that I was voted in primarily for being a good player, and I'm not convinced that's the right criterion. At other clubs, the leaders are determined by senior staff, as when the late Phil Walsh chose Tex Walker to lead the Crows: *You've got the qualities, you're the captain.*

I was proud, but I also don't think I understood the responsibility – not that the responsibility then was what it is now. Back then, we worried about trivial shit rather than the things that mattered, concerning ourselves with people being late to meetings, or early to leave sessions, and we would micro-manage accordingly. When you're young, you think leadership means 'Do as I say', and you think it's more important to punish than teach. Someone would be late to a meeting, and he – as well as the jumpers standing either side of him – would be in for a 5am beach session. Someone would break curfew, and it would mean a 5am beach session for everyone. And then, before you know it, you're waking up in the middle of the night, and driving to Kerferd Road in Port Melbourne, and you're wading into the water in darkness, and you're swimming out to the jet-ski poles in Port Phillip Bay, and you're getting scratched to smithereens by barnacles on the buoys, and you feel like you're swimming back to shore leaving a blood-trail chum-line behind you for the Port Phillip Bay sharks to follow.

Curfew is a great example of how things have changed. We just don't have one anymore. We're adults, and treated as such, guided by a club maxim: *Wide paddocks, strong fences.* The boundaries are vast, but they do exist, and you're trusted not to cross them.

There weren't too many infractions or incidents to manage anyway, certainly not compared to what was going on in the wider football world. The destructive Ricky Nixon saga was in full swing. He had been my manager since I was drafted – I'd joined his Flying Start agency mainly because my cousin Nick was a client – and he was exceptional at his job before his life turned. Flying Start was considered as good a management company as there was, and Nixon a trailblazer in the field. At his highest point, the roster of players he represented was immense. I could list dozens, but naming three – Wayne Carey, Tony Lockett, Gary Ablett Sr – is enough to give you the idea. A day or so before the scandal erupted, I was part of a briefing of clients in Ricky's Docklands office.

'Something's going to come out about me,' he said. 'I just want you to know it's completely not true.'

I was young, and naïve, so I took what he said at face value and moved on. I certainly didn't sense the oncoming media storm, nor did I expect the allegations and rumours to be backed up with tawdry video evidence of my middle-aged manager in his boxer shorts on a hotel-room bed with a young woman. When the dust finally settled, Ricky Nixon was banned from being a player agent for two years for bringing the game into disrepute. The AFL did the right thing by ousting him from football. Ricky had been great at player management and contract negotiations, and was ahead of the curve when interpreting the salary cap and collective bargaining agreements. I respected his business sense and entrepreneurialism. But his personal life had gone off the rails. His judgement was faltering. His decisions were poor. And affected by addictions, he came crashing down.

I did, too, albeit in a completely different setting. Early in the new season we played St Kilda on a Friday night at the

MCG, and something happened that would be replayed again and again for the remainder of my career.

Early in the first quarter I tried to take a screamer but fell backwards and smacked my head on the ground. When I came to, I was struck by the MCG lights – how incredibly bright they seemed, how it was as if I had woken up in bed with those towers beaming down at me and a crowd of thousands writhing around the edges. I had to be carried off and ushered down to our underground rooms by two members of our medical staff. The knock left me confused but also agitated – two common symptoms of concussion. The doctor knew I was in no state to rejoin play, but I argued with him anyway: I thought I was fine to go back out there. With only a few seconds left in the first quarter, I decided to take matters into my own hands, and began crawling up the stairs to the oval, a scene captured by the Channel 7 cameras.

That moment has become part of a kind of running AFL blooper reel, but the seriousness of it isn't lost on me. I had no idea what I was doing. And after finally getting all the way up the stairs, I walked to the interchange bench and sat down, and what most people didn't see then was my continued agitation and annoyance. I started demanding to go back on the ground. The bench refused. Irritable and irrational, I began what can only be called a tantrum, to the point where the medical staff had to take me back down into the rooms again. The doctors eventually calmed me down, and I accepted that I was out of the game. I sat reasonably quietly on the bench for the second half, and the game finished in a draw.

Concussion is scary like that. It can turn you into someone else. Footage of those moments is not something to be replayed for comic relief. I remember when Alex Rance was concussed one day while I was sitting on the bench. His face was caved in by Troy Selwood right in front of me, and I'll never forget the sound of that crunch, or the way he was completely unresponsive a moment later. It was sickening. Or I think of my cousin Nick. He was once knocked out in a head-to-head collision in Adelaide. When he finally awoke, in hospital, his mind was so jarred that he forgot that his sister Maddie had died. Imagine being brained so heavily and hard that you don't remember the greatest personal loss of your life.

Yet, like the entire AFL at the time, I probably didn't take concussion seriously enough. The science was – and still is – evolving, to the point that it's difficult to know exactly what you should be doing to stay safe. I played the following week – which I wouldn't be allowed to do now – and I remember it distinctly because I was fined for giving the middle finger to the Hawthorn bench.

I'd never done anything like that before, and I'll never know if that was my natural reaction to the moment or a lingering side effect of an injury that required further rest.

My actions on the bench, however, weren't taken as an understandable reaction to a heavy blow, but instead as antics, or theatrics, or hysterics, or something in between. I was given my first big whack from a media pundit – former Carlton great Robert Walls.

'Wallsy' had a weekly column in *The Age*, which he wielded as a weapon, using it to smash players and clubs that he thought were underperforming. He didn't seem to do any research prior to writing his thoughts – he didn't call club insiders for background information or quote detailed statistical data. He just wrote from off the top of his head, or from his gut. It felt as though he would just grab that metaphorical rocket launcher and blow a player or club to bits. The column appeared in the Friday edition of the paper, so it often focused on someone who was playing in the Friday night game. In round four, we played Collingwood on a Friday night at the MCG, and Wallsy decided that I needed a clip. His article, which carried the headline 'Tigers' Jekyll and Hyde?', argued that I'd become 'an individual in a team sport'.

'Sadly, but understandably,' he wrote, 'if a footy fan's team is not winning but his full-forward is kicking goals, too much attention can go to that individual. Sometimes, a monster can be created. That is the dilemma the Tigers find themselves in with Jack Riewoldt.'

Now I was a monster? I didn't really care what people like Robert thought of me personally, but I was disappointed in the article all the same. Mainly because it seemed to me just another negative missive from that group of grizzled old men who seemed to be the key commentators within radio and TV and newsprint at the time. Walls was probably the leader of the pack, but there were others who had clearly decided their role was that of the critical curmudgeon, including his Carlton premiership teammate Mark Maclure, and legendary player and coach Malcolm Blight. They were paid to have opinions and had figured out that negative opinions gave them not so much more airtime or column inches but more attention. Their 'expertise' wasn't gleaned from poring over modern match vision, or consulting statistical gurus, or interviewing club tacticians, but instead drawn from their experience playing the game – something none of them had done in roughly three decades. To my mind, it was lazy and reckless. They were the hot-take merchants of the day, paid to be scathing and scolding elder statesmen.

That kind of coverage still happens a bit these days. There are plenty of commentators who seemingly watch little footy and have only a surface-deep understanding of what the teams are trying to do. They see one thing that irks them and, suddenly, they're unleashing a diatribe on that person, coach or team. My advice for today's young players when they cop one of these sprays? You don't want to feed the fire by adding comment and fighting back, but you can't just ignore it and move on either, because it cuts deep, and it does play on your mind. All you can do is go into bat for those you care about and make sure they know the value they add.

It was a frustrating time for an ultra-competitive person like me. We were being beaten handily, and I wanted to win. Indeed, there was never a time in my career when I lost that competitive urge. I'd look at our team each week and no matter who we were playing – the top side or another bottom side – I'd think to myself that if a few things went right, and a few blokes played their role, we could win. That we *would* win. In my heart, however, maybe I was really only *hoping* we'd win. *Expecting* to win came much later.

As the 2011 season wound down, there were some tough days at the office. That happens when finals are no longer a possibility. Players who need it go in for surgery. Young players who aren't ready are given game time to accelerate learning. Inexperience shines through and the losses can turn heavy and hopeless. We conceded twenty-eight goals to Carlton in a 103-point flogging. A month later we trailed Geelong by eleven goals to one at half-time at Docklands. We followed that up with a ten-goal loss to West Coast in Perth. Even for someone like me, who loves playing anywhere, anytime, the dog days of a long and losing season aren't fun.

I guess I found my fun elsewhere. I was still a big kid at that stage and loved having fun with my mates back in Tassie during breaks. We had a party on Grand Final day in 2011, and one of my best mates came dressed as Dane Swan. We used Textas to draw all over his arms, so it looked like he had sleeve tattoos. While we were mucking around playing half-time heroes, he broke his arm and we had to call a cab to take him to hospital. The injury was so bad they had him sucking on a green whistle for the pain, before slipping his limb into a cast. When it came off six weeks later, the faux tattoos were still there. It wasn't the only fracture that day, either. I was mucking around with another mate, kicking a basketball up in the air and competing to mark the thing. I out-bodied him a couple of times, so things got physical, and before I knew it, he'd accidentally – or perhaps on purpose – thrown an elbow into my face. I flew home to Melbourne the next day to get a badly broken nose fixed. And to explain to the club how half-time heroes had turned into half-time zeroes.

Yet in other ways – important ways, I think – I was growing up.

8

PRIMA DONNA

I bought my first house when I was twenty-three. Well, *we* bought *our* first house, pooling together what I could spare with what Carly had saved. It still seems ridiculous to me that we could do such a thing. At a time when most kids our age were leaving uni, or perhaps embarking on low-paying jobs, finding their feet in the world – dating and dancing and travelling, and moving through life with a kind of youthful abandon – I was becoming a property investor and moving in with my long-term partner. It all sounds so grown up. So serious. So staid. We were still in the habit of going for Sunday night dinners at the Daltons, and one such night Rob pointed out a place on a road parallel to them – in Whyte Street, Brighton – a deceased estate with a park close by, a stepping-stone home on a small block. Rob was the smartest person we knew, so we paid attention to his advice, and even asked him to bid for us at auction. Our limit was $990,000 and that was our *outer* limit – if we sweated and scraped together every last dollar.

On the day of the auction, Rob told us not to look at him or talk to him, so as not to seem in cahoots. He had a plan, but didn't let us know all of it. He was late, for instance, which floored me, but that turned out to be intentional. We knew when he arrived by the gunning of his engine. Rob isn't remotely showy or ostentatious, but he appreciates quality, so he showed up in his black Mercedes coupe, pulling up and parking it in the middle of the road, then stepping out in one of those double-breasted suits he would have worn at Ernst & Young, set off by a bright-pink tie. Tall and thin, he leaned on his car door, and joined in the auction from there. It was a pure power play. They had barely begun when he threw out the opening bid.

Someone else bid above that, and Rob threw in a much bigger bid before they even had time to lower their hand. He kept going and going, aggressively outbidding other parties, daring them to match him, but also going past our limit. I looked at Carly in a panic, and she texted Lisa: 'What is he doing? These are our savings! Stop him! The power's gone to his head!' Lisa replied calmly: 'Don't worry about this – we've got you. It's fine.' The Daltons were quietly offering – *insisting*, in real time – to cover our shortfall, free of interest. The hammer came down and we owned our first home, paying $1,015,000 for an unattached fixer-upper in Brighton.

We went inside and realised how much work would be required to live there. Nothing was high enough or wide enough or new enough. We had to gut it and go with it, and so throughout the week – after my training sessions and before Carly's university lectures – we would teach ourselves how to renovate, taking lessons from *The Block* and *House Rules* and

Grand Designs, figuring out how to cut and stain and hammer quad into skirting boards. We made mistakes, too. I hired a sander from Bunnings and worked it so hard that I created a divot in the floor. I accidentally cut the mains power once with a pair of pliers, was thrown across the room by the electric shock, and watched as a wall that had been freshly painted white turned black with electrical soot. But it was a labour of love – the best financial stretch we ever made – and with it the whole idea of spending money to make money came into focus.

We bought a house in Kew after that and fixed it up to rent it out. We bought another house in Whyte Street, right next to the first, and did it up with the help of two builders: Carly's brother Ollie and one of my best mates, Scott 'Devil' Jury. We invested in an old shop front in Brighton, with dreams of turning it into a New York-style loft, but sold it with the plans attached. We made discoveries about planning permits and building permits and council regulations and easements and titles. We eventually bought the place we live in now, our little dream palace a block back from the beach, and began renovating again. All of which is to say, we did a lot of growing up.

It was an exciting time as we sensed the world opening up. Fame and recognition and the spoils of all that come thick and fast in the AFL. One minute you feel as though you're banging on Terry Wallace's door begging for a game, and the next you're playing regularly in front of 85,000 people, and playing well, and the truth of the privileged position you're in can hit you between the eyes. We were driving to the airport one day, and as we cruised along the freeway past the Essendon

DFO complex on the road turning north toward Tullamarine, there was a huge billboard above us advertising Foxtel – 'Every game, every round' – and there I was taking a huge speccy. We drove up Punt Road another day, and there on the corner of Bridge Road was a huge three-sided one, facing all traffic in the busy intersection, again spruiking Foxtel – 'No ad breaks, siren to siren' – and again it's a gargantuan photo of me flying for a grab.

Carly turned to me: 'Who even are you?' I turned back to her: 'I have no idea.'

But other people knew who I was, and that took an adjustment. We'd be out at a café and I'd suddenly have to leave because people would be looking at me, stealing a surreptitious glimpse, maybe trying to place me, or perhaps taking a few glances because they weren't quite sure yet. More than once someone would say: 'Has anyone told you that you look like Jack Riewoldt?'

I can't complain, however. The life I was granted comes with so many perks. Our major sponsor at the time was Jeep, and so I could get a brand-new Jeep to drive, and I could get one cheaply for Carly, too, and when we had done a certain amount of kilometres, we would swap those for newer models. Neither of our families were 'new car' people, and here we were, kids in our twenties with replacement leases twice a year.

So many little things show up at your door. Cadbury do a promotion, and you're somehow tangentially connected to the business, so boxes of gratis chocolate arrive. The haircare company Matrix is a sponsor, and so your laundry ends up filled with orange bottles of bodywash and shaving gel.

(I remember Nathan Foley, Brett Deledio and Chris Newman did an advertisement for them – *they looked like a boy band* – which I can only assume entitled each one of them to a lifetime supply of shaping wax.) Nike was a sponsor, and on a trip to the USA their team set me up with an account at the five-level Nike megastore in Manhattan, and a simple instruction: 'Go in and take whatever you want.'

People talk about how well paid athletes are, and how they have the world at their feet, with so many people there to support their professional growth and nurture them through those early years. But not everyone has exactly the right networks or guidance. They don't all have the Daltons insisting they come over for dinner on Sunday night, nudging them in the right direction, doing them favours as if they were part of the family. Guys come and go from footy clubs, dropping off lists, being dumped, and it's not always entirely their fault. It's no easy thing for young men with means to sacrifice their youth, living with the constant handbrake of professionalism, but you have to if you want to succeed.

We played the Gold Coast in Cairns early that season. These days it's hard to believe, given Richmond has returned to powerhouse status, but the club then was still carrying a lot of debt, so the administration had signed a three-year deal to play a home game each season against the Suns in tropical North Queensland. The first of the games took place in 2011, which was Gold Coast's first year in the AFL. We kicked six goals to one in the first quarter, a howling gale at our back, Bachar Houli taking shots on goal from seventy metres out, and waltzed into our huddle thinking we were going to win by 100 points without breaking a sweat. Next thing we knew, we were three points down at half-time. We managed to lose by fifteen points.

In 2012, the result was even more ridiculous. The game began in bizarre fashion when Dimma subbed out Jeromey Webberley in the first quarter, the coach filthy with the way he was playing. Nevertheless, after Addam Maric kicked his one and only goal in yellow and black, we led by eighteen points with ten minutes left. Josh Caddy, who some years later would become a premiership teammate, kicked a goal for the Suns, then Jarrod Harbrow slotted another one. The ball went back to the centre with twenty-five seconds left on the clock. What happened next was what Paul Roos once called 'the worst thirty seconds of football in history'.

We should've put a heap of players behind the ball, but we were such an immature side and nothing of the sort happened. Our ruckman, Tom Derickx, tapped the ball down to the ground and it was sharked by Shaun Grigg. He tried to get a kick away but it was smothered. In the blink of an eye, David Swallow won possession and dished off a handball to Trent McKenzie. He sent a long bomb into the Suns' 50-metre arc. Alex Rance managed to effect a spoil, before tapping the ball towards the boundary line. Suns small forward Brandon Matera dashed after it, picked it up and spotted former rugby league player Karmichael Hunt on his own about twenty-five metres from goal. Matera's kick was spot on. Hunt marked on his chest in front of Bachar Houli with four seconds remaining. The siren sounded as Hunt was preparing to take his kick. He didn't look at all confident, but it didn't matter. He dropped the ball perfectly onto his boot and it went straight through the middle. As I trudged off the ground, I was convinced that Richmond was cursed. How do you lose to a team that's essentially a bunch of kids (and Gary Ablett) and a bloke who doesn't even know half the rules of our game? I still don't know the answer.

Clearly, we were still doing so many things wrong in those early years under Damien Hardwick. But when I stepped back and looked at the big picture, I was confident we were getting better, even if the improvement seemed painfully slow. And when I look back on the journey we went on as a club – from the bottom of the ladder to the top – a key turning point came late in that 2012 season. We won three of our last five games, and something seemed to click within the group. We started to build the belief that we were doing the right things, and more importantly, we started to understand what the right things looked like and felt like. And if you looked at our win–loss record through those years, we were on the rise. We weren't surging, but we were definitely growing, year by year, making steady, incremental progress. We had won six games in 2010, won eight and drawn one in 2011, and then won ten and drawn one in 2012. A couple of extra wins in 2013, and we'd be on the edge of making the finals.

We were also a team whose best players were approaching the peak of their careers. Trent Cotchin was on the cusp of becoming a full-blown midfield superstar. When the 2012 Brownlow Medal count was held, Trent polled twenty-six votes to finish equal-second behind Essendon's Jobe Watson. Four years later, Trent and Hawthorn's Sam Mitchell were awarded the medal after Watson's victory was annulled following the Bombers' supplements scandal. People often like to place an asterisk next to that Brownlow, but it's worth noting that Trent was the 2012 Player of the Year for *The Age*, and the AFL Coaches Association's Champion of the Year. He was, naturally, an All-Australian selection, as was Brett Deledio. I was picked in the initial forty-player All-Australian squad but missed out on the final team, probably unluckily. I had just won the Coleman Medal for the second time, registering only four fewer scoring shots than two years prior, kicking sixty-five goals.

After enjoying such a promising if tumultuous year in 2012, there was a lot of confidence around Tigerland in the approach to 2013 – a sense that things were coming together and that the younger players were ready to make their mark. A generational change of sorts had begun when Chris Newman stepped down as captain after the last game of our 2012 campaign. Newy had been a great skipper since being appointed in 2009, but it was clear that Trent, who was vice-captain in 2012, was made for the job.

Although I never doubted Trent's ability to perform the role, on the flipside, it was a job I'd always wanted – and now it was being handed to someone who might hold it for the next decade. Unless something went drastically wrong, a longtime dream of mine had just been dashed. It took some getting over.

By the start of the 2013 season, I felt like we'd done the growing we needed, and we'd laid a lot of building blocks. Now we needed to learn *how* to win – to see our hard work rewarded – and we needed to learn what it was like to *expect* to win. We were still placing too much focus on round one, but finally – in front of more than 80,000 people, after being six goals up at three-quarter-time – we hung on to beat Carlton in the season opener by five points.

Yet to start the season we were still playing a game of swings and roundabouts. We won our first three games, filling our boots with confidence, then we lost our next three, and people were writing us off again. One of those losses was to Fremantle – who would go on and play in the Grand Final that year – by one point at Subiaco Oval. It was a match we should have won, and at the end of the game I noticed Alex Rance standing around talking to a few Dockers with a smile on his face. I saw red. I started angrily telling the boys to get off the ground. I was gutted by such a galling loss, and just hated seeing them standing around – particularly Alex – having a casual chat as though it didn't matter.

My first memory of Alex was him walking into the gym at Tigerland, and how massive he was. He was eighteen and could already bench-press more than anyone in the club. And footy was black and white for him. He roared at Matthew Richardson once in an early session – to push through to the cones in sprints – and he and I would lock horns in training, too. We were like twins at times, bulls butting heads, stamping our feet in the same paddock, arguing in meetings and then wrestling on the track. I later learned to love him, to see how we were different sides of the same coin. He was the most competitive person I had ever met – he *hated* losing – and I loved that about him. I came to appreciate his devotion to his religion, and how that faith grounds him. He was funny, too.

I remember once he soaped up the changeroom floor and made it into a slip and slide, and the time he built a raft out of office-water cooler drums and went for a paddle in the downstairs swimming pool. But in that moment after the loss to Fremantle, I was livid. And apparently it showed.

You would think the grumpy old footy commentators would've appreciated the emotion on display. I've heard so many comments over the years about players not seeming to care enough when their team has lost. But this time their reaction was the exact opposite. David King saw the vision and described me as having 'complained and sooked and carried on', and he was far from alone. I couldn't believe it. I had given everything and was bitterly disappointed. That was all. But it became a pile-on nonetheless, so much so that Trent Cotchin found himself having to defend me in his mid-week press conference. Cotch spoke up for me, for wearing my heart on my sleeve, for loving the footy club and the club loving me back, but the questions kept coming, and so did the whacks.

Mark Maclure labelled me a 'prima donna' (adding that my teammates needed to pull me into line). These days I have a better relationship with Mark, thanks to both of us working at Fox Footy, but back then I didn't take his critique kindly. In fact, I managed to get hold of his phone number and gave it to a few of my mates down in Tassie. They started putting up a stack of classified advertisements on Gumtree – things like an iPhone for $100 – with Mark's phone number as the contact. They also started hammering him with phone calls and messages. A few of us at Richmond waged a war on him that lasted years. In 2013 and 2014, for instance, on weekends when we were playing in Melbourne, I used to go over to Brett Deledio's house with Shaun Grigg, to watch Friday night footy together and eat a meal of honey-mustard chicken and rice made by Lids. Occasionally, Maclure would be on the Friday night Fox Footy coverage, and sometimes leave his phone on the desk. We started prank-calling him from a private number while he was on air. We thought it was hilarious. I'm sure he didn't. In the end Mark found out I was the one who was spreading his number around and told me to pull my head in or he'd get one of his friends in the police force to charge us. That put an end to it. 'Sellers' has since admitted that he got it wrong in calling me a prima donna. We can even have a light laugh about the whole saga. I think he's forgiven me. One day, I think I'll forgive him.

Everything clicked for us through the middle part of the season. We won eight of the ten games we played between rounds seven and seventeen. In the middle of that great run, I signed a new contract thanks to some great work from my new manager. I had initially stayed with Phoenix Management Group for a few seasons after the sale of Ricky Nixon's Flying Start business. I had a great relationship with Winston Rous, the junior manager there, but never quite forged a relationship with the general manager, former Essendon forward Scott Lucas. When I booked a meeting and he didn't turn up, I knew I needed to switch. In early 2013, I joined Liam Pickering's company, then called Strategic Management. Pickers had an amazing stable of stars, including Lance Franklin, Dane Swan, Scott Pendlebury and Gary Ablett, so I felt in good company. A good manager is incredibly useful, not so much for those mythical Jerry Maguire 'show me the money' moments, and not even as some kind of professional best friend within a cut-throat industry. A good manager is there to give you simple peace of mind. Their commission pays for the absence of big commercial errors and missteps. That was particularly relevant in these negotiations with Richmond because it was the same story as ever for me with this latest contract: I didn't want to go anywhere, but I wanted to be paid what I was worth.

The negotiations ended up dragging on longer than we would have liked. In fact, they became so drawn out that a few crazy articles bobbed up in the media, including one in which Greater Western Sydney were said to be hunting my signature. (Dustin Martin was also off contract and held out until after our season had finished, going so far as to tour the Giants' training base, which was under construction in Sydney, but that was all smoke and mirrors. Neither of us was ever going to leave a massive club like Richmond and head to Blacktown.)

There were other offers on the table, too. Fremantle found around a million dollars a year to offer me. The Brisbane Lions were waving big money, as well. But I believed in loyalty. I loved what I had come to know of the club and its people – the way they would rev me up each week, and how I felt like I could rev them up, too. It was a symbiotic relationship, and it was just beginning to bear fruit. In some ways, entertaining outside offers made me uncomfortable. I was so averse to the business of leveraging my open-market value that the club would've known I was never leaving. Or maybe they didn't. That's where managers shine.

On July 25, the club announced I'd signed a three-year contract for the 2014–16 seasons. 'I genuinely love this football club and all it stands for, and I'm pleased to be part of the journey we're on,' I told a press conference afterwards. 'I hope to repay the faith shown in me by the club, and I'll continue to give everything I have for the cause.' I meant every word.

Not long after I signed on, we beat Hawthorn in a Saturday afternoon game at the MCG. The second half was played in driving rain. We kicked six goals in the first quarter and six goals in the final term. Our defenders ran forward at every opportunity. Even Chris Newman, who only kicked fifty-six goals in his 268-game AFL career, dashed forward and snagged a goal. After the final siren, on the Fox Footy coverage, Dwayne Russell delivered one of his full-throated calls: 'They haven't just walked into the finals. They've kicked the door down with a win over the top team in the competition.' People were talking us up as a premiership chance.

I rolled my ankle the following week, and carried it through the week after, but the injury soon faded into insignificance. On Tuesday, August 27, the AFL announced that the Bombers, who were seventh on the ladder and assured of finishing in the top eight, were being kicked out of the finals as punishment for a rogue supplement program, which had been under investigation since February. There were other penalties, too, from forfeited draft picks to a $2 million fine and twelve-month suspension for senior coach James Hird. Like everyone else, I was taken aback that something like that could happen in Australian sport. I always think of Australian sport as being clean. I think of us as being a clean nation. It was hard to fathom.

Carlton, North Melbourne and the Brisbane Lions suddenly found themselves in the running to replace Essendon in the top eight. Whichever of them finished ninth would earn a berth in the finals. Carlton secured the berth in dramatic fashion, coming back from thirty-nine points down to defeat Port Adelaide by one point at Football Park. The Blues it was. They'd be our opponent in the first week of the finals.

The build-up to that final was enormous. So many players had waited so long for this moment. It was Chris Newman's 233rd game and first final. It was Brett Deledio's 195th game and first final. It was Daniel Jackson's 146th game and first final. It was my 134th game and first final.

When I look back on my career, the grand finals are the greatest highlights for sure, but the other thing I'll never forget is the noise when we ran out of the rooms, through our banner ('The roar is back where we belong') and started jogging towards the Punt Road end on that gloriously sunny Sunday afternoon. There were almost 95,000 people at the game (a record for an elimination final), and it was an over-whelmingly Richmond crowd. As the theme song played, it felt like a wave of noise was reverberating through every bone in my body, and when it reached its crescendo and the fans belted out 'yellow and black', the sound was simply deafening. It made the hairs on the back of my neck stand up. The Tiger Army was with us.

There was another massive roar as the umpire bounced the ball to start the match, and I then learned that the first ten minutes of your first final is like the opening ten minutes of your first game. You run around like a headless chook, just trying to get a touch, and you end up gasping for air because you expend so much physical, mental and psychic energy. As the game started going our way, I was desperate to have an impact, but my opponent, Michael Jamison, wasn't allowing me any space. Thankfully, my fellow forward Ty Vickery was on target and started well, kicking a goal in the first quarter and another one early in the second term. Trent Cotchin, Brett Deledio and Dustin Martin were on fire in the middle of the ground, Ivan Maric was dominating in the ruck, and Alex Rance and Chris Newman were leading the way in the backline. When I finally snared my first goal at the twenty-one-minute mark of the second quarter, we were twenty-six points up and the Richmond supporters were going crazy in the stands. The margin was still twenty-six points at half-time, then Aaron Edwards kicked the first goal of the second half, which gave us a thirty-two-point lead. Everything was going to plan. We were on.

But games of footy can turn in an instant. Just as it looked like we were on our way to the second week of the finals, everything started to unravel. We certainly didn't consciously take our foot off the gas, but maybe some complacency crept in, maybe a few guys started thinking we were going to roll on to a ten-goal win and cruise into a semi-final. Instead, the opposite happened. The Blues rolled the dice. They started charging forward at every opportunity and we weren't ready for it. We became anxious and went into our shells. I'm not sure our coaches had a Plan B either. And when they did try and change things, their messages seemed to get lost on their way down from the coaches' box.

Perhaps most importantly of all, Chris Judd, an all-time great of the game, came to the fore in his team's hour of need. He was incredible. Judd cut a swathe through the middle, his side surged with him, and we stumbled onto our back foot. The passage of play that best sums up how it all went wrong for us took place with fourteen minutes remaining in the third quarter. There was a boundary throw-in, Ty Vickery made it into position, and there was no Carlton player there to contest with him. Ty should have been able to grab the ball unopposed and dish it off to one of our running players, but for some strange reason, Shane Tuck ran up to the contest and went up in the ruck against Ty. Maybe in the white-hot heat of the moment, Shane thought Ty was a Carlton player. Whatever the reason, we were a player short on the ground, and the ball landed in a sea of Blue. Bryce Gibbs accepted the donation, dished off a handball to Marc Murphy, and soon enough Jarrad Waite had kicked their first goal of the second half. It was the start of an avalanche. In the space of eight minutes our lead was reduced from thirty-two points to one. We still had our noses in front at the last change, but we were running on empty.

Following that Waite goal, the Blues kicked eleven goals to three during the remainder of the game and won by twenty points. Nick Duigan, who came into the Carlton team only after midfielder Brock McLean injured his thigh with his last kick in their warm-up, kicked four goals. Jarrad Waite killed us. Eddie Betts kicked three. Modern footy is so much about momentum swings, and once we lost that momentum we couldn't get it back, no matter how hard we tried.

Momentum is bizarre like that. It's almost like the wind. You know the precise moment that it shifts, and it feels as though nothing you can do will ever shift it back. It's elemental, lifting up everything around you into one great wave, an unstoppable tide that can sometimes be kind to you – sweeping you along and taking you where you want to go. Or it can just as easily turn cruel – carrying you far from the place you want to go, instead crashing you onto the rocks below. Momentum has a way of making you feel utterly helpless, and in the closing minutes of that game – when it was clear we could no longer win and the Carlton supporters were dancing in the aisles – it made the MCG into a hollow and unforgiving place, a cold colosseum from which there was no escape. We were shattered. It might not have seemed obvious for another few years, given our finals appearances in the subsequent two seasons ended in tears as well, but we learned lessons from that defeat. We learned firstly that in finals, the stuff you think you know goes straight out the window – the pressure stops you from thinking straight. We promised ourselves we wouldn't make that mistake again.

But it was such a heartbreakingly Richmond thing to do – to lose to a team that actually finished ninth. As people queued up to tell us, only the Tigers could manage something so ludicrous. I know there were heartbroken fans out there saying, 'I wish we didn't even make the finals', and I couldn't begrudge them that sentiment. I'd been a Richmond man for less than a decade; they'd been Tigers all their lives.

9

A LION IN
A CAVE

Losses in September almost always have consequences. Inside
Richmond, the disastrous loss to Carlton meant scrutiny for
those in charge, including me. I ended up outside of the leadership group ahead of the 2014 season, and I understood why.
I'd been placed in that group when I was only twenty-two
because I had football intelligence, because I was opinionated
in team meetings, and because I had just won a Coleman
Medal. Yet I'm not sure I responded well to that official tag of
leader. In hindsight, I perhaps charged into the role with too
much confidence, too much bluster, too much surety. I got a
few things wrong.

I became too forceful with my feedback, and too demanding around the standards I set. There's a fine line between
asking for excellence and punishing mediocrity. I was too
commanding and insistent with the former, and too vigorous
and open with the latter. In meetings I talked too often and
for too long, and on the field I allowed my body language

125

to betray my emotions. At the same time, key defender Troy Chaplin and ruckman Ivan Maric had arrived at the club from Port Adelaide and Adelaide respectively and were clearly better leaders than I was. They were elevated into the leadership group and I was taken out. And I was embarrassed.

I'm a proud person, and a competitive person, so a public demotion of sorts was tough to stomach. I knew there was a raft of other reasons I was left out, unrelated to me directly – that sometimes it's worthwhile to mix and vary the voices you elevate, for instance, and that it's often smart to let your talented young players focus solely on producing their best footy – yet I couldn't help but take it personally. The media narrative – that I had been 'dumped' from the leadership group – a pejorative word that made it sound like some kind of admonishment or whack – made me angry, too. I was confused and upset to be left out, but I could also see how the revamped leadership group was a positive story for Richmond. We had recruited two truly great people – one in Chaplin (who is today talked about as a likely senior coach) and the other in Maric (who later became emblematic of our entire club culture) – and instead of recognising them, the whole footy world was talking about me. Or so it felt to me, anyway.

I tried to do as instructed – appreciate that I was being given time to work on my own game, and learn more about leadership, with the aim of being elevated back into the group in the future. I assumed that after a couple of days the story would become old news and the media would leave me to concentrate on my footy. But in truth I felt as though anything I did on the oval or in the public eye could (and would) become a story, and that began to niggle and gnaw inside me.

I became so worked up over the media's treatment of the story – and the constant questions about my perceived demotion – that I enacted a self-imposed media ban. I quit my regular radio spot on Gold 104 and stopped appearing on *The Footy Show*. I was earning good money for those things, so it was quite a financial sacrifice, but it was what I felt I needed to do to turn all eyes away from me and back onto what we could achieve as a group.

Unfortunately, going into that season, I suspect many of us naively believed we were on a course of natural progression. Six wins in 2010, eight wins in 2011, ten wins in 2012, then fifteen wins and a final in 2013. In that light, 2014 seemed easy – turn up and take home the four points in sixteen or seventeen matches, stroll into the top four and take matters from there. We got caught in the trap of thinking it was all going to happen for us. How wrong we were.

Our season opener that year was against the Gold Coast in the humidity of Queensland, and the dewy ball felt like a bar of soap, slipping through our fingers – along with the result. We rebounded to defeat Carlton in round two, but that proved a blip. We slumped to 2–4 after an eleven-goal hiding from Hawthorn in round six, followed by a bye. Richmond's greatest coach, the legendary Tom Hafey – who led the club to four premierships – passed away, and although we wanted to play well in tribute to him, we lost to Melbourne, who were themselves a rabble. Brett Deledio fronted the media for us afterwards but was at a loss to explain the results.

'If I had the answer to that I'd be a coach myself,' he said. 'We're searching. We're trying to find it. We're training hard. We're definitely staying united and getting around each other. I can't explain it and I can't put my finger on it. If I could, I'd be a genius, I suppose.'

In such times you find yourself talking to people about what's going wrong, and why. You search for those elusive answers in all corners of the club. On the Wednesday before our round-ten game against the Giants at Sydney Showground Stadium, I chatted to a staff member who pointed to statistics and patterns, and had a general read on the situation as it stood: *Maybe we were trying to play too much like Hawthorn?* The idea stuck in my head – because I thought it was right. Our game plan *did* seem built on calculated movement and transition, predicated on precise passing, ball control and a high kick-to-handball ratio.

The problem was that while this plan suited the Hawks, whose list-build and strategy development had happened in sync, we'd simply fallen in love with a style that seemed to be a winning one. As a former lieutenant to Alastair Clarkson, Damien Hardwick has an enormous amount of respect for Clarkson, so it wasn't hard to make that connection and assume the apprentice was aping the methods of the master.

With all of this in mind, I fronted the media that week for a regulation post-training press conference, designed mainly so the TV stations would have an audio grab or two for that night's news bulletins. You're asked to do these kinds of pressers a few times each season, and you're trained how to deal with them. The rules are simple: *Don't give anything away. Be as boring as possible. Give the chooks some scraps. Get in and get out without getting dirty.* I was asked if I had any thoughts on why we were playing so poorly, and without thinking blurted out the Hawthorn theory.

'Unfortunately, we went one way with our game, and the game went the other way really,' I said. 'We probably tried to copy Hawthorn a little bit too much with our kicking style. We probably need to rely a little bit more on natural progression, which I think we'll get back to, actually I know we'll get back to. You try new things and unfortunately you learn from your mistakes. We've learned from it as a playing group, as a coaching group and as a football club as a whole.'

When the press conference concluded, I thought nothing of it, but the journos all looked like they had won TattsLotto. An hour or so later, the following headline appeared on the AFL website: *Tigers 'tried to copy Hawks' admits Riewoldt.* The nightly news bulletins all led their sports reports the same way. I still was largely oblivious until dinner that night, when I sat down with a few friends at Koko in the Crown Casino complex.

My phone rang. It was Dan Richardson, our football manager. You don't usually get calls from the footy manager in the evening, so I quickly ducked out of the restaurant and took the call.

'What did you say in the presser?' Dan asked. (He hadn't seen the comments yet, but journos were ringing him about them.)

'Nothing too bad,' I replied.

Dan took me at my word and hung up, so I went back to dinner, but he quickly called again. He'd now read the comments, as had Dimma. I was in trouble.

I sat in Dimma's office the following day, and he was wild. Not just furious either, but emotional, having taken the comments as a personal slight, as me saying he wasn't a good coach, that he had no ideas of his own. It made sense. What does a coach have if not their ability to come up with tactics and to execute them with the talent at his disposal? Calling all that intellectual property and process and planning into question was – to him at least – tantamount to a personal attack. I had hurt him. Dimma said he was thinking about dropping me from the team for the game against the Giants, and I nearly fell off my chair.

Then it was his turn to front the media. Again, it was nothing more than his regular weekly pre-game press conference, but with the clickbait I'd given the footy media, there were now fifteen journos in front of him, instead of maybe three. He explained to them all how the club had just spoken to me.

'We caught up with him this morning and removed his foot from his mouth and my foot from his arse,' Dimma said. 'Obviously we were pretty disappointed with his comments. We talk about being a united footy club, and Jack went outside those boundaries. Unfortunately, he's learned a harsh lesson from that. We've got match committee this afternoon,' he added, scowling. 'His form has been okay. Whether we take any of this into account we'll see this afternoon. Like anything, with every action comes an equal and opposite reaction. We obviously have some standards that we abide by here and he went outside those.'

I wanted to hide under a rock, or at least from waiting media. Today, almost no matter what has happened in my life or at the club, I can walk past a microphone and camera without blinking. The doorstop interview is to be accepted, and they're simple enough to decline or ignore until you close the door to your car and speed away. But something on this day – my bubbling hatred for the way my intentions and actions were being skewed and amplified and twisted by reporters and commentators and columnists – led to one of the silliest episodes of my career.

It wasn't my decision, but I was encouraged by the club to get away from Punt Road Oval without having to speak to anyone – without waving them away or even walking past them – by sneaking out the back door. I did as instructed – and hatched a plan. John Vickery, our weights coach (and father of key forward Ty Vickery), moved my car from the players' car park around to Brunton Avenue, closer to the MCG, so that I could sneak out of our training facility undetected. Once I was done for the day, wearing thongs and a Richmond backpack, I jumped the barbed wire fence at the Richmond station end of the oval, only to look up and see a reporter sitting in his car staring straight at me. I stared back and swore. *Shit.*

More reporters and camera operators came scooting around the corner, so I ran across Punt Road itself, ducking behind cars, trying to hide. I wasn't thinking straight at all, and out of desperation decided to run up to the train station. I reached the gates and realised I didn't have a ticket, and the cameras caught it all, including me shaking my head while I bought a Myki card to get through the gates and onto the platforms.

In the end I didn't catch any train. I just sat on the platform, facing north, pondering how I ended up in such a pickle.

It would have been comical – and clearly was to some – had it not been so upsetting. Once all the waiting media had left, I picked up my car and started driving home. It's a strange thing to turn on the radio and hear your own name in the mouths of people trying to interpret your day, explaining why and how you've lost the plot, criticising you for this and that, or laughing at your expense. It's the most bizarre feeling – to be studied so carefully and yet be completely misunderstood; widely known yet basically alone.

Still, it's easy to see how my immaturity was responsible for much of the frenzy. If I'd made the same gaffe years later, I know exactly how it would have gone. I would have walked out the front of Punt Road Oval, stood in front of the cameras and the journalists – 'Righto, what do you want to know?' – and they would have asked me to explain myself. I would admit my mistake, explaining how we all make mistakes but I was prepared to own this one, and that would have been that. I would have smiled for the obligatory footage of me getting into my car, and I would have driven away, leaving the moment behind me instead of dragging it out into a sorry saga. You learn later just how quickly an issue can burn out, but only if you let it – only if you cut off the oxygen and let the flames die down. You can't keep opening your mouth to breathe new life into the fire.

It needs to be said that a lot of my decision-making at that time was based on what I thought other people wanted me to be. Sometimes when I did silly stuff – like the media ban – I was just doing what I assumed was expected of me. In that example, I took the idea of the club not wanting me to speak out of

132

turn to mean I shouldn't have a voice at all. They got it wrong, I got it wrong, and it all went wrong. I know I have to accept responsibility for putting my foot in my mouth (comparing us to Hawthorn), but the club has to accept responsibility for the way it responded. As hurtful as it was for Dimma to hear me questioning his tactics, I felt that the way he treated me was worse and that he'd hung me out to dry. I felt like a kicked dog.

The story did have a funny ending, however. A year later we held a comedy day at the club to raise money for charity and to cover the footy-trip flights for the younger guys at the club who find it harder to afford such things. I was the master of ceremonies and auctioneer, selling footy boots and training gear and framed pictures. I still had the Myki card in my wallet and Shaun Grigg told me I simply had to put it on the block. I signed the card and prepared to sell it at the end of the auction, as a joke item to close proceedings. I took the piss out of myself, called for bids, and suddenly there were hands in the air all over the room. A lady ended up with it for the princely sum of $450.

Things cooled down quickly, too. Dimma kept me in the team for the match against the Giants, which was Brett Deledio's 200th game. I was so relieved to get on a plane and get out of Melbourne for a few days. I began to feel better about myself, and I repaid the faith in the best way possible. I had a day out, kicking the first goal of the game, then my seventh just before half-time. I kicked my eighth during the early stages of the third quarter, and there was Dwayne Russell on the broadcast, sounding like the soundtrack to my career: 'No one expected him to make this big a statement. It's huge.'

I kicked three more goals in a five-minute burst at the end of the third term, giving me eleven straight for the match. I could have finished with an even bigger bag, but I missed both my shots in the last quarter, and dished off a pass to Trent Cotchin after taking a mark only twenty metres out from goal with four minutes left. I wanted to show that I was a team player, and the coach appreciated it. In his post-match press conference, Dimma highlighted that passage of play as his favourite of the game. 'For him to actually come back and give the ball to Cotchin when he could have kicked more goals is probably testament to the kid he is.'

After the game, I was interviewed by former St Kilda, Sydney Swans and Western Bulldogs player Barry Hall. Inside my head fireworks were going off, but I had to play down my happiness. Rather than carry on about how well I'd played, I was careful to ensure that everyone understood I was a team player and sorry for causing such a fuss. I remembered the rules – *Don't give anything away, be as boring as possible, give the chooks some scraps, get in and get out without getting dirty* – but I also hated the rules. And I felt it was important to highlight that people make mistakes. That they aren't robots.

'It was a pretty emotional week, Baz,' I said, with a furrowed brow, all seriousness and solemnity. 'Obviously, it blew out of proportion. I was pretty devastated with how it came across. Let the coach down, let the side down. Today, I just came with the mindset of trying to repay the faith from Dimma and the boys and the footy club.'

But we were still a side filled with immaturity and prone to inconsistency. Those fluctuations in form and mood weren't mine alone. The following week we lost the Dreamtime game to Essendon by fifty points, and Dimma went berserk, his voice echoing around the meeting room as he told us he was 'sick of this shit'. We lost our next three games as well. Most years, you are guaranteed a spot in the finals if you win twelve games. But we had won only three, and there were nine remaining in the home-and-away season. Things looked hopeless.

But we played the bottom two sides, St Kilda and the Brisbane Lions, in rounds fifteen and sixteen, and although we didn't play well, we won nonetheless. A week later we knocked off third-placed Port Adelaide – and started to believe. We defeated West Coast in Perth in round eighteen, then the Giants and the Bombers. In round twenty-one, we travelled to Adelaide and beat the Crows on their home deck. A week later, we beat St Kilda again, taking our winning streak to eight.

With one round remaining, the task ahead of us was simple: beat the Swans in Sydney and we would claim a very unlikely berth in the finals. When I look back across my career, that game at Stadium Australia is my favourite home-and-away match. It was Chris Newman's 250th AFL game, and Newy gave us an inspirational pre-game speech.

'When you're confronted by a lion in a cave,' he said, 'you can either run from it, or you can stand there with a spear and charge straight at it.'

We charged straight at the Swans, smacking them early, then hanging on to win by three points. I managed to kick four goals, while Brett Deledio produced an unbelievable performance in which he tallied twenty-nine disposals and kicked three goals. Down back, Alex Rance came of age with a heroic performance. Try as they might the Swans just couldn't get past him in the frantic final minutes. Dustin Martin capped off the day with a show of strength and balance to seal the win. It really had everything.

The elation after the game was similar to winning a grand final. It was difficult to believe that we had truly won nine games in a row and barnstormed our way into the top eight. But the key reason it was one of the best moments of my footballing life was because we were able to win for Chris Newman, a great Richmond person and a great captain.

That left us full of bravado and confidence when we travelled to South Australia to play Port Adelaide in an elimination final at the Adelaide Oval, but the game was a disaster from before the first bounce. Trent Cotchin won the toss, then elected to kick into what proved to be a howling gale. I need to take a bit of the blame for this. Trent would usually ask me which way we should kick, and on this day, when he asked, I pointed towards the scoreboard end. Maybe the breeze had dropped off a bit at that point, but I pointed straight into the wind. Trent was the captain, so he had the final call, but we each played a part in getting it badly wrong.

When I think about it now, deep down we probably knew that our wave of energy had run out. We had burned through so much emotional effort during our nine-game, do-or-die, win-or-bust streak. The AFL's new weekend off before the finals also conspired to rob us of momentum. We got hit between the eyes, and by quarter-time, Port Adelaide led by eight goals to one.

Over my career, we had some great moments at the Adelaide Oval, usually playing competitive football in a standout stadium where opposition teams often go to die, hounded into submission by the most parochial of home crowds. Unfortunately, that 2014 final was one of our worst efforts. The final margin was fifty-seven points, and our failure to compete at any stage undid all the remarkable work of having saved our season. It was also fodder for a new story the media were only too ready to write: the Tigers are flaky in finals.

10

FIGHT LIKE MADDIE

When you've been granted a good go at life, as I have, you sometimes slip into a mindset where you don't believe that bad things – really bad things – will ever happen to you. Tragedy and calamity just never seem to touch the sides of your life, or the lives of those to whom you're closest. But then, sometimes, you get a reality check.

My cousin Maddie was diagnosed with aplastic anaemia, a bone marrow failure syndrome, back in August 2010. I knew that Nick was desperately worried about his sister, but I have to admit I don't remember the significance or seriousness of the situation engulfing me as it should have. When you're surrounded by peak physical fitness and constant competition, you're largely removed from the bad luck that can befall anyone, almost sliding into this blind faith, a 'she'll-be-right' mentality. But the truth eventually catches up with you.

I hadn't spent a lot of time with Maddie, but you have a bond with all your first cousins, formed in colourful childhood memories, like the time we spent together in Queensland when I was thirteen. We went to the Wet'n'Wild theme park on the Gold Coast, and I forgot to wear sunscreen. My pasty Taswegian skin was roasted red, and I was so embarrassed that I wore long-sleeved shirts for days to cover up my sunburn. The T-shirts stuck to my skin, which made me miserable. Maddie thought it was hilarious.

I see her in fragments of memory all the time. Maddie was a foodie, for instance, and we would always go to Chinatown when she was in Melbourne. I recall going out to eat a delicious family banquet of spring rolls, lemon chicken and beef in black bean sauce, but I also remember the medical tubes in her arm, intravenously supplying her with the drugs she needed to fight the disease. I remember chatting to her about Richmond versus St Kilda games, and how, as a Saints fan, she was willing to hate the opponent who was playing on me, but she still wanted St Kilda to win. She wasn't about to compromise her footballing faith for my ego. She was great at keeping both Nick and me grounded, calling out our bullshit, and never dishing out praise unless it was warranted.

Maddie played footy herself in her younger years on the Gold Coast. I'm told she had no fear. Her dad, Joe, says she played football like Joel Selwood. While playing on a boys' team, she kicked the only goal for her side in a losing semi-final, then reached that age when girls weren't allowed to play in the boys' teams anymore. Joe vividly remembers her reaction when she learned that news. Maddie just looked around the room at the boys she had played alongside, and started pointing at them: 'But I'm better than him, and him, and him!'

Maddie fought aplastic anaemia for more than four years, meaning everyone around her had ample time to adjust to the challenge she was facing. The slow passage of time had this effect of lulling you into a false sense of security, so it caught me completely off guard in 2013, when her family asked if I would be tested to see if I could become a platelet donor for her. I agreed, of course – my O negative blood type made me compatible – and then the process began, and with every little medical step the reality sunk in a little deeper. I needed steroid injections to maximise the harvest of my platelets, for instance, and that meant I needed WADA permission to take injections during pre-season. Two days later I was walking into a hospital past terminally ill people and those requiring transfusions for dire ailments. They strapped me to the harvesting machine, with a drip in either arm – one pumping my blood into the harvester, the other returning the blood to my body – and I sat there for four hours, surrounded by people trying to stay alive, like Maddie, and people trying to keep them alive, like me.

There were other procedures, too. She had two bone marrow transplants in 2014, responding well to the first one but reacting terribly to the drugs the second time. She ended up in the intensive care unit at the Royal Melbourne Hospital in July and stayed there for 227 days. She had a third bone marrow transplant in November that seemed to have the desired effect, but other things conspired to make her very sick again. Visiting that space was so emotionally fraught. The catchcry of the ICU is that 'You leave when you're well or you're dead', and the impression I got was that you tend to know which one will happen to you quite quickly. Spending two-thirds of a year in there was a strange and sad kind of suspended reality.

I found out Maddie most likely didn't have long to live on Boxing Day. Carly and I had been celebrating the festive season with my parents and brothers in Hobart, but Maddie had fluid on her lungs and the doctors were worried that they wouldn't be able to save her. Harry, Charlie and I decided we would fly to Melbourne that day to see Maddie. On the way to the airport, we went to see my grandparents, Oma and Opa. They'd lived through the Second World War in Germany and saw, in their younger years, more than their fair share of suffering and death. But the thought of losing one of their grandchildren had left them utterly bereft. Opa, who was usually such a powerful character, found it difficult to speak, and when he did, his words were timid, fearful whispers. It was heartbreaking.

We flew to Melbourne that afternoon and went to the hospital. Joe and Fiona asked the people who visited her to tell her stories about the good times, to celebrate her life and not spend the time left with her on maudlin, morbid goodbyes. To the doctors' amazement, Maddie started recovering over the next few days, and by early February it seemed she might soon be well enough to leave ICU and be cared for on a regular ward. Hope can be cruel like that. Before she could leave intensive care, she contracted an infection, and her condition deteriorated swiftly. On Tuesday, February 24, 2015, Maddie passed away. Her brothers, parents, maternal grandmother, sister-in-law and her young nephew were by her side. She was twenty-six years old.

I was on my way into training when Dad rang to tell me the news. I was sitting in traffic on Punt Road, waiting for the lights at Swan Street. I drove into the club car park minutes later and just sat for a while, reeling with sadness and shock. Right up until the end, I had kept wishfully thinking she would be fine. I picked up my bag, walked into the club, and didn't tell anyone in the first hour or so. Then I bumped into Dimma in the stairwell, and he asked if everything was okay. He could tell something was up. I told him Maddie had passed away.

We did a cultural session in the club only recently, in the days immediately after Dimma left, during which each player wrote down a moment when Dimma had touched them in some way. Jayden Short, for instance, wrote down how much it had meant to him that Dimma would text him every single year on the anniversary of the death of his father, to make sure Shorty was all right. The moment I wrote down was that moment in the stairwell in 2015, when Dimma hugged me, close and tight – 'What are you even doing here, mate?' – and I shook my head and cried, 'I need to be somewhere.' Football clubs are great places to be in terrible times, offering a distraction, a beacon of safety, the comfort of familiarity, and a touch of normalcy in the most abnormal moments.

Clubs aren't strangers to suffering. Often, they welcome troubled souls in through the front door, whether a family grieving the loss of a loved one, or a patient suffering from a terminal illness. From the first year you're inducted into the AFL system, you end up in the critical-care wards of so many hospitals, using your spotlight to warm an otherwise gloomy

setting. I can't think of many – any – other professional organisations that make a point of bringing their people into contact
with the neediest members of the community, but that's what
happens, regularly, and it becomes part of your life. You hear
harrowing stories. You meet the bravest young souls. You get
introduced to them in team meetings or get up close and
personal with them as they run water to the team during a
weekday training session. You develop a side of yourself –
a sense of perspective – that not many eighteen-year-old men
would know is there. You might be little more than a fleeting
moment in someone's journey, but you come to understand
how you can use your fame to bring them a smile. It's one of
the great levellers.

Throughout my years at Richmond there were so many
people in need of our attention and time, but there was one
little boy in particular – Nate Anderson – who stood out from
the rest. Nate was battling leukemia, and had to have one of his
legs removed, and became our unofficial Western Australian
mascot. He became truly connected to the club, a great little
mate to his favourite player, Jake King. He would run out onto
the ground with us, bouncing along on a prosthetic carbon-
fibre leg, crashing through the banner at speed. After a win in
the wet at Subiaco one night, I lifted him onto my shoulders
to join the circle and sing the club song. It's funny how certain
people come into the club and guys are just attracted to their
energy, but that's exactly how it was with Nate. He was a young
man who needed something – maybe a little love or hope or
happiness – beyond what his family could provide. Being able
to give him that is a responsibility, a privilege, and a gift.

People like that make you think differently about life. And Maddie's death did something similar for me. It made me remember that every day you're here on earth is a good day.

I think it changed Nick, too, and certainly the public perception of him. He was always so driven that footy fans probably saw him as an automaton – a bulletproof superman, always saying and doing the right thing. A perfection myth come to life, really. Now they saw him consumed by grief, humanised by his vulnerability, and lauded for his dignity. I was sitting in the front row inside the Medallion Club at Marvel Stadium when Roo addressed the audience for the launch of what would become Maddie's Match. It was only six weeks after she died, and he was so raw, but there was this awesome sense of pride emanating from him – pride in her. His ability to rouse people to the cause and get them believing made me feel like he was going to change the world.

Meanwhile, I found myself back out on the MCG for the opening round of the 2015 season. It was only a month after the funeral, when I had blasted the photographers hanging around the service, taking photos of a family trying to grieve. I struggled back on the field at first, but halfway through the second quarter I crumbed the ball off a pack and snapped a goal. Tears welled in my eyes as I pointed to the sky. That one was for Maddie. I ended up kicking four goals in all and we won by twenty-seven points, but I was emotionally drained. In the rooms after the game, I saw my old man, gave him a hug and just broke down. It was captured on camera – this grown man collapsing into his dad's arms – and I began to understand how much I'd been living in a pressure cooker.

In some ways it was hard to build myself up for yet another season, given how trivial sport had come to seem. I comforted myself with the knowledge that Maddie loved watching me and Nick play, and that she would want me to focus on becoming the best player I could be.

It was another up-and-down season for the Tiges. We trailed the Western Bulldogs and lost by nineteen, then headed to the Gabba and thumped Brisbane by seventy-nine. We lost terribly to the Demons on Anzac eve, then stormed home against Geelong a week later but fell short anyway. In round six we played North Melbourne at Bellerive Oval – an opportunity I built up too much in my head. I'd gone down to Tassie a few days early, visited my old school, and got caught up in the hype of playing on the oval where I learned the game. Not many people get that chance. It was the equivalent of Brett Deledio getting to play a game for points at Kyabram, David Astbury running out for the Tigers in a match at Tatyoon, or Shaun Grigg suiting up for Richmond at the City Oval in Ballarat.

My dream homecoming became a nightmare. We didn't give a yelp after half-time, allowing North to kick seven goals to one in the third quarter and win by thirty-five points, slumping to 2–4, and copping criticism from all corners. My old mate Mark Maclure led the charge. 'They don't shepherd, they don't block, all they do is play individual football,' he told ABC radio. 'I think we have found out that they are just not a very good side. This team can't take them to the promised land, I can assure you. The coach knows.'

Was he right? With that exact group of players, and that exact game plan, yes. But twelve of the players who were out there – more than half the team – formed the nucleus of a premiership side less than two years later. Commentators know a few things, but they don't know everything, and they don't know half the things they say they do. We like to say that footy is an opinions game. It's often a guessing game, too.

In the days after the loss, I was asked to attend a meeting with Trent Cotchin, Brett Deledio and Shane Edwards. They sat me down and told me a few home truths. They were unhappy with the defensive side of my game. I wasn't applying enough pressure. I wasn't working hard enough to close down space. I wasn't emptying out of the forward line fast enough to defend the field and block the corridor. As an older player, you often sense when those sorts of conversations are coming, but in this instance I felt nothing but blindsided, and a little confused. Nevertheless, I pledged to work harder when I didn't have the ball, and they were mollified and impressed when my tackle count rose in the following month.

The loss to the Kangaroos seemed to give us the jolt we needed. We beat Collingwood by five points in a great game the following Sunday, and that victory set us off on a barn-storming run of form that saw us win thirteen of our last sixteen home-and-away games. The second time we played the Magpies for the year we beat them by ninety-one points. I had signed a new three-year contract extension that tied me to the club until the end of 2019. Everything was clicking.

A couple of weeks after signing my new deal, we played St Kilda in the first Maddie's Match to raise money for our new charity, Maddie Riewoldt's Vision (MRV). We promoted the game using the hashtag #fightlikemaddie, which was a tribute to the way she tried everything to get better, fighting her illness at every step. The hashtag was also recognition of her wish that we all do everything in our power to try and cure bone marrow failure syndrome. Today, MRV is supporting countless research projects, and I'm incredibly proud to have been a board member and helped set up the foundation.

The lead-up to the match was emotional. Almost 46,000 people came to the game at Docklands and there was purple – Maddie's favourite colour – everywhere in that crowd. It was a wild game, too. Brett Deledio was on fire as we dominated the second and third quarters and led by fifty-two points at three-quarter-time. The Saints then piled on some quick goals early in the last quarter before we steadied at the finish to win by sixteen points.

Entrenched in the top eight, we had a few 'Richmondy' moments in the run home – including an after-the-siren loss to Fremantle courtesy of a David Mundy set shot – but we finished fifth, making the finals for the third year in a row. It was the first time the club had done so since Tommy Hafey was coach – a big achievement, yet after two elimination-final losses, we needed to win one.

The Tiger Army turned out in force, with 90,186 people in the stands, the vast majority supporting Richmond. Our average attendance across all our games that year was 49,764, almost two thousand more than the next-best club, second-placed Collingwood, and five thousand more than Hawthorn, which was about to win its third straight flag. Richmond had long been known as the sleeping giant of the game, but our fans had well and truly awoken. Now was the time for the players to repay them.

Hindsight makes it clear that we were far too focused on the outcome of that game. People were telling us that we needed to win a final to justify our place among the good teams, and to justify Dimma's position as coach, and we foolishly listened. We didn't know it at the time, but we were clearly held captive by the commentary, stressing about what the world would think of us if we stumbled again. We were the club that had finished ninth six times. We were the club that sacked coaches and wasted draft picks. We were the club that lost a game to lowly Gold Coast, defeated by a kick from a rugby league player. We were a club carrying thirty-five years worth of baggage. We didn't just have a monkey on our back. We were carrying a gorilla.

Yet we started strongly. Chris Newman, who at thirty-three was hoping to play in his first finals win in his 268th game, began up forward and kicked our first goal. By the six-minute mark of the second quarter, we led five goals to one. I kicked three goals in the second quarter, the third coming after I was wrestled to the ground by Michael Firrito. I wanted to snap the ball through, and I was sure the North players were encroaching on the protected area, so I put the ball on the ground and measured it out myself. The Richmond fans loved it, the North fans not so much.

The game seesawed during the third quarter, and our boys made some bad mistakes, none worse than when Troy Chaplin tried to evade our former teammate Robin Nahas, who wrapped him up in front of goal and converted the free kick. Two goals from Drew Petrie put them in front. We regained a narrow lead in the last quarter but faded. Boys would talk about that day in meetings months later, describing how heavy their legs felt, how drained they were in that last stanza. We lost by seventeen points.

The media made a beeline for the Richmond players of yore – the heroes of the golden era of the 1960s and 1970s – and they whacked us. It would be nice if we could say we understood, but the truth is their comments bred a very real resentment among the current crop towards those old guys. Instead of backing us, they had fed the unfolding narrative that we were mentally and physically weak, not like them, the Tigers of old, the strong and the bold. We had tried and failed, and there would be enough humiliation from outside of Punt Road. The last thing we needed was recrimination from club elders, too.

Trent Cotchin bore the brunt of the flak, after being tagged out of the game by Ben Jacobs, finishing with nine disposals, only four of them deemed effective. Amid the avalanche of crap thrown at Trent that week was a column from Mark Robinson, suggesting I should replace Trent as captain. I was miles off when it came to leadership. I wasn't even in the leadership group. Trent had a bad game, but that didn't make him a bad leader.

Our loss to North brought the magnificent career of Chris Newman to an end. Newy played his first game in 2002, the year after the Tigers made a preliminary final, and retired two years before our era of success began. Yet so much of what we became can be traced back to his passion, and the way he became a bridge between generations of players, connecting the old and the young. He was old school, grabbing you by the throat to get you going, yet also modern, understanding the flexibility and sensitivity required to manage the differing moods of forty-four young men. Long before we started using the term inside Tigerland, Newy was a *connector*.

We speak often as a team about our pride in the Richmond jumper, and he started that, too. Fans would remember him clutching the sash on gameday, showing his righteous pride, but they mightn't know how much he revered the colours. Newy was part of the group who decided we shouldn't wear our official jumper in pre-season matches – that we should wear it only when we were playing for points. And Newy set the standard in terms of how we cared for our jumper, things like never chucking it on the ground. That became the Richmond way.

I've stayed close to Newy, too. I hear from him all the time. I'm in an NFL Fantasy league with him. He's got four girls and I've got two, so we bond over that. And I've got a sneaking suspicion that he'll end up back at Tigerland at some point. I think there's a connection there – a thread that will one day bring him back. He'll be drawn to return to the place, perhaps as an assistant coach, or as the senior coach, or a board member, maybe. However he finds his way home, I don't think his Richmond journey is done.

11

ADD, KEEP, DELETE

I was now deep into my career – a full decade, in fact – and my disdain for the media was well known. I found too many reporters predictable and tedious, too many columnists reactive and misleading, and too many commentators foolish and false. No matter how I consumed my footy, it felt like the Fourth Estate found a way to distort the truth of what we did on the field every week. I just didn't trust them to interpret tactics or mindset or motivation. Maybe I just didn't trust them in general.

All of which made it doubly strange to receive a call from Gerard Whateley, the host of Fox Footy's flagship TV show, *AFL 360*. He had a pitch for me, both compelling and brief.

'If the Jack Riewoldt currently perceived by the public is not who you are,' he said, 'we can provide an environment in which the real you can shine.'

The show had a segment every Tuesday called 'Players' Night', he explained, and they wanted me to replace Western

Bulldogs skipper Bob Murphy in the hot seat, riffing on the issues of the day in a weekly public forum. It felt like the perfect forum for me to correct the record, to explain myself – to show people I was more than a heart on a sleeve, a grin after a goal or a pout after a loss. The way the role was described to me, the more it felt like a chance to offer perspective and nuance, and to remove myself from the vicious cycle of one-liners and hot takes. It felt safe, too. The *AFL 360* team gave me confidence that I could be quintessentially myself – that I wouldn't be thrown to the wolves, or under a bus, and that their questions wouldn't be designed to coax out a headline but to elicit insight.

In hindsight, what a gift that was! What a fork in the road it became. It was touching to be hand-picked for the job, and believed in. Gerard, in particular, was strong on helping me correct the public record, wanting me to be me: 'Toe the party line of the club, of course, but let your personality shine.'

Of course, I picked perhaps the worst year to join the punditry. Insight is easy when things are going well, but it's not so simple when things are going poorly. And in 2016 things went incredibly poorly, and incredibly fast. For the third year in a row we staggered through the early rounds. We were 1–6 after round seven, then we beat the Swans by a point at the MCG thanks to Sam Lloyd kicking a goal after the siren. We clawed our way back to 6–7 then fell away badly from there.

Nothing went right. Bachar Houli missed months of football through injury. Dylan Grimes was still struggling with his recurrent hamstring problems. Brett Deledio, who had been Mr Durable up until then, played only eleven games for the season. Our depth was tested and it didn't hold up. Daniel Rioli, who had turned nineteen during the early weeks of the season, should have been eased into AFL footy by playing no more than a handful of games. Instead, he was called upon most weeks. Injuries are a legitimate explanation for a faltering team, but cited by one of its players, they never sound like anything more than an excuse.

Our struggles weren't confined to the field either. Another developing problem was our leadership culture program, which was run by Gerard Murphy, who'd arrived at the club following the 2014 season. He introduced us to the type of feedback sessions that he'd used at Geelong to great effect. One person sat out the front of the group and everyone was invited to give them feedback on things they should 'stop doing', 'start doing' and 'keep doing'.

Gerard had seen the exercise – one of a suite of offerings used by the group known as Leading Teams – work wonders. Gary Ablett Jr received an infamous dressing-down in 2006 when senior Cats savaged his work ethic. Apparently shaken by the serve, he went on to win three consecutive AFLPA MVP awards and two Brownlow Medals. While the method is still used at several clubs, many others have stridently rejected it as giving players licence to bully and degrade. Whatever, it was a complete failure at Richmond.

The sessions opened the door to a kind of mob mentality. As humans, we're programmed to go to negativity in difficult moments, and at Richmond at this time, it led to an outsized emphasis on what people needed to stop doing. Once a fortnight or so, a player would have to enter the auditorium, knowing that his teammates had been divided into groups to discuss and critique him. It was my turn midway through 2016. I entered the room alone and sat on a stool in front of forty-three teammates, who'd gathered in private to list my shortcomings, as well as behaviours for me to add, keep or delete. They came up with words to describe me, and a seemingly never-ending list of feedback nuggets.

Stop speaking over others. Stop feeling the need to be the matchwinner, instead of just playing your role. Start critiquing your own game. Start finding solutions instead of pointing out problems. Start condensing your comments in meetings. 'What you have to say is really important,' said Alex Rance. 'The first ten seconds of it, anyway. But then it loses impact the more the message goes on.'

Even though it was largely silent in the room, it felt noisy, because my mind was racing.

They said I was trying too hard to be an individual – wearing the older Nike-branded gear to training, rather than the newer BLK apparel. They wanted me to be more respectful in dealings with all people – and to watch my body language on the field. They said they wanted 'consistency', but I wasn't sure what that meant, so I asked them, and Dylan Grimes answered. 'We feel like one week in our personal relationship with you we love you and we'll go to war with you,' he said, 'and the next week something will happen and it feels like we're a piece of shit to you. It's a bit of a rollercoaster.'

There were positive pointers, too. Keep asking questions and challenging the group. Keep educating forwards and backs by showing them your tricks. Keep showing interest and care for your teammates. 'You're really relatable now,' said Rance. 'Everyone loves spending time with you, and you show a lot of genuine care and a better connection.'

Steven Morris showed me some love: 'Playing against you as the opposition in training, it just feels like you're leading this increase in camaraderie in the forward-line group really, really well.' Shane Edwards did, too: 'More than half the time you're the perfect leader,' he said. 'It won't take long or much tinkering for you to be the most influential player here.'

We had so many kind and authentic people in my time at Richmond, but that feedback forum had a way of changing everyone. I can freely admit those sessions brought out the very worst in me. I dished out some terrible feedback, and I doubt any of it helped anyone. If anything, it tore holes in the fabric of the team psyche. I was senior enough to cope with the criticism, but young fringe players just trying to make their way? Such attacks must have been devastating. We had a young key forward named Liam McBean, who was struggling at the time. Liam was told that he was weak over the ball – just weak in general. I hate to imagine how that must have felt to him alone up the front. Liam was delisted at the end of the 2016 season, having played just five AFL games. I look back now and it's no wonder he didn't succeed. He had no chance in an environment like that. Those sessions weren't about constructive feedback. They were a pile-on.

AFL clubs spend so much time thinking they can copy what's been done at other clubs. I'm sure that's what happened when we hired Gerard. His appointment as our leadership consultant was sold to us as a massive coup: the guru who had turned the Cats around was going to do the same thing for us. Everyone became so infatuated with the idea that one man had the secret sauce that would automatically make us better leaders and better players, and it was bullshit. It backfired spectacularly, and even spread into the rest of the club.

Instead of just players, our player development manager, Bronwyn Doig, a bubbly and enthusiastic young staff member, was put up in front of the group, too. Bron was the person who nurtured draftees and rookies when they first arrived at Punt Road, helping them acclimate and assimilate. She was the person who helped you find lodging and bedding and transport. The person who made sure we all had adequate literacy and numeracy – that we knew how to pay our bills and had a plan for our careers (and our lives) after football. Bron helped us develop and grow up as professionals and people. She rode with us in the back of the ambulance when we broke a leg or punctured a lung, and called our parents when things went wrong. Bron felt she had to buy into the new cultural program, and was encouraged to sit up the front one day and receive her own barrage of 'add-keep-delete' feedback, framed as an opportunity for her to enhance her relationship with the list.

The criticism came – a laundry list of faults and deficiencies and limitations – and she listened and watched as the boys read from their critique sheets. Blindsided, gobsmacked and dumbfounded, Bron finally walked out. She left the club in tears that day – not over the judgemental things that had been said to her, but for not having had the courage to speak up and voice her concerns about the program. The feedback she was given is her story to tell – I think she's largely blocked it out – but it also honestly wouldn't have mattered what was said, because the method we were taught for delivering any message was so brutal, devoid of sensitivity or nicety. It was as though you had parliamentary privilege to say whatever you wanted without consequence, and that kind of radical honesty was ingrained in everything we did. Given all we now know about mental health, it's a wonder the dangers of the blunt feedback approach weren't raised immediately.

After a bad loss during the first half of 2016, in the Anzac eve game against Melbourne, Dimma was ferocious with us in the rooms. Gerard also gave us a spray. We had all made a commitment during the week to play for one another, and now that we hadn't backed that up, he called us out on it.

'You talk about that jumper. You're full of shit. You're fucking seriously full of shit,' he said. He pointed to Trent Cotchin, praising his work rate up to the final siren, and lambasting us for not doing the same. 'Which one of you was coming with him? It's fucking disgusting. It's fucking shit.'

I wasn't in the leadership group at that stage, but I'd had enough. I went to see Brendon Gale. 'This isn't working,' I said. 'This can't go on.'

The playing group was told in July that Gerard was departing. He still works in this space. But the work he did with us was never the right fit for our group. In a way, how poorly it worked almost became his parting gift. Richmond went through such turmoil that season that perhaps we worked out what we *didn't* want to be as a club. Perhaps the first seeds of the fun, friendship and success that were yet to come were sown in those dark times.

We had some horrendous losses that year. We lost to West Coast at Subiaco by eleven goals and lost our two matches against Hawthorn by a combined tally of 116 points. For the second year in succession, we played North Melbourne at Bellerive Oval. This time the game was played on a Friday night, so everyone was watching, and we lost by seventy points. Even when we won, we did it hard. We trailed Gold Coast by two goals at three-quarter-time at the MCG in round twelve, and just barely managed to get our act together and scrape home by seventeen points. God knows what the Richmond fans would have done if we'd lost.

Behind the scenes, the board instructed Brendon Gale to undertake a full review of our football department, and it was clear that no one was safe. With that kind of distraction hanging over our heads, it's hardly surprising that our form deteriorated even further. We conceded eight goals to zip in the first quarter against the Giants at Manuka Oval and went on to lose by eighty-eight points. Alex Rance held Jeremy Cameron to two goals and won twenty-six disposals of his own, in one of the greatest individual performances I ever saw. Without Rancey we would've lost by 200 points. Our score of 3.5 (23) was – and still is – the lowest ever by any team against the Giants. But the lowest of the low points came in round twenty-three when we lost to the Sydney Swans by 113 points at the SCG. At the end of the game, Rancey went ballistic. Buddy Franklin had kicked seven on him, and the pain was showing. 'Blokes don't care! I'm down the back getting killed and no one wants to help me!'

Those results tested our love of the game, and the club. So many questions were running through my mind. Is this the end of the coach's career? How many players are going to leave? Will anyone want to come to the club? Our recruiting department had spent all year trying to lure gun midfielder Dion Prestia to Richmond from Gold Coast, and they were confident he was over the line. I worried he would now think we were a rabble and look elsewhere. Dion has since admitted to me that the scale of the loss to the Swans made him think twice: was he just going from one basket case to another?

Football's only a game, but when you get belted like we did against the Swans, you find yourself walking down the street with your cap pulled down low. You don't want people to see you. It's hard not to let it affect the rest of your life. Sometimes I just didn't go out – didn't want to be bailed up by people telling me how shit we were.

The media had a field day. They said we needed to start another rebuild. They said I should move clubs and chase a premiership somewhere else. They said the two-year contract extension for Dimma at the beginning of the year was foolishness. They said Dimma had *lost* the players, too.

That couldn't have been further from the truth. There was never a moment that we didn't want to play for him. To be honest, I'm lucky enough not even to understand how coaches *can* lose their players. I've never been in a situation where that's happened. Even when Terry Wallace was in his last season, it wasn't as though we hated him. It was just that he had chosen a certain method of coaching, and it didn't work. For a coach to 'lose' the players, he would have to say or do something provocative or destructive – something he couldn't walk back. That was never the case with Dimma. Not even close. There's no doubt he needed to change some aspects of his coaching. He needed to lighten up a bit at times, and not worry so much about how the rest of the world perceived Richmond. He had, as he acknowledged at times later, become a stress head. But there was never a moment when I believed he should lose his job.

Another long off-season began, and legendary Richmond ruckman Neville Crowe died. Neville was famous not only for his work on the field in the 1960s; he later became Richmond president and led the Save Our Skins campaign that rescued the club in 1990. His death thickened the pall that hung over Tigerland, a sense of doom magnified by the impending results of the Ernst & Young review of the football department. Key leaders would later describe the exercise as a review *for* football rather than a review *of* football, but the findings were no less dreaded for that. Handed down on September 12, the key outcome was that Dimma kept his job, which was a massive relief, but several of his assistants were let go.

Mark 'Choco' Williams, the former Port Adelaide premiership coach, and one of the key people to welcome and settle a young Dustin Martin to the club, was moved on. Choco was an energetic figure who always wanted to help more and more, and in a way that might have been his downfall. He was almost always offering some inventive solution or left-field suggestion, but these were problematic, too – we didn't always find his constant thought bubbles that helpful.

Greg Mellor isn't a name most would know, but I always found him a quiet and caring coach, someone who was easy to talk to and always invested in making people better.

In the more recent shift toward sensitivity and authenticity in football, Greg would have been an ideal development coach. He was always flanked by Mark 'Wilba' Williams, who was passionate and bubbly, a 'yes' guy always looking to help, never to create friction. He coached the forwards and valued what the players had to say. I always felt heard by Wilba.

Ross 'Jacka' Smith was let go, too. That would have been hardest for Dimma. They'd been assistants together at Hawthorn, and Jacka was in many ways his right hand – that old-school coach who was committed to toughness, defence before offence. And he was a challenger, too, that forthright voice, unafraid to debate the senior coach and be a voice of opposition – a necessary check and balance.

Brendon Lade left, too, taking up an offer to join Port Adelaide under Ken Hinkley. Ladey is one of my best mates, as close as I've ever had to a big brother. Fun and funny and charismatic, I would have dinner at his house once a week. He was an exceptionally kind man who never failed to see the best in his players. He struggled with the decision to leave, but it was also a different club then. It was somewhat frowned upon by Dimma, for instance, for coaches to fraternise with players. Those kinds of relationships do need to be carefully calibrated, because there's an obvious power dynamic, but Ladey did that beautifully. Carly and I used to babysit his kids. At a time when I sometimes felt hounded by the footy department to grow up, grow up, grow up, Ladey was always playful, and plenty of players need those figures around them. He would have been eminently suited to the 2017 version of Richmond, and the irony of that is not lost on him now.

The life of the assistant coach can be nomadic like that – your position chopped and changed on a whim, your life turning suddenly on what happens each weekend. In many ways it's no different to life as a player. A handful or more are traded or delisted or retired from every club every year. We moved on from 2016 without Troy Chaplin, Adam Marcon, Liam McBean, Reece McKenzie, Andrew Moore, Ty Vickery and one other player, Brett Deledio. (More about Lids in a minute.)

There was a major restructure of the football department, too, with Neil Balme recruited to lead the new set-up and Dan Richardson now his offsider instead of the man in charge. It all seemed reasonably positive. However, I still had some thinking to do. I was disillusioned, like a lot of guys were. It felt as though we were never going to become the successful team and club that we wanted to be. Playing in a grand final was unimaginable.

I asked my manager, Liam Pickering, what my options were, and he told me exactly what he was hearing: I was being thrown up as a trade option. I asked Richmond list manager, Blair Hartley, about it, and he said I wasn't. That same game of ducks and drakes plays out every year at every club, and it does make for a strange working life, with an odd kind of conditional trust. Regardless, the media had dubbed me as potential 'trade bait', and that has its own effect – plenty of clubs made inquiries based solely on the perception that I was gettable. The Brisbane Lions came hard again. And the Bombers were unequivocal about their interest. One day, I was in the bedding section of Myer at Southland when my phone rang, and Essendon coach John Worsfold was on the other end. There I was, lying back on a nice new mattress, chatting to the coach of an arch-rival. Brendon Goddard called later to give me a feeling for what was happening at the Bombers, doing his level best to see me swap a yellow sash for a red one.

Throughout it all I felt dirty – *There's just no way; I couldn't, could I?* – almost as if I were cheating. It was such a strange and disorientating period, and yet at the same time, I was by now mature enough to manage myself and have those grown-up conversations. Over time, when enough deals have been put to you, you learn how to talk about money, and identify your self-worth, and stand by your value without sounding like a wanker. You understand the salary cap, and how everybody in the side needs to be paid fairly. I knew when other players were coming off contract, and that what I asked for would impact what they got. I was never interested in any deal that would see my teammates ripped off.

I never came close to leaving Richmond. I couldn't. It was ingrained in me to be loyal. Instead, I sat down with Trent Cotchin, who himself had had a big heart-to-heart chat with Dimma after Neville Crowe's funeral, and we made the decision that we needed to stick by the club. We had coffee at St Rose café in Essendon, and spoke about what we wanted our legacy to be. We wanted to leave the club in a better place than we found it, and that meant we needed to try and finish the job we'd started. Were we hopeful that we could compete for a premiership in the coming years? I don't think so. We were just hoping we wouldn't be shit. We were hoping the sun would come up the next day. At the core of our conversation was an acceptance that Trent and I were most likely never going to win a premiership. Given that, we needed to invest our time in creating a great club, so that the likes of Daniel Rioli could taste the success that we would never enjoy.

I remember watching the 2016 Grand Final in the Coca-Cola corporate box at the MCG. I had a paid gig doing some analysis of the game during the quarter breaks. I took my mate with me, a mad Swans supporter named David 'Flash' Lithgow. He was flat at the end of the game, but I was in awe of what the Bulldogs had done. As I watched them run their lap of honour, I didn't allow myself to imagine that one day I might be down there, jogging around the boundary with a premiership medal around my neck. It was never going to happen. We weren't going to live the fairytale – it wasn't worth even dreaming.

I think that's why Brett Deledio decided to leave. He couldn't see that the Richmond curse was ever going to be broken. He wanted to go to a club in premiership contention. For a couple of weeks, it looked like he was headed to Geelong. His dream was to live in Torquay and play for the Cats, a club that just about always makes the finals. He was briefly linked to the Western Bulldogs, who were coming off their famous premiership, but ended up reuniting with his old teammate and fellow Richmond stalwart Wayne Campbell at GWS. Wayne was the Giants' footy manager at the time. The deal went through in the last few minutes of the trade period on October 20.

Lids had always been indestructible. He played 140 consecutive games between round eighteen, 2007 and round two, 2014, and he was such an important piece of the Richmond puzzle every week. There was a time in his career when the stats showed that if he didn't play, we couldn't win. The only dilemma was where to play him. He could light up your midfield. He could stand at full-forward and take contested grabs in the goal square. He played a season in defence once and should have been an All-Australian half-back flanker. He was so damaging all over the ground.

He was a boy from the bush who loved camping and pig shooting and dirt bike riding and golf – a guy with a healthy sense of humour and attitude and ego. If you asked Lids why he never fell for the trend of tattoos, like so many other footballers of our generation, he would offer a wink and a nod and a trademark word of wisdom: 'You don't put bumper stickers on a Ferrari, mate.'

But Lids became disgruntled with everything that was happening at Richmond, and I couldn't blame him. I still can't. He had been at the club a dozen years, through so many hard times, and after weathering false dawns and then growing excited by the recent climb, the steep fall and crash of 2016 must have shattered him. A couple of Lids' best mates, Chris Newman and Troy Chaplin, had only just retired, which might have been a factor as well, but in essence he wanted a premiership and he knew the clock was ticking.

Lids is a great friend of mine, so we went out for lunch, just around the corner from where he lived. He had news, and I think I was probably one of the first people at the club that he told. Even though I knew he was unhappy, it caught me off guard a little. We'd never had a star player quit the club during my time at Richmond. He asked me what I was going to do, and I told him I was staying. He looked at me, and he wasn't smiling, or frowning. His face wore an expression that told me he was resigned to the only option left: 'I'm going.'

12

WHY NOT US?

When we came together to start pre-season ahead of our 2017 campaign, the familiar face of Damien Hardwick was right there, but he was flanked by a lot of new blood.

Justin Leppitsch had played in three premierships with the Brisbane Lions, then been an assistant coach at Richmond between 2010 and 2013, before enduring a tumultuous stint as senior coach at the Lions. And now he was back at Punt Road as our forwards coach. It was great to have him.

One of Leppa's best qualities is that he's always challenging you, always questioning how things are done, and at an AFL football club, that's an important – possibly crucial – trait to have. The easy way to settle in on a coaching panel is to go with the flow set by the senior coach, but if you do that then everyone can become a yes man. The fundamental point of the group is to come up with the best idea, and you get that only with push and pull.

Leppa was a technician, too, particularly with key position players. He was obsessed with aerial contests, so it's no coincidence that 2017 became one of the best years I've had in the air. He would take you through a new 'Master Class' every week, homing in on footwork, or protecting the drop zone, positioning from the front of the contest, then finding a way to the back of the contest. He would talk it then train it – thereby training us.

Former Adelaide Crows defender Ben 'Truck' Rutten took over as our backline coach. I'd played against Truck, and although mainly in the latter part of his career, he had been a serious lockdown defender – All Australian in 2005 – so he had tricks.

He was still relatively early in his coaching journey, but maybe that helped him bond with the core of our defence. Alex Rance and Nick Vlastuin, yes, but more so Dylan Grimes and Dave Astbury, who were country boys and seemed to speak his language. Truck coached the fundamentals while bringing an expertise and enterprise that our defensive unit hadn't been exposed to before. An analytical person, Truck didn't make things all about feeling; he knew the importance of quantifiable data.

He had ideas, too, which he knew how to execute. Protecting the spare defender became of paramount importance. If the talls on the team looked like elite interceptors that season, taking MOP after MOP (marks from opposition), that was partly down to the emphasis Truck placed on that element of the game. He ran our overall team defence, too, and that famed Richmond hunger to defend seemed to start every week with his Thursday meeting, where he showed exactly the right edits, one after another, so we knew what it felt like and looked like, so we knew how to SUBA (set up behind attack) and suffocate.

Last but certainly not least was Blake Caracella, a premiership teammate of Dimma's at Essendon in 2000. Blake had made a name for himself as an assistant coach at Geelong, where he worked under Neil Balme, and Balmey's arrival paved the way for his move to Richmond. Blake was put in charge of our midfield and offensive ball movement, and externally at least, he is often lauded as the man who created the game plan, who revolutionised Richmond ball movement. I would never put that down to one person, but Cara was certainly crucial.

He's a quirky cat, too. Witty. Wry. Dry. A football nut and a sporting savant. He was also an offensive thinker, always searching for holes and gaps and seams. His simple philosophy was to play to the fundamentals, but also play the percentages, and he did that by asking questions. How do we isolate this player? How do we get a two versus one, or a one versus none? How do we attack in a way that gets someone running through 50 by themselves, either to dish the pass or have a shot? Under Cara, protecting the corridor was everything, and that required smart footballers. Not smart as in those wily old guys who can read the flight and predict the bounce and turn that perception into a mountain of possessions – but smart as in knowing how to collapse in on the unguarded space and close off options. Smart like Shane Edwards. People often talk about the Lambert-Martin mid-forward swap – and Cara certainly had a lot to do with those kinds of positional ideas.

171

Together, the coaches cooked up a completely new game plan, and the idea of trying to copy other successful teams went out the window. Rather than attempting to build a playing list to suit a specific style of play, they looked at all the players at their disposal – their strengths and weaknesses, abilities and limitations – and retrofitted a strategy and style to suit them.

This new strategy focused on speed, and stylistically it was all about chaotic football, with an attacking use of handball. Embracing our imperfections – and our mistakes – was a key plank of the plan. We no longer cared about playing perfect footy. We wanted to flick the ball around swiftly, with abandon and instinct, and put our opponents under extreme pressure. The philosophy was best encapsulated by the structural shift in the forward line, which would now consist of myself, Ben Griffiths and a heap of speedy smalls at our feet.

The coaches weren't the only fresh faces either. When it came to our playing list, we'd secured three incredibly strong recruits in Dion Prestia, Toby Nankervis and Josh Caddy.

Although there was a worry about his persistent knee problems, we all knew Prestia was a gun. He had twice finished inside the top three in Gold Coast's best and fairest and had been the Suns' vice-captain for his last three seasons there. Dion brought gut running – as a genuine contest-to-contest midfielder – and fun. He fitted seamlessly into the new tactical structure but also loved the social side of being around the boys, bridging the young and old players. Some guys don't say much, and they're in and out of the club each day, there to do the job. But Dion was open and approachable, and always around.

None of us knew exactly what to make of Nank. He looked thirty years old – maybe older – but was only twenty-two. He's a Tasmanian, so I connected with that straight away. We'd been lucky to have Ivan Maric there for a few years, setting a new standard for us and building a culture, but he was slowing a little, and we needed a man in the middle. We knew Nank was tough immediately. I remember he lit up Cotch with this tackle at pre-season camp on the Sunshine Coast, absolutely smashing Trent and sending him to the ground. Everyone stepped back – 'Oh shit' – wondering what to do next, as Trent struggled to his feet, but in that one act Nank showed the group what they could expect from him. From then on, if you were the AFL opposition, or had the misfortune of being on the other team during an intraclub practice game, that was your shitty luck, because hurting the opposition was his job. Toby Nankervis is the biggest white-line fever player I've ever met.

Caddy, meanwhile, was a player with a stack of talent and confidence. He'd been one of the priority selections the Suns were able to make outside the draft prior to coming into the AFL, but had spent the previous couple of seasons at Geelong. Cads was the interesting one, because he was floated as a trade piece had Brett Deledio gone to Geelong. When that deal didn't eventuate, Cads would have felt as though he was on the Cats scrapheap, until Richmond decided to sniff around and see if he was gettable. He and Dion were drafted to the Gold Coast together, and that helped make him more comfortable at Tigerland. Cads can be a hothead, and a talker, but he became a valuable piece of the puzzle. The Lambert–Martin duo was at times almost a tripod, with Cads as the third leg. He could manage that role because he was a smart footballer, entering a team that was beginning to show some maturity. He was a deadly forward, too. It was always a nice feeling when the ball landed in his arms inside 50. You knew he would walk back behind the mark with purpose, and stride in to kick with intent, threading drop punts and curling snaps and spinning bananas. Cads was a genuine sharpshooter.

The other thing that changed markedly in the lead-up to the 2017 season was our mindset, and the person who spear-headed this cultural change was the amazing Emma Murray. These days Emma consults with the club but also runs a very successful business called High Performance Mindfulness. But when I first met her at the club in early 2017, she'd been working one-on-one for some time with Dylan Grimes, Sam Lloyd and Steve Morris, only now she was given a chance to work with the entire playing group. Her focus was on 'the intentional quadrant' – training us to utilise yogic mindful-ness, guided meditation and attention control to be our best selves on the field.

That kind of new age, eastern, Zen approach could easily have fallen flat with a few dozen smart-arse young alpha males, but her approach was so matter of fact and straightforward – no bullshit whatsoever – that it immediately struck a chord with all the boys. She worked with us on letting go of Rich-mond's past failures – the 'heavy legs' most guys remembered from those elimination-final losses to the Blues and Power and Kangaroos – and concentrating instead on what made us all great. She helped us understand that the mind is filled with emotional goat tracks we walk down time and again, but that the mind is also a muscle, and it can be strengthened and trained and directed to do what we want it to do. She taught us how to critique without criticism. Emma's approach was so different to the relentless negativity built into the model used by Gerard Murphy. She was a breath of fresh air for a club and a playing group that was crying out for positivity. She was exactly what we needed.

I had always been open to alternative thinking, and I think because the experience was so new to everyone, we all went on that same journey together. We lay down in darkened rooms and listened to guided visualisation exercises, and no one batted an eyelid because it all felt right. You can't attribute a percentage increase in performance to what Emma did for us – there's no Champion Data stat for connection – because it's largely immeasurable. But in a game of inches, if you improve attention control and decision-making even a fraction, isn't that enough? It's hard not to draw a correlation between us playing good football on a spiritual level, and that coinciding with Emma coming to the club.

In terms of personal performance, she helped us all find 'anchor' words that we could say to ourselves on the field, to bring us back to our best football. Trent Cotchin used to say 'Jokey' because he felt best when things weren't tense. People have seen the way Daniel Rioli writes 'Run – Chase' on his wrist strapping, and that's Emma, too. Shane Edwards' word was 'Angles' – to remind him to look for them. Mine was 'Walk Taller'. When I said that to myself, I would begin to look at the tops of other people's heads on the field, so that I was almost walking above them. My posture would improve, and my outlook would change. It's not so much about gaining an advantage but just dragging your attention away from things outside your control – like the crowd, the umpires, your opponents, the scoreboard, the stakes – and it gave me just the slightest sense of superiority, which is everything for key forwards. You need to have a presence.

Emma also became something of an unofficial counsellor for the players. Female figures in footy clubs, particularly those in positions of power, are so important. They humanise the entire environment. Young players who move to the club from interstate often look for strong female figures, but in many cases there are none to be found inside the furnace of the football department. Emma was a light for them, someone you could seek out for a conversation. One player used to have sessions with her that were often little to do with visualisation but more just a 'brain dump' – a chance to vent anger or fear or anxiety. And it would be wrong to think of her as a shoulder to cry on, or a soft sounding board. She wouldn't just listen; she would formulate a clear plan of action for you to implement, then stay on you to stick with it and succeed. She wasn't a counsellor – she was part of the high-performance staff.

Another key person who arrived at Richmond in the lead-up to season 2017 was Shane McCurry, who was appointed our leadership and culture consultant, and was a perfect fit alongside Emma. Shane drew us away from the constant sporting analogies into more general knowledge and history. He would talk about Napoleon one day and the Spanish conquistadors the next. He loved fables and allegories – things that aren't in the average footballer's wheelhouse. And the lessons he shared tended to stay with you, breaking you out of the building and sending you into the beyond.

He came up with so many methods for connecting us as a group. We did exercises on butchers paper, where we'd sit around in groups and draw our journey, perhaps what we imagined the year ahead was going to look like, or what we thought the year had looked like so far. Not just words and lines and bubbles either, but drawings, with a story – with obstacles and stick figures. You would draw an injury. You would draw the rain at training in winter. You would draw the Covid bubble. The losses were always valleys, and there always seemed to be a squiggly image of a mountain somewhere in the distance.

Voting for the Francis Bourke Award changed under Shane's watch, too. One of the great honours the club bestows each year is the Francis Bourke Award, named for the legendary Tigers wingman and later defender, who played in five premierships for Richmond between 1967 and 1980, and is an Immortal in the club's Hall of Fame. Francis is the nicest man you could ever meet, but on the field he was as tough as they come. And the Bourke Award is the result of a weekly player vote (3-2-1) for the people around the club – players, coaches and staff – who most epitomise the team's trademark values.

Inside the Richmond Man sessions Shane led, the process of nominating someone who best upheld the club's values became more public. The importance of off-field acts seemed to grow in importance, too. I remember a 2019 game at the Adelaide Oval, where play had stopped for a Crows player to be taken from the field by stretcher. Nathan Broad walked over to console the injured opponent – which was gracious in itself. But we noticed something else on the footage later. Adelaide captain Taylor 'Tex' Walker had dropped some strapping on the ground, tossing it as a piece of rubbish, and Broad picked it up. It was a little thing, but something we'd learned in our cultural sessions. We'd heard about the legendary All Blacks and their sweep-the-sheds mentality, and Shane McCurry had done a presentation to us about a Japanese World Cup soccer team that was renowned for leaving their changerooms spotless after every match. Little acts of care like that would be highlighted in our open meetings, and strangely enough, when we were absolutely flying on the field – humming as a team – our off-field nominations seemed to increase. Reward and recognition bred better habits, and more and more guys would go above and beyond. It was no longer just about how an individual played but how he carried himself, and what he did for others. And the value of the award seemed to rise, too, as we gradually drilled down into what was most important to the group.

Then there was the 'bucket of love', which is little more than a black plastic gardening bucket, filled with $5 notes, and a handful of questions. Once in a while, when Shane thought we needed it, he would bring out the bucket of love, and we would each take $5 and walk to a café with another player – someone you mightn't normally grab a coffee with – and you would do exactly that: have a cappuccino or whatever while asking each other set questions, like 'What do you aspire to be?' and 'What do you feel like when you're at your best?' and 'What are your goals outside of footy?'

Shane is a fascinating man, and he also brought a key mantra to our club. *Celebrate what you're good at, celebrate your unique gifts, skills, attributes and strengths, and bring them to the fore, day after day.* It's been more than six years since he introduced us to that way of thinking, and it's now grown into the fibre of the footy club. Shane has become something of an idol of mine, for the way he lives his life and goes about his work. He does things differently, and is never afraid of his ideas failing. In my time as a player, he opened me up to the power of connection, and how that goes hand in hand with high performance. But the lessons I learned from Shane extend far beyond football. He's taught me how to have a better connection with my family, friends, and the people important to my life.

The proudest moment for me in the lead-up to the season came when I was voted back into a slimmed-down leadership group. There were only three members of the new group: Trent Cotchin, Alex Rance and myself – with Cotch as the captain, and Alex and I as vice-captains. Leadership groups can sometimes grow too large and unwieldy in this league, but a set-up of a single captain and deputy can mean there are too few voices leading the long playing lists that make up a modern AFL side. Three leaders, however, seemed perfect. There was a beautiful symmetry to the new structure, too: a single skipper leading from the centre, flanked and backed by tall lieutenants in attack and defence. The media were still fixated on our shambolic 2016 – and so they lambasted the club for taking too long to decide on a leadership group. We were one of the final teams to name our group that year, just weeks before the 2017 season opener, but we didn't care about the delay. We took our time. We did it right.

My reinstatement to the leadership group also saw one of my surviving superstitions take on a new meaning. On gameday, I'd always loved to run out last. It was one of the few superstitions that lasted my entire career. I don't really know why it started, but in those years when I was a vice-captain and Cotch was captain, it felt symbolic to me that he ran out first and I ran out last. Trent led the way, while I was at the back making sure everyone was there. We were like bookends. Like sheepdogs. Like sentinels. I loved that feeling.

We were a bit scrappy in our first two games, against Carlton and Collingwood, but we won them both. The downside was my fellow key forward Ben Griffiths suffered a bad concussion against the Pies. Griff had a long history with concussion, dating back to primary school when he fell backwards from a backyard rope swing and knocked himself unconscious on a tree root. By the end of his playing days, the most innocuous head taps or high bumps would rattle him. Sadly, he never played another AFL game. And from then on, our forward line was me and the mosquito fleet – one tall target with speed demons like Dan Butler, Jason Castagna and Dan Rioli buzzing around below. The doubters said we couldn't contend for the flag with such a small forward line, but we didn't listen. Over the coming weeks, as we extended our winning run to five on the trot, we were convinced that our combination of speed and pressure and spread was not only unique but devilishly hard for anyone to stop.

Things went briefly off the rails. We were flogged by the Crows in Adelaide in round six, and then came a challenging three weeks. We lost to the Western Bulldogs by five points. We lost to Fremantle by two points. And we lost to Greater Western Sydney by three points. But there were lessons and takeaways each time.

We led the Bulldogs by four goals at quarter-time, for instance, having taken the game right up to the reigning premiers, on their deck – a ground where we've traditionally struggled – and lost only on the turn of a fleeting moment or two.

Against the Dockers, we played like shit for the first three quarters, then kicked six straight goals in the last to hit the front with twenty-one seconds to go. The Dockers, who hadn't kicked a goal since the nineteen-minute mark of the third quarter, rushed the ball out of the middle and it was marked by David Mundy close to goal. Alex Rance took some blame for this in our post-game review. Rancey had been standing with Mundy deep in defence, but assumed Freo would bomb the ball long into the forward line. Thinking he should be the spare man to crash the pack, Rancey called in Dylan Grimes to pick up Mundy while he waited deeper. But instead of bombing the ball, Lachie Neale made the most of another mistake. (Usually, we would've had a player – Bachar Houli – guarding space at the back of the centre square, but Rancey had called him back into the fifty-metre arc, meaning Neale could run unopposed into attack.) Neale delivered a beautiful pass out in front of an unguarded and leading Mundy, who marked on his chest, with ten seconds left, while Rancey stood by himself just outside the goal square. For the second time in his career, Mundy beat us with a goal after the siren. You couldn't make it up. But a lesson was learned.

Our loss to the Giants was my fault, but there was at least a little bad luck involved, too. Shai Bolton played his first game that day, and with a minute left on the clock he kicked his first goal – the sealer, a magical moment – at least until they were about to bounce the ball in the middle, when a score review cruelly showed that Shai's kick was only a behind, the ball having grazed a solitary GWS finger. The ball was in the Giants' hands when commentator Cameron Mooney summed up the situation: 'Richmond all week have been talking about what they do in red time when they have a lead – they've practised this situation. Let's see how they go.' We didn't go well.

The Giants launched their winning play from the kick out at full-back, but they were able to race the ball so easily into the middle of the ground only because I forgot to man the mark at the top of the goal square. Nathan Wilson saw the gap I'd created and kicked to himself (which you had to do back then to play on from a kick out), then he sprinted for twenty unguarded metres and launched a long bomb that reached the centre circle. We didn't have anyone out the back protecting the space if we lost that contest either, so when Phil Davis fisted the ball forward it landed in the lucky lap of Jeremy Cameron, 'The Emu', who picked it up and nailed his running shot.

But we learned from that, too. Watch any close Richmond game in subsequent years, and there would always be a Tiger sitting behind the long kick in, protecting that exposed space. The lesson learned against GWS saved us later. In fact, you could draw a direct line from that loss to us winning the 2020 Preliminary Final against Port Adelaide, thanks to a spare player – Tom Lynch – rolling around to protect the space and take a big defensive mark at the death.

Still, from a 5–0 start, we were now 5–4, and the commentators imagined a mass of fans putting feet through television screens. Jonathan Brown laughed and shook his head: 'Who would want to be a Richmond supporter?' To the media – and probably the football public – we seemed the same old Richmond. And I couldn't blame them for that. Same shit, different year – that's how it looked. But inside the club, so much was so different. The game plan, yes, but also the mindset. We *knew* we could pick ourselves up and go again without stressing about what everyone else thought of us. We didn't remotely act like the world was coming to an end every time we lost a game, or even a few, which was exactly what had happened in 2016. We analysed our losses and moved on.

The next six weeks were a rollercoaster. We had some good wins but some terrible losses. We kicked the first five goals against the Swans in round thirteen, and were still twenty-five points up at half-time, but lost by nine points. In round sixteen, we trailed St Kilda fourteen goals to one at half-time and lost by sixty-seven points. St Kilda were talked up as a premiership chance after that game, but they didn't even make the finals. In previous years, these losses would have crushed us, emotionally and spiritually. Yet we kept getting back on the bike and fronting up and doing more than just showing up but rather playing brave and manic footy. We beat the bottom-of-the-ladder Lions at Docklands in round seventeen, then gained some revenge against the highly fancied Giants in round eighteen. I remember Dimma's pre-game speech. He showed us a photo of him wearing a spearmint-green wool jumper his family had made for him with a message across the front: 'Why not us?'

Just a month out from the finals, I got accidentally poked in the eye by Mabior Chol during the last drill at training on the Thursday before our round-nineteen game against Gold Coast – which was also my great mate Shane Edwards' 200th game. I went to pick up the ball from the ground and Mabior came from the opposite direction, missed the footy and poked me straight in the eye. All I could see was red. I honestly thought I'd lost my sight. I put my hand over my eye, then looked down at the pool of blood in my palm, and half expected to see my eyeball there, too. There was a crew at training from Channel 7 news who'd been filming for a cancer fundraiser and weren't supposed to be filming any of the training session. They saw me coming off the ground with my hand over my eye, and I remember going ballistic at them when the lens was pointed my way, telling them to piss off. Looking through that eye was like looking through bloody frosted glass.

The club doctor rushed me up to the Royal Victorian Eye and Ear Hospital, just off Victoria Parade, and I sat there in the waiting room, wearing my full Richmond training kit. I was diagnosed with a tear in the sclera (the medical term for the white of your eye) and a bad graze on the cornea. The pressure in the eye was three times more than it's supposed to be due to all the blood. It took six hours for the injury to settle down to the point where I could see again, and then I went in for surgery. As is often the case before an operation, the surgical team gets a marker and draws an arrow on your skin, pointing to the area in need of repair. In this case, a nurse drew a big arrow on my forehead, pointing to my crook eye. I had to laugh at that. I really don't think the arrow was needed – but still appreciated the fail-safe approach.

I wasn't put under a general anaesthetic, which is not unusual but still extraordinarily disquieting for this procedure. It meant I was lying there, fully conscious, while a surgeon put tiny stitches in the torn sclera. He did a wonderful job, but the experience of someone sticking a needle in your eyeball while you're awake isn't one I'd recommend.

As soon as I got out of hospital, I began telling myself that I was going to be right to play against the Suns. Shane Edwards was one of my best mates and we'd enjoyed such similar foot-balling journeys since being drafted in 2006. I had to be out there for his 200th. Of course, this was merely the delusional thinking of a professional athlete who thinks he can bend the realities of the world to suit himself. I was never going to play against the Suns, yet I was still furious when the doctor told me I'd have to take the weekend off.

We played Hawthorn the following week, and again I was certain I'd be right to play, but the surgeon would make the final call. I was able to drive myself to his practice in Kew, which was an adventure in itself, with a crew from Channel 9 news trailing me through the streets. I actually waited at a set of lights – the intersection of Burnley Street and Bridge Road – until the light turned orange, and then gunned it in order to lose them. They went straight through the red light anyway. When I walked into the eye doctor's practice, however,

I noticed that there was Hawthorn memorabilia all over the walls. I convinced myself that his allegiance to Hawthorn would cloud his judgement – that he would keep me from playing to give his boys from Glenferrie an advantage. Sure enough, the surgeon advised against playing, so I rang our club doctor, Greg Hickey, and let him know my suspicions.

'I cannot take this guy's word for it,' I said. 'He's a bloody Hawthorn supporter.'

I'm certain Greg rolled his eyes on the other end of the call, but he was good enough to book me in with another doctor for a second opinion. You can bet what the first question I asked was: What team do you support? It was Essendon. The second doctor came to the same conclusion about my eye as the first, and I let go of my paranoia, but I was still annoyed to miss any footy.

We beat the Suns and the Hawks, then headed down the Princes Highway to take on Geelong at Kardinia Park. It seems amazing now that a club with the drawing capacity of Richmond was fixtured to play a game at a venue that barely seats 30,000 people. Collingwood never play there. Nor do Essendon. Or Carlton. It felt like punishment from head office to send us down to Sleepy Hollow. That, or the league expected us to be a basket case again in 2017, and no one would want to watch us. As it was, both teams were in the top four, so the stands were packed. It felt like an old-fashioned 1980s Saturday afternoon game at a suburban away ground.

Dimma was at his storytelling best during the build-up to that game. His inspiration this time came from a tale about how the Tampa Bay Buccaneers had motivated themselves before they won the NFL Superbowl in 2003. During their training camp, defensive line coach Rod Marinelli told his linemen to 'pound the rock'. The theory was that if one person keeps hitting the rock by themselves, they'll tire and never break it. But if one person hits it, then the next person hits it, then another and another, it's bound to break in the end. Buccaneers coach Jon Gruden ended up adopting the motto for his entire squad, and even the Tampa Bay fans caught on in the end, with T-shirts appearing in the stands with 'Pound the rock' emblazoned on them.

They're not the only sporting organisation to adopt the motto. The San Antonio Spurs follow the same principle, only they point to the history of the phrase: 'pound the rock' is the sporting shorthand version of 'The Stonecutter's Credo' – a truth written by Danish-American journalist and reformer Jacob Riis. His exact words are more poetic, and part of a longer personal manifesto.

> *When nothing seems to help, I go and look at a stonecutter hammering away at his rock perhaps a hundred times without as much as a crack showing in it. Yet at the hundred and first blow it will split in two, and I know it was not that blow that did it, but all that had gone before.*

Dimma was so taken by the credo that he organised for a humongous hunk of granite to be placed in our changerooms before the game against Geelong as a prop to go with his story. We loved his address to us, but it didn't change the outcome. We matched the Cats for most of the game, only for a lapse in the second quarter to cost us in the end. The final result was a fourteen-point defeat. Harry Taylor, who was essentially playing as a defensive forward on Alex Rance, was the difference between the sides, kicking four of Geelong's eleven goals.

We knew we had played well, though, and more importantly, we'd learned a lot about how to play the Cats. We had just faced them at their home ground, which is much narrower than the rounder MCG. 'Just wait until we get them on the width of the MCG,' Dimma said. 'Just wait.' He told us we had their measure, but if you looked at the recent history between the clubs, it was a curious statement. Richmond hadn't beaten Geelong for eleven years. Worse, we hadn't beaten them at the MCG since 1999. But that was our mindset. We willed ourselves to believe. At the end of his speech, he looked at the big rock and grinned, then turned to Giuseppe Mamone, our property steward: 'Sepp, on your way back up the highway, you can throw that fucking rock out the window.' We roared with laughter, and left Geelong smiling.

In our second-last home-and-away game, we played Fremantle in Perth, and an injury to Josh Caddy in the loss to Geelong had opened the door for Jacob Townsend to play his first AFL game for the season. His job was to play as a defensive forward on Michael Johnson, a backman responsible for launching a lot of the Dockers' attacking forays. Dimma spoke to Towner in front of the group, telling him he trusted him with the task. 'If you kick six,' Dimma added, chuckling, 'you'll keep your spot.' Towner duly came out and kicked six. Freo actually jumped us early on and led by four points at quarter-time, but we got on a roll after that which felt impossible to stop. We could do no wrong. We kicked twenty-two goals to four in the last three quarters and won by 104 points. I kicked one of the best goals of my career when I soccered the ball to myself and then snapped it through off my left boot. The funniest part of the game was when Dimma swung Alex Rance into the forward line for a bit of fun. Rancey kicked a goal (just his ninth in his 171st game) and we all went crazy. Meanwhile, Towner was kicking his goals from everywhere. After the game, Dimma looked at him and nodded. 'You've set the bar high, mate. Now you just need to kick six again next week.'

Sure enough, Towner kicked five goals in our round-twenty-three win over St Kilda and sealed his spot in the team for the finals. He had nineteen kicks in those two victories and kicked eleven goals and one behind. If Josh Caddy hadn't been injured, Towner would have been playing in the VFL. He was in the right place at the right time, had a dose of luck and made the most of that chance.

The win over the Saints was my cousin Nick's 336th and last AFL game, and Alex Rance had the job of playing on him. During the final quarter, when we were about eight goals up, Rancey decided he was getting bored and thought he would try and repeat his goal-kicking heroics from the game against the Dockers. He jogged forward, looking to get in the play, but we lost the ball and the Saints ran it down their end and kicked a goal. It's funny to us now, but it wasn't funny to the coach at the time. Dimma grabbed the phone in the box and yelled down the line to our runner. 'You go and tell Alex Rance that he's a fucking defender! Get behind the fucking ball!'

Everything came together for us as a team at the back end of the 2017 home-and-away season. We got everything right.

We found ourselves in such a sweet spot. All our meetings ran like clockwork. How your team meetings play out is a great guide in terms of how you're travelling as a team. If they flow nicely and the vision is great, you perform well. Why? The information is succinct. The vision illustrates exactly what you're supposed to do. And it all becomes so simple that everyone finds himself on the same page. There are no convoluted ten-point plans – you walk away from listening to your coach with one or two fundamentals ringing in your ears. In this case it almost became a mantra. 'Our defence takes away their offence. Our defence takes away their offence. Our defence takes away their offence.'

And then you perform well on field, meaning you've got great fundamentals to focus on in your meetings, so you play well again. It's a circular argument, a chicken-or-the-egg situation. There was no one moment or action that ignited our run. Our training was faultless. Every one of Dimma's stories hit the mark. Perfection seemed to breed perfection. Even though I played in two more premierships, I never experienced anything quite like it again in terms of being in such an untouchable sweet spot. Something magical just happened, and once we got ourselves on a roll, that momentum kept building on itself like a snowball. Week after week, game after game, we became bigger and better and faster – review and perform, rinse and repeat.

Inside the club, we have these video clips that are called 'Keep Forever' edits. They're great snippets of game footage that sum up how we want to play. They can – and are – used again and again. They help you understand the goal, and as you watch them unspool on the big screen with your team-mates in match review or a line meeting or opposition analysis, you remember what it was like during those games, when the team is pressuring and harassing and shutting down space, and you begin to *feel* what that was like at the time, and you want that feeling again.

Planning becomes fun. You're watching edits of your team playing brilliantly, and you can't help but be excited for the next game, confident and eager to do it all again. Could we do that in finals? Could we keep it up in the cauldron of September? The coaches kept telling us we could, that our brand stacked up, that other teams would fold under the blast of our blow-torch. It became easy to believe. Easy to imagine. Someone was going to win the premiership. Why not us?

13

HAPPY VALLEY

It was the end of my tenth season playing for Richmond, and I had never played in a win against Geelong. Indeed, the Tigers had beaten the Cats just once in the new millennium. There was so much history to overcome, yet we didn't feel burdened by that. I know that must sound strange. And I knew at the time what it must have felt like for the Tiger Army, many of whom had known only shellackings and misery at the hands of the blue and white hoops. But we were living in the moment, not the past.

We were buoyed, too, in the lead-up to the game, when Dustin Martin signed a new contract. North Melbourne had thrown an unfathomable amount of money at number four, and on the eve of finals, he still hadn't signed. The numbers being bandied around – $10 million over seven years, according to one report – would have turned anyone's head, particularly someone who hates the limelight and isn't likely to have a lucrative media career in retirement. Two weeks prior to finals, I thought he was leaving. His demeanour seemed to have changed. I remember chatting to Shaun Grigg about it, wondering about this shift in mood, this sense that he was closing himself off a little. 'He'll be fine,' said Grigga. 'It'll sort itself out.'

We did wonder, though. If he genuinely wanted to leave, then we didn't want him to stay. But if it was just about money, then the question became, 'How could we open his eyes, and let him see that there were other ways of recouping those earnings, without shifting clubs?' I thought of all the signed and framed merchandise that would be sold with his image in yellow and black, and went as far as to call Russell Taylor, a specialist in memorabilia sales, who rang Dustin's manager, Ralph Carr, who in turn rang celebrity agent Max Markson, and together they evaluated the difference in value between Dustin Martin in a Kangaroos jumper and the same man in a Richmond jumper. No one had really talked to Duz about that – about the power of playing an entire career in that guernsey, and the power of winning versus losing – which I found baffling. Because the difference wasn't a gap – it was a chasm. I don't know if my phone call had anything to do with the decision he made. He never walked us through his reasoning.

I suppose if Duz had become a little more shy than usual, it only made sense. It's easy to forget how 2017 thrust him into bona fide superstardom, playing arguably the greatest home-and-away season ever, combined with him being out of contract, combined with us surging up the ladder and into contention, combined with the fact that he hates being in the

194

public eye at all. There was the constant thirst that year for Dustin Martin content, and the less he provided, the more the world wanted it. Then we gathered one night at Cotch's house in the inner north to watch *The Footy Show*. They had the scoop – a pre-recording of an interview with Dusty – in which he declared he was staying. It was such a lift, and so well timed.

Our mindset was all about growth and opportunity, and the way I saw things, Geelong's mindset was poor. They had finished second on the ladder, while we'd finished third, so the game should have been their home final, but was played at our home ground because theirs was just too small. I understood how that must have grated on and aggravated them, but I was still surprised they would make their displeasure public. It became almost a full fortnight of bleating about how they should be allowed to host finals at their tiny boutique stadium in regional Victoria. Their recent finals record at the MCG was terrible, too, and their complaints only served to highlight that fact. Damien Hardwick always hated playing at Docklands, and he would complain about it publicly, and pundits would rap him on the knuckles for that, suggesting that he contributed to our poor form at the venue by continually spouting what became a self-fulfilling prophecy. Maybe so. But if that's true, the foolishness of whingeing about playing a final at the home of football is even truer.

We bought into the belief that we had one over the Cats before they even ran onto the ground. And that belief only grew after they did. The crowd was 95,028, a record for a qualifying final, and it felt as though the Richmond supporters outnumbered the opposition fans by ten to one. We were doing our stretches in the goal square at the Punt Road end when the Cats hit the grass, and loud, long and lingering booing filled the entire stadium. After the game I remember Craig McRae marvelling at that moment: 'Did you hear the crowd when Geelong ran out? I've never heard anything like that. Never.' We drank it in, and felt ten feet tall, like we were playing a home game against a minnow from interstate.

Jacob Townsend soccered the first goal of the game. 'He's done it again, hasn't he,' Bruce McAvaney told the viewers at home. 'A miracle man.' That took Towner to twenty kicks and twelve goals for the season. We were all over them early, too – our pressure rating was elite – but we wasted chances. Maybe it was the confusion of the occasion: we could hardly hear one another, but we could hear the fans. Whenever the Cats had a shot on goal, jeers echoed in the night. Every time they missed, there was a roar like we'd just scored. And when we *did* kick a goal, the roar turned deafening, and the hairs on the back of my neck stood up. Geelong didn't kick their first major until twenty-five minutes into the second quarter. Patrick Danger-field then slotted a running goal with one second left on the clock, and at half-time our lead was just nine points. It was disappointing to have such little reward for our dominance.

We were under the pump early in the third quarter, and fifteen minutes in the scores were level. The old Richmond would have collapsed in this situation, but we'd developed a habit of finishing games strongly, and the wheel began to turn in our favour. I put my stamp on the game by laying a big tackle on Patrick Dangerfield about sixty metres out from

With my dad, Chris, after his 300th game for Clarence, 1991.

My paternal grandparents, Helga and Heinz Riewoldt, with their grandchildren. From left to right: Harry, Maddie, Alex, Nick and me.

Me and Harry with our grandfather, Ivan, on Christmas Day.

Living up to the Riewoldt family motto: life is for living!

Montagu Bay Primary School sports day under the Tasman Bridge.

Dressed for my Grade 6 leavers dinner with purple hair!

Playing junior footy for Clarence.

Sprint tests at the 2006 AFL Draft Camp at the Australian Institute of Sport.
© GSP Images/AFL Photos

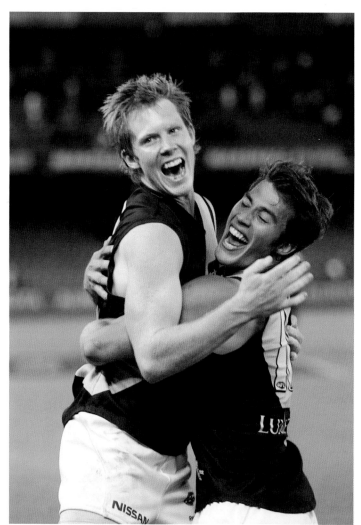

Celebrating a win with Alex Rance in 2009. © Greg Ford/AFL Photos

Happy as a pig in mud after a goal in 2010. © SMG/AFL Photos

Carly and I outside our first home, which Rob Dalton bid on for us.

Carly and I with Rob
and Lisa Dalton, our
Melbourne family.

Me and my cousin Maddie, who sadly died from aplastic anaemia, a bone marrow failure syndrome, when she was just 26.

Pointing at the sky and blowing a kiss to Maddie after my first goal during the opening round of the 2015 season. © Michael Willson/AFL Photos

Trent Cotchin and Alex Rance supporting me after an emotional loss in July 2015.
© Michael Dodge/AFL Photos

From tears to triumph! Richmond's magnificent 2017 Premiership. © Scott Barbour/
AFL Photos

Celebrating the 2017 win with Damien 'Dimma' Hardwick. © Scott Barbour/AFL Photos

Singing 'Mr Brightside' with Brandon Flowers and The Killers after the 2017 grand final. © Scott Barbour/AFL Photos

Celebrating the 2017 Premiership with my family, Carly's family and the Daltons.

Our wedding, 4 November 2017, in Tasmania.

Talking to my cousin Nick after Maddie's Match in 2018. An annual tradition that helps raise awareness and funds for bone marrow failure syndromes.
© Adam Trafford/AFL Photos

Poppy's first game, 2019. The team sang the song in a whisper to not upset her!

Celebrating with fans after Richmond's 2019 Premiership win. © Darrian Traynor/
AFL Photos

Winners are grinners! Me and Tom Lynch after the 2020 grand final.
© Michael Willson/AFL Photos

Celebrating Richmond's 2020 Premiership with family. ©Bradley Kanaris/AFL Photos

There was something extra special about having my girls out on the ground with me to celebrate the 2020 Premiership.

Being chaired off after my 300th game in July 2021. The stadium wasn't as full as usual due to COVID restrictions. © Albert Perez/AFL Photos

My family had to celebrate the milestone at home in Melbourne.

Enjoying some time off with my girls, Poppy and Hazel, on top of Mt Wellington in Hobart.

Tommy's first game, July 2023. © Michael Willson/AFL Photos

Posing with my family after announcing my retirement. The end of an era.
© Morgan Hancock/AFL Photos

One last hug with Trent Cotchin (left) and
Dustin Martin (right) as Tigers on 19 August,
2023. LEFT: © Michael Willson/AFL Photos
RIGHT: © Daniel Pockett/AFL Photos

I am so grateful for my time with the Tigers and have so much to celebrate.
© Daniel Pockett/AFL Photos

It was an emotional farewell. I'll hold these memories close as I embark on the next chapter of my life. © Michael Willson/AFL Photos

our goal, and the free kick set up a goal for Shane Edwards. Nailing opponents that season became almost more important to me than converting set shots or riding high for a pack mark. I remember talking to the boys about it during our forwards line meeting, in a little room under the stadium, an hour before the game had even started.

'Accept that there are a few people out there watching a game of footy. It's a fact. But remember that our one wood is our chase and tackle,' I said to the other forwards. 'Every single one of them will hesitate at some point, and then we are just going to mow them down. Let's run these fuckers off their feet.'

With just twenty-eight seconds remaining in the third quarter, Dusty won a crucial one-on-one against Tom Stewart, and took off down the wing, had a couple of bounces and poked a low drop punt in my direction. I nudged my man out of the way and grabbed the Sherrin, raked a long kick to Dion Prestia in the goal square, and the stands shook with a kind of happy, violent abandon. The buffer at three-quarter-time was three goals. Our confidence jumped right over the final break, keeping the momentum with us in the last. Dusty again found the ball, and flushed a long bomb forward, which carried and cleared the bubble, landing in the goal square on Shaun Grigg's chest. The more goals we kicked, the louder the crowd grew.

Tiger fans were dancing in the aisles by the time Trent Cotchin kicked the best goal of the game, with about five minutes left. I'd tried to take a screamer over Geelong ruckman Zac Smith, but the ball spilled off my hands and hit the ground. Cotch arrived, running flat out. He picked up the ball in one take, spun blind past Cats midfielder Mitch Duncan, took two steps and threw it on his left boot as he was being knocked down. The kick was a floater but went dead straight, sailing right through the middle for a lead of forty-five points. We were heading to a preliminary final.

After a weekend off, I was filled with excitement when preliminary-final weekend rolled around. If we were going to play in the big one, we needed to get past Greater Western Sydney, and that meant coming up against Brett Deledio. This set up an intriguing battle. As some people saw it, if the Giants won then Lids would be proved right for leaving Richmond. While if we won, he would become the man who walked away at exactly the wrong time. To my eyes, Lids left to join a club in contention, and he had achieved exactly that. The previous weekend, he had played in his first-ever winning final, when the Giants defeated West Coast by eleven goals at the Sydney Showground Stadium. Yet his recurring calf injuries were a constant throughout the year and his form was patchy at best. In our planning before the game, we didn't put much time into him. He was an incredible player, hobbled by his body.

Our preparation for the game was unique. In the middle of the week, our leadership and culture coach, Shane McCurry, spoke to us about the power of connection. Then he walked us over to the old changerooms in the base of the Jack Dyer Stand, where we found sixty Senegalese drums and a handful of instructors. Every single player and coach sat within a pair of concentric circles, each learning how to whack the skin of the *djembe* – which translated means 'Gather in peace' – in sync with everyone else, until we were smashing and thumping those instruments and falling into rhythm with one another. Near the end, Bachar Houli decided he wasn't done, and set off on a frenzied tear, pummelling that drum while we clapped and cheered and danced. Who thinks of stuff like that?

We played the Giants at the MCG on a Saturday evening. It was a twilight game – the first bounce was 4.40pm – and it felt strange for a final, starting in the daytime and finishing under lights. When the siren sounded to start the game, you could feel so much energy pulsing through the crowd and through each Tiger waiting to play. I felt like I could have run through a brick wall.

We made an incredible start, with Dustin Martin setting up Kane Lambert for the first goal of the game in the opening twenty seconds. Shortly after, Josh Caddy marked in the pocket and snapped our second. It might seem repetitive to mention the noise and the crowd so often, but the Tiger Army was such a part of our journey. They were crucial to our success. And they were gathered that day in a way I suspect will never, ever be repeated. The official crowd was 94,258, and more than ninety per cent of those had to be Richmond supporters. Never before in an AFL match has a team played in front of roughly 90,000 of their own fans. The social media meme of that week was all about the 'Big Big Sound' coming to the MCG, but the biggest sound of all was the crowd after those early goals. Channel 7 suspected it might be and had arranged to measure the volume. 'It has landed at 122 decibels,' said Cameron Ling at quarter-time. 'Just below a jet aeroplane and just above AC/DC on the *Back in Black* tour.'

The members of the Tiger Army had always been incredibly passionate, but I think prior to 2017 they became, in a way, part of the club's baggage, carrying that burden with them, so it was almost never left behind. It became a millstone around everyone's neck – a collective ball and chain we were all forced to drag. Many of the fans seemed to love playing up to the stereotype, flooding talk radio after a bad loss to pay out on the club, players, coaches and administrators. The angry-fan stereotype had been built over a long period. Kevin Bartlett needed security to keep irate supporters out of the rooms after a bad loss to Fitzroy in 1991. There was the idiot who spat on Danny Frawley in 2004. And the supporter who backed up and dropped off a load of manure at the entrance to Punt Road Oval. It all meant that the club was forever trying to please the fans, doing things that might appease them – recruiting messiahs like Ben Cousins and Nathan Brown. In 2017, however, we created a game plan and culture that worked for the people already inside the club – fit for purpose, distinctly ours – and the fans fed off the fun we were having. They seemed to understand that we were sick of carrying that baggage, too, that it wasn't ours to lug from year to year. We were on an adventure, and by preliminary-final day I had no doubt that the fans completely understood that. Win or lose (there are no draws in finals), there wouldn't be any scarves burned or membership cards microwaved.

As we knew they would, the Giants hit back. They kicked the next three goals and hit the front, before Daniel Rioli and Jason Castagna gave us a six-point lead at quarter-time. Dan played a great game. He kicked our only goal of the second quarter, then kicked our first in the third term when the contest was in the balance. With about ten minutes remaining in the third quarter, we led by seven points. Daniel Rioli then ignited the charge that gave us control of the game. He kicked his fourth – half of our eight majors for the day – but we loved even more that he was the leading tackler in the game to that point. Shane Edwards added another, before Dustin kicked three successive goals, two before three-quarter-time, and another one in the second minute of the final quarter. The Giants had one last gasp, narrowing the margin to twenty-three points, midway through the last quarter. A couple of minutes later, I hit the scoreboard after a brilliant long pass from Dusty, snapping the Sherrin around my body. We were twenty-nine points up with seven minutes to go. Not even Richmond could cough up the win from there.

When the siren went, the camera panned to me, because I looked emotional and overcome. I was actually trying to get a fly out of my throat, but was also in tears. I've watched the finish of that game a few times over the years, and it makes me smile every time. Twelve months earlier I had resigned myself to the fact I would never play for Richmond in a Grand Final, and now we were in one. Whatever happened next, the Richmond curse was buried.

Our skipper was our best player. Cotch finished the game with twenty-six touches and nine tackles, although he would later find himself at the centre of a media frenzy due to a collision with GWS midfielder Dylan Shiel. Trent and Dylan had been competing for a disputed ball in the first quarter, and in winning the contest Trent made contact with Dylan's head and concussed him, leaving the Giants a man down for the rest of the game. But it just wasn't fair for that incident to over-shadow everything else Trent did in the game. He was so cool and calm when we needed those qualities. He was also unbe-lievably tough and courageous in the way he attacked the ball and the opposition. I was so happy for Trent because he was able to show his true colours. He had copped more flak than anyone for our elimination-final losses. Now he was leading from the front, playing a pivotal part in two of the biggest matches you could imagine. And he did it with class. Straight after the game he hugged a few of us but then sprinted the length of the field to shake the hand of Brett Deledio, who was weeping. Lids finished the game with just eleven touches. I can't imagine the pain and regret he must have felt, taking our commiserations while watching our celebrations.

It's hard to stick to your regular routine during grand-final week. You don't want to walk on eggshells, but you do anyway. We were all novices, but Dimma nailed it for us early in the week, sharing his experience from three grand-final weeks as a player. He told us simply to enjoy it all. 'If you don't *want* to do something, say no,' he said. 'Just don't say no because you're scared to embrace the week and the occasion.' Having been given a licence to enjoy the week by the coach, we did exactly that. My parents, who had come up from Tassie for the preliminary final, decided to stay for the week. My brothers were both in Melbourne as well, and some of Carly's family came over. I had to organise twenty Grand Final tickets.

For the Monday recovery session after the preliminary final, there were cameras everywhere and people hanging off the fences at Punt Road. Having our training ground in the middle of Melbourne, right next to the MCG, meant we were smack bang in the heart of the Grand Final precinct every day. In previous years the club had hired out Punt Road for functions, but it was now off limits, transformed by a ring of cyclone fencing and bollards.

Monday was a huge day. The media were in a lather about Trent's collision with Shiel, but the Match Review Panel decided that he had no case to answer, which was a great relief for us. Trent and I had a chat about the episode a few hours later, over a few glasses of water at the Brownlow Medal count. If we needed more evidence that the footy gods were on our side, it came when Dustin Martin took home 'Chas' after polling a record tally of thirty-six votes.

The rest of the week was a blur, but open training was a highlight when thousands of Tiger fans packed into Punt Road to watch us have a light run in the sun. Although we were going into the game as outsiders, we didn't feel like underdogs except in the sense that we were being underestimated. Adelaide had finished on the top of the ladder, handily defeated the Giants in week one of the finals, then smashed Geelong by sixty-one points. Their offence was the most vaunted tactical tool the league had produced in years – a kind of surgical stealth built on articulate overlap handball and precision kicking. They'd kicked 400 more points than us during the home-and-away games, yet we knew we could blunt them with our backs.

We were the elite defensive team in the competition, and that was the message for the whole week. I remember sitting in Ben Rutten's meeting, and him telling us how our greatest strength would take away their greatest weapon, and after that, they would have nothing left to fall back on. Think about the defenders we had at our disposal. The three big backs were Astbury, Grimes and Rance, three of the greatest defenders of their generation. We had Nick Vlastuin, one of the best interceptors in the league, and Nathan Broad, who was rarely beaten on the ground or in the air. Then there was Bachar Houli, a player who with a bit of luck could have ended up with two Norm Smith Medals. It was a phenomenal six that made us almost unbeatable behind the ball. And when it came to the key statistic in modern footy – forward-half turnovers – we were record setters.

On the Friday, we were part of the Grand Final Parade through the streets of Melbourne, and we embraced the festival atmosphere. Sitting inside the Old Treasury Building before going out to hop in the back of a motorcade of Toyota Hilux utes, we were relaxed and happy. As we crawled along Spring Street, I looked out at the crowd and tried to pick out the people I knew. When we got on stage, Trent Cotchin joked with a few of us older boys that he was going to hold on to the premiership cup longer than Adelaide captain Taylor 'Tex' Walker. It actually got a bit awkward. Trent can be very headstrong when he sets his mind to something, and he's never been afraid to embarrass himself. Cotch simply wasn't going to take his hand off that trophy before Tex did. In the end, Tex let go first and we all roared. I don't think anyone gathered there knew what we were carrying on about. Trent did the same thing prior to the 2019 Grand Final. By then he had even come up with a tactic to make it work. While holding the cup with one hand, he put his other hand out for a handshake with Greater Western Sydney captain Phil Davis. Phil let go of the cup to shake Cotch's hand and we all laughed and high-fived. It was gold.

We went into the game with no one in football expecting us to fire. I was nervous, too, playing the game out in my head more than a few times. In our pre-game meeting, Dimma spoke about the Hillary Step, the final challenge on Mount Everest – a twelve-metre vertical ice face you need to scale slowly and carefully before reaching the summit. Slip, and you fall three kilometres to your death. He spoke to us about the concentration you need to make it, and how you need to keep looking at your feet, because if you get distracted by the sight of the summit – *thinking about where you're going instead of what you're doing* – you can fall and die. The theme fitted perfectly with the job we had at hand. Before we walked out of the rooms, he wrote four words on the whiteboard: '40 feet to go'.

We ran out and were ushered straight to a row of seats to have our pre-game photo taken. We'd spoken beforehand about embracing that moment by smiling. A lot of teams sit down and want to look serious. We wanted to show how much we were enjoying ourselves. In contrast, the Crows had become hung up on things like their infamous 'power stance'. We knew it was going to happen, and we worked with Emma Murray on our response. We decided to lower our gaze, and just not engage with it. It wasn't like a Maori haka where we had to show respect to another culture and make solemn eye contact. They stood still, arms out by their sides like cartoon characters, while we locked arms and grinned, then just walked off. I thought their approach was so stupid that it was almost funny, and I suspect most of their players didn't buy into it either. The Crows didn't have their whole group on the same page like we did.

Adelaide kicked the first goal of the game four minutes in, then Eddie Betts kicked another one a minute later after Nick Vlastuin slipped over just outside the Adelaide goal square. 'Hang on,' I wondered. 'Are we going to get blown away early?' The Crows were the sort of team that could easily kick seven goals in ten minutes – they had flogged us in exactly that manner in round six at the Adelaide Oval. I was desperate to get my hands on the footy soon, to settle my nerves with some action, having been quiet during the win over the Giants. I took a big pack mark within range and missed my shot at goal. I kicked our next two scores of the game as well, but they were behinds, too. Still, I was in the thick of things, my nerves were gone and my confidence was up.

The Crows were a free-running team, so we knew we had to deny them space to move. By applying pressure, we were able to force them into errors. Rory Laird had been one of the favourites to win the Norm Smith Medal, and I was stoked to lay him out with a big chase-down tackle. Things like that – little and big – happened all over the field, gradually shifting the mood. And there were moments that no one noticed except us. Adelaide kicked a goal, for instance, and a few of the Crows players started sledging Toby Nankervis. Big mistake. Nank is a competitive beast, so getting stuck into him was like waving a red rag at a bull. He started smashing in harder than

206

ever – both malicious and marvellous – our driving force as we started to gain control.

We felt like we had the game on our terms during much of the second quarter, but it wasn't until late in the term that our dominance was reflected on the scoreboard. Jacob Townsend, Jack Graham and Dustin Martin all kicked goals in the last ten minutes of the second quarter and we went into the long break nine points up. Those goals were great, yet my favourite moments during the first half were Jacob Townsend's bone-crunching tackle on Matt Crouch and Alex Rance's desperate dive to touch a Taylor Walker shot on the line. Andrew 'Mini' McQualter, who would step in as caretaker senior coach when Dimma left the club, was excited by what we had done. Adelaide, Mini told us, had played both their finals – and most of their season – in control of matches from the outset. For them, going in behind at half-time would have been a foreign experience. It would have frightened them. 'They haven't seen this, boys,' said Mini. 'They have *not* seen this.'

We kicked the first three goals of the third quarter, which meant we'd booted seven in a row, and we soon led by twenty-eight points. Those of us who had been part of the elimination-final losses to Carlton in 2013 and North Melbourne in 2015 knew what to expect. We knew that in this time of desperation, Adelaide would roll the dice and go on the attack. We needed to be ready and to stand tall when the onslaught came. Trent Cotchin was playing as a defensive midfielder. He knew he needed to sit back behind the play and make sure Adelaide couldn't stream forward unopposed. Everyone else knew we needed to clog the corridor. We were mature and calm; those elimination-final losses had prepared us. By three-quarter-time, we led by thirty-four points.

I kicked a goal at the start of the last quarter, which put us forty points up. Then Dion Prestia added another one. The Crows hit back briefly, before Towner marked an Adelaide kick-out after a behind and slotted his second. Soon after, small forward Dan Butler brought a huge smile to our faces by slotting a checkside goal. That kick was something we practiced fifty times after every training session. Despite all the practice, he didn't get a single chance to have a shot like that all season, until this moment, his moment, in the Grand Final. He was never going to miss. It was after Butler's goal that a Channel 7 camera panned to Brendon Gale and Peggy O'Neal up in the stands, their faces a mix of tears, disbelief and joy.

Even late in the game, when it was clear we were going to win, we didn't slacken off. We were yelling at one another to watch certain players and deny the Crows space. We were all over them. With fifteen minutes left we were so far in front that it was inevitable we were going to win. But it had been ingrained in my head that Richmond could lose from anywhere. I found myself watching the clock tick down. It was the greatest few minutes of my life, yet I wanted them to disappear so we couldn't somehow fall at the last hurdle. It wasn't until the final siren blew that I truly believed we were going to win. When it sounded, we all started running around like crazy. I embraced Grigga and Dusty – I remember that much – but the rest was a daydream. Even now it seems hard to believe it really happened. We had gone from a rabble to a premiership team in twelve months, and Grigga and I were screaming at each other, not just to celebrate but to make sure we both understood: 'We just won a fucking premiership!'

Dustin Martin was a deserving Norm Smith Medal winner, but Bachar Houli could easily have won it, while Alex Rance was possibly the best player of the first half, repelling everything. Prior to the presentation of the medals and the premiership cup, I thought of Maddie. She would have been proud of me for living out my dreams. Dimma and Cotch hoisted the premiership cup and we all charged forward to get a piece of the action. On our lap of honour I spotted my former teammates Troy Chaplin, Kel Moore and Chris Newman, and it dawned on me how close so many players had come to being part of our success. They left in 2015 and 2016, so they were only a year or two away from what I was enjoying. Timing is everything. That couldn't have been made clearer to me than by the guy I was running around the oval with – young Jack Graham, who had just played his fifth game, tagging Rory Sloane out of the match while helping himself to three majors as our leading goal kicker.

Then there's the story of Brett Deledio. Lids wasn't at the game that day. He felt so terrible about Richmond making a grand final without him that he took his kids to Taronga Zoo in Sydney. I don't doubt that he loves Richmond deep down, but I doubt he'll ever get over the fact that he left when he did. That can be the harsh reality of sport. Sometimes you lose old people and bring in new people, and your culture changes. One group isn't better than the other – the new lot just fits with the dynamic of the time. I would've loved to have played in a premiership with Lids, but his leaving also opened the door for others to step up. Dan Butler and Jason Castagna were given opportunities because he'd gone. They played crucial roles in our success, and I would never deny them that.

That year shines so bright and warm in my memory, probably because we found ourselves laughing so much more than we had in the past. It was in 2017 that we adopted a new warm-up tradition, where Grigga, Duz and I would sit around in the players' change area before each game, listening to music. We created this custom, where we would sit around chatting, play 'True Blue' by John Williamson, 'I Still Call Australia Home' by Peter Allen, then 'Waltzing Matilda'. It became such a routine that it even had its own choreography. When I heard the lyric 'Down came the squatter, mounted on his thoroughbred', I knew to get ready for the next line – 'Up came the troopers, one, two, three' – because it was my cue to gallop into the space, pretending I was riding a horse. As players, I guess we're born performers, too. And that's not even counting the craziness of finding myself onstage with one of the biggest rock bands in the world.

The Sunday before the Grand Final, my mate 'Flash' Lithgow – the Sydney supporter who I went to the 2016 Grand Final with – told me he thought it was huge that the AFL had booked The Killers to play at the post-match concert. 'I can see it now,' he chuckled. 'You up on stage with The Killers.' That innocent comment planted a seed in my mind. 'If we win,' I laughed, 'I'm going to make it happen.'

There are rules about never getting ahead of yourself in football, and I broke them all, asking the club's media and social media staff if they could put the feelers out, to see if it was a possibility. We were supposed to be a humble group. (If we'd lost, I would've blamed myself for putting a mozz on us.) But it was such a wild time in Richmond's history, and in my own life, that it felt as though I could take the risk and have it pay off.

After our win, Nicky Malady, our media manager – the person who sets up interviews and pressers, and gives you pointers on what to say and especially what *not to say* in interviews – came up to me and said, 'If you want to get up there with The Killers, you've got to come now.' I told her I couldn't leave. When the coach is going to say something, you need to be there.

I was glad I did. Dimma's speech was so heartfelt, emotional and proud. We then sprayed a heap of champagne around the room before we started lining up to go out on stage. Suddenly, Nicky was back: 'If you want to do it,' she said, 'you've got one more chance.' I didn't need to be told twice. We were directed around one side of the stage while the rest of the boys went the other way. By this time, Carly had joined Nicky and me. No one knew I was going up except them. Suddenly, a roadie was in front of me with an instruction: 'Walk up the stairs. They know your name,' he said. 'They might pass you a mic, but just have the time of your life.' As I walked on to the stage, the lights were blinding, and a smoke machine was pumping. I couldn't see a thing, and then I could see everything – the band, the crowd, the lights, even the Richmond players who hadn't played that day, all standing there in their suits on an elevated stage platform, going absolutely mental.

Brandon Flowers looked at me and turned to the crowd: 'Want to do a little "Brightside" with Jack Riewoldt?' I knew all the words, so I pumped my arms in the air and gave Brandon a hug. During the first few bars of the song, he sang while I danced around like an idiot. Then he gave me a mic. I was a rockstar, apparently. I looked down and saw my teammates Taylor Hunt and Shaun Hampson getting into it while I sang and danced and waved the mic above my head. At the end of the song, Brandon looked out at the crowd again. 'Give it up for Jack Riewoldt!' We hugged, then the band smashed out some big notes to end their set. It's hard to believe the entire event took place at all, and yet it might well be the thing I'm best remembered for now that my playing career is over.

That night and the next day were all about quality time with teammates and family and friends, at a special reception in the Palladium at Crown Casino, and in the Maurice Rioli Room at Punt Road. We necked beers. We watched the replay. We necked more beers and watched the replay again. Our jumpers and medals never came off. I remember talking with Shaun Grigg about how far we'd come in the space of twelve months. We both had the same question: 'How the fuck did we end up here?'

When I look back now at how that premiership side came together, it's amazing to think it was built during that period when the Gold Coast and Greater Western Sydney were getting so many draft concessions. The extra picks they were handed meant that the early rounds of so many drafts were stripped bare. With what was left for the rest of us, you had to get every selection right to stand a chance. Take the 2011 draft. We were at close to our lowest ebb as a side. In any other year, we would have had a top-five draft selection, but the expansion clubs ate up the prime picks. Greater Western Sydney alone had eleven picks inside the top fourteen. With pick fifteen, we chose Brandon Ellis.

Clubs also had to be a bit more creative, and look a little deeper in the national draft, or the rookie draft, and then put more time into developing those players. Our premiership team had so many late draft picks, like Jack Graham and Dan Butler, and players who had started out on our rookie list, like Jason Castagna and Kane Lambert, and even pre-season draft selections like Dylan Grimes. It was also built on clever targeting of players from other clubs, from Bachar Houli and Shaun Grigg, to Dion Prestia, Josh Caddy and Toby Nankervis. Although it seemed such a shock to so many people that we won the flag, much of that shock was based on our implosion in 2016. When you look past that aberration, you see a steady, linear progression before our triumphant surge.

Given we'd won the premiership, the footy trip had to be a celebration of the highest order. Grigga and I loved planning these events. We went to Cairns three years in a row between 2014–16, but in 2017 we decided we wanted to go overseas. We wanted all the players to come, too, including the youngest of them, meaning we didn't want to go to the USA where you need to be twenty-one to be properly let off the leash. I ended up arranging for us to go to Hong Kong.

Camaraderie is part of the secret sauce of winning. I know quite a few clubs have drifted from the idea of letting their whole list go on a trip together at the end of the season, and I think that's short-sighted. You end up with players travelling in cliques instead, and those cliques can be hard to break up when the squad comes back together. That's what it was like when we first arrived at Richmond – various small groups doing their own thing.

It's true that taking 40-odd players away together can be fraught with danger, but if the majority of the people in your group have got their heads screwed on, everything works out fine, and the bonds you form help hold the list together. Not everyone comes, anyway. Footy trips aren't Bachar Houli's thing, and Trent Cotchin wasn't really into them either. But I have no doubt that time together helped the bulk of us build our culture of connection.

Arriving in Hong Kong, we were going to be presented as special guests when we went to the races at Happy Valley, and we'd have our own security detail when we went to the races again at Sha Tin. But before all that, at the airport, after passing through customs and into the arrivals hall, we had to find our tour company. The driver held up a sign so we could locate him, with two simple, glorious words: 'Richmond Premiers!'

14

MERCY RULE

Life kept getting better and better in late 2017. On November 11, Derby Day, I married the love of my life. We were in Tasmania, surrounded by family and friends. It was important to us to tie the knot there – to show people where we're from, and to celebrate that place. Many mainlanders consider our island home an afterthought, and it's important for us to correct the record. We are the little state that punches above its weight – the poor state with incredible natural riches – and we're fiercely proud of our patch.

Our wedding was held at Freycinet Lodge, which is located on a stunning part of Tassie's east coast, with the pink-hued boulders of the Hazards mountain range above, and the cool clear water of Coles Bay below. Guests made a trip out of it, and we helped them experience the place. We sent out itineraries that would direct them to drive up the Great Eastern Drive, visiting vineyards and cheesemakers and lookouts. One group of mates hired a ten-seater minibus to bring five couples – the

Newmans, the Griggs, the Lades, the Foleys and the Deledios –
and we emailed the wineries to let them know 150-odd people
might be stopping by, giving them a chance to get ready. A
group would stop in, and the winery would call up the next
winery on the route – 'Yep, they just left, and had a bit to eat,
so they'll probably just want a tasting and nibbles.' I loved that
our guests got to experience a little of that Tasmanian quirki-
ness and charm. (They were probably cursing us the next day,
though, on the winding, three-hour drive home after a big
night. There would have been a few heads out the window.)

Our ceremony was in the late afternoon, and we wrote
our own vows. Carly spoke about how she loved my curiosity – the way I always valued learning over knowledge. I spoke
about meeting her in Year 11 English class, and how we both
thought we were such clever scholars because we knew how
to use the word 'juxtaposition'. That word came to represent
us, me the jock with the footy in hand, bouncing around the
school, and her the bookish girl with a schedule and a plan.
But our differences can't compare to the way we complement
each other. At the reception we ate locally, with Coffin Bay
oysters, blue-eye Tasmanian trevalla and crème brûlée with
Freycinet honey and Pyengana clothbound cheddar.

It was a day filled with joy, but it also went so fast. Once
the party got going in the evening, it began to feel like a
continuation of our flag celebrations. Richmond didn't hijack
our wedding – they were an integral part of it, as our chosen
family. When do you ever get a whole room of your nearest
and dearest all in one spot, all at once, there to cap off such a
memorable few months?

Around 1am, as hotel staff were starting to pack up the show, I found myself chatting with Alex Rance and my cousin Nick. A couple of months earlier, Nick had retired, and now, with quite a few beers under our belt, Rancey and I decided that Nick had more footy left in him. We were going to bring Roo out of retirement, to play alongside me in the Richmond forward line. We were going to get him the premiership he craved. At some ungodly hour, we rang Blair Harley, the Tigers' list manager. Nick left him a voice message: 'I'll come across as a rookie,' he said. 'And I'll play for a pittance.'

It was one of those moments of drunken folly that vanishes in the night. When Blair rang me the next day, I couldn't remember who we had called, or when, or why.

'How about you boys last night,' he said. 'What?' I replied, laughing.

'You've signed Nick up as a rookie for next year.'

We both cracked up, fumbling around in hysterics. It was just a joke, of course, but still . . . imagine if we could've pulled it off, and Nick had run around in yellow and black for a year. It could have been magnificent.

Instead, Nick began doing special comments for Fox Footy, and showed a real affinity for the role. My work with *AFL 360* had already shown me that I was comfortable in front of a camera, too. I think I knew by then that whenever I finished my playing career, I would find my way to a microphone to talk about football. Some players come into training, dutifully attend meetings, play on the weekends because they're competitive animals, then watch no footy whatsoever, listen to no commentary, and read no stories. Some hate the way the game is covered, and some are just indifferent to the whole circus. And then there are people like me – footy heads – who get sucked in by the minutiae and the mechanics, the drama and the story, the sound and fury.

I could talk footy for days, but at this time I was still playing. The 2018 pre-season competition began, and we played with such confidence through those early games in summer. Our two games in the JLT Community Series were like glorified training drills. We beat Essendon by eighty-seven points in Wangaratta, then thumped North Melbourne by seventy at Princes Park. We were flying. Our group had such hunger, and we were rarely challenged through the first half of the home-and-away season. We beat the Brisbane Lions by ninety-three points, Fremantle by seventy-seven and Essendon by seventy-one, and the supporters turned out in droves to see us put on a show. Our average home-game crowd in 2018 was a touch over 61,000. Compared to the rest of the league, it was Richmond then daylight.

I enjoyed one of my best seasons, which was hardly a surprise given how often the ball was in our forward line. Against the Swans one week I reeled in twenty-one marks. I kicked ten goals against the Suns. I ended up booting seventy goals in all, and won the Coleman Medal for the third time. I also won my second Jack Dyer Medal – the award given to Richmond's best-and-fairest player. Back in 2010, when I won my first Jack Dyer Medal, we were a rabble as a team. This time around, I'd been adjudged the best player in one of the best teams in the competition.

And my role was much different now – far more team-oriented. A huge part of what the coaching staff asked me to do was to set up goals for my teammates by crashing packs and bringing the ball to ground. More important than goals was a display of aerial power, even when outnumbered. If our midfielders were under the pump and needed to release the pressure by kicking blindly, blasting or dumping it forward, they needed to know that I would be there to stop any interceptors. The ball simply had to hit the ground, even if I was outnumbered in the air. It's called halving the contest, and I was good at it. In short, I was asked to sacrifice part of my game for the good of the team, and I fulfilled the brief.

It was amazing how this new role changed people's perceptions of me. Where once I had been castigated as a petulant forward who cared only about how many goals he kicked, I was now considered to be a player devoted to a system within a team. In the middle of the 2018 season, former Sydney Swans and Melbourne coach Paul Roos, who was working for Fox Footy, called me 'the most selfless player in the competition'. It was a far cry from the days when Mark Maclure and Robert Walls were smashing me in the media every week. Winning will do that. I was trying as hard as I ever had, working with as much diligence as ever, to do what my coaches wanted me to do, and yet in my early seasons I was branded a prima donna, and in my later seasons I was suddenly a paragon of magnanimity. Neither characterisation is true – both are just interpretations, coloured by results on the field. My entire career I've tried to do everything I could for my teammates and my club. That's all I've ever wanted to do. But when we were losing, I was seen as selfish, and when we were winning, I was suddenly selfless.

People began to praise this 'growth' they had seen in me through my career, the way I'd 'matured' and found myself – and it was so patronising. Sometimes they even put it down to Maddie passing away – they said losing someone close to me had made me wake up and put others first – and that angered me. I've never wanted anything but success for the guys I run out with every week. It's always – *always* – been about the win. If people think that's a realisation I made halfway through my career as a result of personal trials and tribulations, they're flat wrong. The drive, camaraderie and passion have always been there. Maybe that's why I see a future for myself working in the media. Maybe I like to think I can do it a little better, with more nuance, paying a little more attention to context, instead of prejudging or assuming.

When I look back on 2018, it still burns that all our hard work and sacrifice for one another didn't carry us to the promised land. Of the twenty-three weeks of the home-and-away season, we spent fifteen of them on top of the ladder, including the last eleven. In the second half of the season, however, we started losing our way. The signs that we were getting shaky were there when we beat eleventh-placed Essendon by only eight points in round twenty-two. A week later, in the final round of the home-and-away season, we played the thirteenth-placed Western Bulldogs. We were eighteen points up late in the final quarter but ended up falling over the line by just three points.

We had fallen into some bad habits that would end up catching us out. Things like players getting overconfident and running forward of the ball too often. They would end up two metres ahead of where they were meant to be, and if the opposition was suddenly able to create a contested situation, those players would be out of the contest and basically ashtrays on motorbikes. We were playing as if we were going to win every contest, which just isn't possible in an unpredictable game like Australian rules football.

Our bad habits were understandable, in a way. We dominated so many of our matches in 2018, and I think players started looking to fill their own boots rather than do the right thing by the team. And we probably didn't tinker with the structure of our team or our gameplan much as the season went on, because we just kept winning. In 2017, there was still an uncertainty heading into the tail end of the season and finals. We blooded and then retained pivotal players like Jack Graham and Jacob Townsend. Those sorts of infusions can give a side a jolt. By changing things up you're showing that no one is secure, that we're still in a fight, still searching for answers. In 2018, it seemed as though there was no necessity to change, and that meant we became predictable. We weren't asking enough questions. Not only that, our opponents had a free hit to try different things against us. They weren't expected to win, and therefore they had nothing to lose. We were no longer hunting – we were the hunted.

After a week off thanks to the pre-finals bye, we played Hawthorn in a qualifying final at the MCG. The Hawks, who had won three premierships in a row through 2013–2015, had squeezed everything out of their list to make the top four in a season in which they were expected to tumble down the ladder. We certainly didn't believe they were a genuine top-four side, and went into the game brimming with confidence. A crowd of 91,446 turned up, and the vast majority were wearing yellow and black. The first half was a slog for everyone except Dustin Martin, who kicked an unbelievable goal from the boundary line in the right forward pocket, city end, late in the second quarter. You can find the goal on YouTube. The clip on the official AFL YouTube account is titled 'Dustin Martin breaks the internet with impossible goal'.

Dustin was in the thick of the action as we put the Hawks away, kicking five unanswered goals in the third quarter to set up a thirty-one-point win. We were just one more victory away from a second consecutive grand final. We were excited, but the win had come at a cost. Dusty had copped a severe corked thigh during the match.

There was so much speculation swirling around him – so much written and said – in the lead-up to our Friday night preliminary final against Collingwood. Dusty looked after himself expertly over the fortnight leading up to the game, doing everything he could in terms of rehab, and was ultimately declared fit to play. But he'd hardly trained, and come the game he was a shadow of his usual self. His leg just wasn't right. And that wasn't the only drama. The night before the game, David Astbury ended up in hospital due to illness. Despite all that, we were confident heading into the game, and had every right to be. We had won our previous twenty-two games at the MCG.

The build-up to the match was enormous. Richmond and Collingwood had not met in a final since the 1980

Grand Final. We had great respect for Collingwood as a team. Their coach, Nathan Buckley, had almost lost his job the year before, but the Magpies had climbed back up the ladder by playing an aggressive brand of attacking footy. We'd beaten Collingwood twice during the home-and-away season, both times by a handy margin, and yet they'd challenged us in both games. When I look back, I have no doubt they were the best team we played that year. I think they copied us, too, not only in the way they played but also in their attitude. You could tell they were a very happy group.

There were no signs in our changerooms that we were anything but switched on. And when the game started, with 94,959 people watching on, we registered the first three scores, though they were all behinds. Collingwood landed the first major blows, kicking a couple of early majors, then I stemmed the tide with a mark and goal. It was an arm wrestle until the Magpies kicked three quick goals late in the first quarter. Suddenly, we found ourselves five goals to one down. Still, there was no panic at quarter-time. We had such confidence in ourselves to bounce back.

That confidence sustained us until everything went sideways in the second quarter. Collingwood started killing us in the middle of the ground, and the beneficiary was their American forward Mason Cox. I found that hard to fathom – as Cox probably did, too. The lanky Texan was outgunning us, leaping and marking like John Coleman. He kicked three goals and was killing David Astbury. I didn't realise Dave had been in hospital sick that week, but you trust your leaders to say when they're right to go, and I don't think there was any correlation between his illness and the night Cox had. Sometimes the stars align and the tallest man in the league happens to catch a ball a few times.

Before long we were trailing by fifty-three points, and our dream of playing in another grand final was in tatters. I think we were in shock for a lot of the first half, looking around at one another, unable to comprehend what was happening to us. I think a lot of our players were hoping someone else would be the person to kick-start a comeback and get us back on track. But none of us seemed in a position to wrest back the momentum, so we found ourselves jogging on the spot and hoping, instead of moving, doing, playing.

We were forty-four points down at half-time, but we never gave up. I kicked three goals in the third quarter and one early in the last as we steadily narrowed the deficit. When Jack Higgins kicked a goal seven minutes into the last quarter, we'd reduced the margin to just twenty-one, but we'd used up too much energy on the chase. Collingwood soon took control again, and the Magpie fans went wild as their team ran away with the match.

In moments like that, when you know it's all over, when the other team is alight with energy, their fans jubilant – in this case chanting that slow droning 'Cooollll-ing-woooood' at full volume – you wish you could be anywhere else. You wish there was a mercy rule. You almost understand the few Richmond fans who choose to leave that little bit early. The opposition cheering begins to feel something like jeering – like taunting or trolling – as if the point of it all is to revel in your public discomfort and private shame. I know exactly what I was thinking at that time: *Just blow the siren.* Your pure footballing instincts remain intact – to keep trying, to do everything you can to put something positive into play – but it seems so hollow when the outcome is already decided. Even great play feels meaningless, like too little too late, because it is. Once the Tiger Army has been silenced, you're almost friendless. And when you know you're about to lose an important match, the mighty MCG – filled to the brim – is the loneliest place on earth.

I found myself wondering what it was all for: why had we won so many games and finished on top of the ladder, only to blow up so badly? That question rattled around in our heads all off-season, and in the wash-up, we realised two key things. We needed to get rid of our bad habits and return to playing team-first football. And we needed to rethink the way we approached the length of an AFL season. In other words, we had played too well too early in the season. Hitting top speed in February and sustaining it all the way to September is impossible. You need to grow and prune, adapt and develop, while experimenting and tinkering with your personnel and playbook until you find the right combination at the right time of year.

For everyone at Richmond, the 2019 season would be about making amends for the preliminary-final loss to Collingwood. Fundamentally, the story I tell myself is that we took one step back to take two steps forward. I don't think we would have enjoyed the success we did later without the pain of that loss. It gave us a kick up the arse, and a thirst for more susccess. Kane Lambert best summed up our attitude when he spoke at the Jack Dyer Medal night mere days after our season ended, in his speech after finishing second in our best and fairest. 'I think it's going to be the year of redemption,' he said, 'and I can't wait to tackle that.'

15

TWO HANDS, TOO CUTE, TWO SECONDS

The footy world moves fast. If our spirits were low at the end of 2018, they picked right up again when it was revealed that key forward Tom Lynch wanted to be traded from Gold Coast to Richmond. This was a colossal – and consequential – recruiting coup. Lynch was twenty-five years old, had played 131 AFL games, won two best-and-fairest awards, skippered his side, and was heading into the prime of his career. He was the biggest free-agency signing since Buddy Franklin left Hawthorn for Sydney, and yet the Lynch move seemed more important, not just for whom he chose but whom he didn't. Remember that his biggest other suitor was Collingwood. Imagine what might have happened in 2018, or any other season since then, if he'd gone to the Magpies instead of us.

I knew Tom would make our team better, and I knew he would love being part of our culture. The latter was a key talking point for us when we first met. We were at Dimma's house in Caulfield East, with Trent Cotchin, Alex Rance, our list manager Blair Hartley, and Tom's agent, Paul Connors. We had a catered dinner, and then sat down to a presentation from Blair, cast from his laptop to the TV, running the prospective recruit through what the side looked like, and how he would fit into the structure. I had never met Tom before, but when it was thrown open to us, I told him I was excited to have the chance to play with him, and to go from being the key forward to a sidekick of sorts. I spoke about the workplace as a whole, and then he asked me what being a Richmond player was like. What I knew by then with absolute certainty was that so much needs to go right to win a premiership. So many things had fallen our way and gone well before we won in 2017, and then in 2018 one or two things had slipped and that was that – we stumbled and fell. The lesson? The prize is no certainty, and the journey is the whole point. I said I couldn't promise him that we would win the flag or play finals every year, but I could promise that he would enjoy coming into the office every day.

'We can't guarantee success. No one can,' I said. 'But we can guarantee you'll have fun. We guarantee you'll come to work – and work hard – and leave with a smile on your face.'

I couldn't wait to play alongside him. The AFL had just introduced the new six-six-six rule, ensuring that teams had to split their team evenly between midfield, defence and attack at every centre bounce. The rule denied teams the option of playing a permanent spare defender, and it would make players like Lynchy extra dangerous. If you could win a centre clearance and surge it forward, a figure as towering as him – standing 199 centimetres, with a strong leap, superb timing and soft hands – would become a near-impossible one-on-one match-up, and a potent weapon for us. Selfishly, it would also mean that the biggest, baddest defender from the opposition would go to him every week, leaving me with a more manageable opponent. Having someone of Tom's calibre and character in our forward line had the very real potential to extend and enrich my career.

I had a few ups and downs during the lead-up to the 2019 season. I was on restricted duties during the training block before Christmas, after having shoulder surgery, but I managed to get myself fully fit by the time the AFL staged its second AFLX competition. During the previous pre-season, all eighteen clubs had taken part in the experimental games, played on a rectangular field with only eight players per team on the field, rather than the usual eighteen. This time around, the AFL decided to create a whole new competition. They invented four teams – the Bolts, Flyers, Rampage and Deadly – and held a televised draft to allocate players to each team. I was offered the chance to captain the Rampage, and even though the competition was nothing more than a bit of fun, I took the opportunity with both hands. It would be a novel experience. I heard that Riewoldt philosophy ringing in my ears again: life is for living.

My team included Carlton star Patrick Cripps, Giants midfielder Lachie Whitfield and Adelaide's Rory Sloane, along with Isaac Smith, who at that time was a triple-premiership player with Hawthorn but would later add another flag to his collection during his time at Geelong. We weren't together long as a group – only two or three days – but we had a great time and ended up winning the competition. The AFL ditched the concept shortly after, meaning we will forever remain 'the reigning AFLX premiers'.

There are more opportunities to meet players from other sides than you might imagine, and there's more crossover in friendship groups than people would suspect. The AFL may be Australia's biggest sport, but it's made up of many small communities, and in Melbourne more than anywhere else, those communities naturally overlap. You go on footy shows together. You speak at panel events together. You do media calls promoting one thing or another for the league together. And you connect through common sponsor events, or within the same management stables.

Even before that, guys come up through the ranks together, playing for the same private-school teams, and the same state representative teams, and they become friends before embarking on their own AFL journeys. I look at the guys I got drafted with and there's a natural bond. You can't help but monitor them as the years go by. Early on, perhaps, you watch with envy – 'He's getting a game and he was drafted after me!' Or sometimes with bafflement – 'He was such an amazing player; how is he falling out of the system?' You can't help but find common ground, and for me the standout point of comparison was always Tom Hawkins. We were drafted in the same year, in the same position, our career statistics and honours are almost identical – and in many ways our lives are almost identical. I swapped jumpers with him one game in my final season because I wanted to recognise our tandem careers. Fans want players from rival clubs to hate one another, but there's often too much mutual respect for anything so petty to take hold.

I was becoming a more rounded person. I had turned thirty a few months earlier, but as personal milestones go, my birthday was far less important than that of our daughter, Poppy, who came into the world on March 16, 2019. She changed our lives forever. Carly and I had been convinced that the baby would be a boy. My cousin Nick already had three boys. His brother Alex had two boys. I'm one of three boys. Dad's one of four boys. Carly has two brothers, and her dad is one of four boys, too. We had a boy's name picked out, assuming we'd be using it. Poppy was our 'break glass in case of emergency' back-up name. But we didn't care one bit whether we had a boy or a girl. The overwhelming emotion was love, as well as relief she was healthy and that Carly was feeling well.

I didn't have long to settle into life as a new parent. Only six days after Poppy arrived, we kicked off the 2019 season with our traditional Thursday-night blockbuster against Carlton at the MCG. It was a milestone match for me and for one of my best mates, Alex Rance. I was playing my 250th AFL game and he was playing his 200th. We did quite a bit of media in the lead-up and enjoyed reminiscing about how we'd butted heads early in our careers.

I remember playing against him in an intraclub match in the middle of summer: AFL forwards on AFL backs. From the night before the game, you would see your names on the team-sheets and know it was on. Even in the warm-up there was a different kind of tension. It sounds dumb, but we almost tried harder against each other than we did against real opponents. This day in 2015, when he was at his peak, I got on top of him early, kicked a few goals, little goosey ones where he'd tried to impact the contest and I'd snuck out the back. He hated that, especially when I got lippy: 'Don't trade up the ground, mate, or I'll sneak off out the back.' I was always more verbal – his weapon was his physicality. He just picked me up and ragdolled me, particularly at stoppages, with this combination of technique and strength. I kept pissing him off, until I was running out of defensive 50 and he smacked me in the back, knocked me over, and an umpire caught it. When he mouthed off in response, they paid a 50-metre penalty. I kicked seven goals on him, and he was filthy afterwards. Icy. But he was over it by that afternoon. There was never any personal animosity – we were always just two bulls in the same paddock, competing in drills against each other, steel sharpening steel. What is it they say? Game recognises game.

Looking past the competitive cauldron of football, we forged a personal respect, too, through care. When Maddie died, it was Alex more than any other player who recognised the impact that had on me – who sought me out to make sure I was okay. That's when we started becoming truly close. Later he wrote a children's book about me – *Rabbit's Hop* – and it's still one of the nicest gestures anyone has made for me. The book was about my entire journey. The rabbit had to get from Little Island to Big Island – Tassie to the mainland. There was a rabbit companion – that was Carly. The purple whale that took me across the water was my purple Combi van. 'Roo the kangaroo was my cousin Nick, Duz was a gorilla, and Alex himself was a Tiger. Maddie was represented, too, in that I had to 'fight like mad' to get across the sea. When Poppy was born, he presented us with an artwork of the two rabbits with a baby rabbit, drawn by his illustrator. You're not thinking about those things in round one, but you never forget them either.

Early in the match against the Blues, the world was a happy place. Tom Lynch started his career as a Tiger by kicking the first goal of the game, and early in the second quarter we led six goals to zip. Things began turning sour when we allowed Carlton back into the match early in the third quarter. With five minutes left in the term, disaster struck. Rancey flew for a mark deep in our backline and landed awkwardly after the ball slipped through his hands. His right knee buckled as his foot touched the ground, and he lay on the ground in agony, clutching his leg. The crowd was hushed and stunned as he was carried from the field. A few quick tests by the club doctor all but confirmed he'd suffered a serious knee injury of the sort that ends a season.

As a team, we pulled ourselves together enough to kick away in the last quarter and win with comfort. But the feeling in the changerooms afterwards was one of mourning, like attending a wake. One of our best players – who'd become one of the greatest defenders in the history of the game, a five-time All Australian – was likely to miss the rest of the year. I was gutted for him, and for us. Yet he quickly showed us how selfless he could be, making every effort to ensure his personal adversity didn't drag the group down into despair. On the Monday after he was injured, he came to the club to address the playing group. It was only an hour after the doctors' gameday prognosis had been confirmed: he'd ruptured his ACL and his season was all but over. Alex said to us that he wanted the letters ACL to take on a new meaning. 'From now on,' he said, 'they mean Always Celebrate and Laugh.'

A week after Alex was injured, the playing group came together for a few beers to celebrate our 250- and 200-game milestones, as well as Poppy's arrival in the world. We had a few laughs and spun some yarns, but that hollow feeling was still nagging inside. How on earth were we going to compete with the other top sides without the best defender in the game? Dimma made this point much later, too, in the Fox Footy documentary *Redemption*, summing up how we felt at that point. 'It was a traumatic period, the loss of Alex,' he said, 'because to us he was Superman.'

Dimma mightn't realise how deeply he had ingrained that superhuman perception of Rancey in his own mind. Before the qualifying final against the Hawks that previous September, the coach had worked with the presentations team at the club for his story of the round. That week the story was superheroes. The idea was to 'be a star at your role' – to bring your own unique superpowers to the field, and to know that you would be out there with twenty-one sidekicks. Dimma had considered the traits of every player on the team, and tried to find a comic-book character that suited their personality. When we returned to our locker after the pre-game speech, we each found a bobblehead doll of that superhero, as well as a small card with our face photoshopped onto the body of some caped crusader, with our strengths listed.

Dylan Grimes, known for his speed and acrobatics, was Spiderman. Athletic, gifted Indigenous leader Shane Edwards was Black Panther. Bachar Houli was The Flash, while

Daniel Rioli was The Reverse Flash. Kamdyn McIntosh was Cyborg and Nathan Broad was Daredevil. Jason Castagna was The Green Hornet and Toby Nankervis was Beast. Kane Lambert had every right to feel sledged after being named as Ant Man, while in the wise-cracking running utility Jayden Short, Dimma saw Deadpool. (Traits: 'Work rate to contest, kicking, decision-making, spread.') Dimma saved a few of the biggest names from the Marvel and DC universes for the leaders of the side. Our clean-cut skipper Trent Cotchin was Captain America. Dustin Martin was The Incredible Hulk. Nick Vlastuin was Ironman. I was Thor. And Alex Rance? Yep, he was Superman. (Listed traits: 'Calm. Clear. Proactive. Physical. Dominant.')

Back in those early rounds of 2019, Alex's injury proved to be the first of many suffered by key members of the team, and we struggled to find our best form. We played Collingwood on a Thursday night at the MCG, and we were desperate to make a statement after the preliminary-final debacle. Instead, the Pies thrashed us again under lights. Making matters worse, I hurt my wrist and my knee, and ended up missing our next three matches. I returned for our round-six match against Melbourne – the much-hyped Anzac eve game – only to suffer another, more serious, knee injury. This one was a strained posterior cruciate ligament.

I was sidelined for almost three months, although there was an upside: I was able to spend a lot of time bonding with Poppy as she started to smile and laugh and generally grow cuter by the day. I also spent a lot of time with Rancey in the rehab group, too, and we managed to find a way to bring some fun to a tough time in our careers. Going to the footy each week to watch the boys play was a reliable source of frustration, not because they did anything wrong but because we were helpless to assist. The team also kept losing more players to injury, while struggling to find any kind of consistency of form.

In the middle weeks of the season, when we were thrashed by Geelong on a Friday night at the MCG and then easily beaten by Adelaide on a Thursday night at the Adelaide Oval, it seemed that our dream of winning another premiership was over. After the bye round, we had a 7–6 record and sat in ninth place. Having gone too hard too early in 2018, we had planned to start at a steady pace in 2019. 'Steady', however, *not slow*. Not faltering. Not stuttering. Not stumbling, either. But that's what we were doing. Alex had been such a crucial part of our defensive structure – and our ability to intercept the ball when the opposition was attacking – that we were almost lost without him. There were definitely some players – including some of Alex's fellow backmen – who found themselves doubting that we could win the flag if he wasn't out there with us. It was as if we were suffering a crisis of identity.

Yet the belief within the group ran deeper than our anxieties about missing players. We were a system side, and we knew we could count on that. We knew that if we didn't lose hope we could resurrect our season. After all, we'd been decimated by injuries and suspensions, robbing us of the chance to field anywhere near our best team. Along with losing Alex, we'd been without Trent Cotchin for much of the season due to repeated hamstring injuries. The leadership group sensed – or knew – that if we could just get the band back together, we could turn things around. We simply needed to chip away, chip away, chip away, and we could do some damage. If we dealt enough blows, we could put a crack in the competition. We could pound the rock.

History tells you that to win a premiership you need to finish the home-and-away season in the top four. When we resumed our campaign against St Kilda in round fifteen, we knew we couldn't afford to lose another game. We beat the Saints and then flogged Gold Coast, and by the time I returned from injury to face the Giants in round seventeen, you could feel our confidence building. We were getting closer to having all our best players available, and the last seven home-and-away matches would be played at the MCG. We won them all – including an epic six-point win against the Eagles in the wet – and charged into the top four, finishing in third.

In most seasons, Damien Hardwick identifies a pivotal string of four games in which we simply must stand up and be counted. He used to call this 'Big Boy Month'. In 2015, Big Boy Month was July. 'It's a make-or-break month, not only for our football club, but most football clubs,' he said at the time. 'It's when the contenders step up and the pretenders step away.' In 2017, Big Boy Month was a series of matches in the front half of the year. But from 2019 onwards, there was only one Big Boy Month, according to Dimma, and that was August. August, he said, was the month when the premiers stood up, and all others were sat down. August was a month of eight-point games – a cutthroat chance to gather four points while denying four points to others. We were on a nine-game winning streak through Big Boy Month, which was why Dimma found a new name for finals, too.

'September,' he said, 'is Bigger Boy Month.'

It felt as though we had an ace up our sleeve, too. Rancey was training the house down, sprinting and leaping, going through full-contact training and running jagged lateral patterns – cutting at full speed. It usually takes at least a year to get over a knee reconstruction. Alex was flying after four months. He could have played in the finals, but ultimately the coaches felt it just wasn't worth the risk. Our system was holding up, too. The defence was covering for him. And there was a part of Alex, too, that knew he'd be taking a risk not just with his body but with the team. If he came into the side, then someone would go out. And if his leg buckled during the first quarter of a pivotal final, and the team was forced to play at a disadvantage, and lose, he would never be able to forgive himself.

Trent Cotchin was back in our side and feeling good by the time we travelled to Brisbane to face the second-placed Lions in the first week of the finals. Now coached by a wise and calm Tasmanian, Chris Fagan, the Lions had been the competition's big improver, finishing fifteenth on the ladder. More than 30,000 success-starved Brisbane supporters turned up to the game (along with an impressive number of Tigers fans) and they roared as the Lions started all guns blazing. A fast and attacking team, they were difficult to stop, but we were lucky. They were prolific but profligate, wasting numerous chances. If they'd kicked straight in the first quarter we might have been six goals down at the first change.

Instead, they led 4.6 (30) to 3.0 (18). In the second quarter, we slowed them down, holding them goalless while kicking four of our own. In the third quarter, Dustin Martin blew the game open. We kicked seven goals to two and ended the contest, while Dustin finished with six goals. We were on our way to another preliminary final.

We played Geelong, and still felt as though we had a point to prove against them. Knocking them over in the 2017 qualifying final erased nothing. These were still the Cats that had eviscerated us for years and treated us with contempt in the process. We felt, too, that their coach, Chris Scott, had no respect for us. Chris is a well-spoken man who chooses his words carefully, so when he goes on radio and responds to a question about Geelong's significant home-ground advantage by throwing flames at Richmond for its 'inordinate' run of matches at the MCG, it's tantamount to a declaration of war. 'If you told someone in the US, for example, that a team could play at the grand-final venue for its last seven games in a row, and then not qualify for a home final but still play at the MCG,' Scott said, 'I think they would laugh at us.'

The game was played under lights on Friday, September 20, in front of 94,423 fans, and the MCG was like a cauldron, bubbling and hissing and hot. Preliminary finals are such different beasts. Unlike the grand final, for instance, there are far fewer corporate seats, so the house is filled with the most faithful of followers. These are the people to whom the win means everything. Many won't be able to afford a ticket to the decider the following Saturday afternoon, and in a strange small way, getting there – by winning the prelim – is more important than what happens on the last Saturday in September. Losing a grand final is a lifelong heartache, but the retired players will tell you that no loss burns so badly as the sour sting of a preliminary final defeat, when that chance to play on the biggest stage just slips away. We had an entire year in which to sit with that experience, and let it burn in our guts. We were ready.

We knew Geelong would want to employ a careful and slow style of play, so we set ourselves to take them on. It worked well for the first ten minutes, in which we kicked three goals to one, but the Cats then took charge, and their wall of mature bodies just began to feel like something we couldn't climb over or crash through. At half-time we trailed by twenty-one points.

In the team meeting during the break we spoke about getting back to playing our way. We were a great pressure team, but we had let Geelong play the game on their terms in the first half. We needed to bring the heat. When the game resumed, our skipper, Trent Cotchin, showed us exactly how it was done. The Cats looked set to win the first centre break when Rhys Stanley received the ball from his captain, Joel Selwood, then took off towards the wing. Suddenly, Cotchin arrived on the scene. In one ballistic motion he stripped the ball from Stanley's grasp and drove the big man into the turf. The ball spilled free, then Dion Prestia delivered a lace-out pass to Tom Lynch inside 50. Lynch kicked the goal and we were back. Football is like that. Big acts, big moments, with big consequences.

That tackle by Trent should go down in folklore as one of the most important moments in the club's history. It's certainly regarded among those who played in the game as the turning point. When we're old men, sitting around enjoying our premiership reunions, we'll talk about the moment Trent showed us why he was our leader. Someone had to set the tone – to show us the way and open the door – and he did it. He turned words into deeds.

A couple of minutes later, Trent created another crucial turnover, when he smothered a Joel Selwood kick inside the centre square. The ball bobbled loose, Bachar Houli trapped it, handballed to Jayden Short, and Shorty took off – dodging and weaving, sending one of his trademark long bombs into our attacking 50. I had to fly for it against three Geelong defenders, but out of the corner of my eye I saw Dustin Martin lurking to my left. I made a split-second decision to tap the ball towards Dustin, instead of marking it. The yellow Sherrin slapped the meat of my palm, deflecting perfectly into Dustin's path, allowing him to seize the ball and the moment, and roost the footy through an open goal. We were back in the contest. That goal exemplified our success as a great team. Most of the competition is regimented and risk-averse, while we played with freedom and creativity, acting upon inspiration, looking for solutions that mightn't seem likely at first but are sometimes staring you right in the face. When I was a kid, and even in my early years at Richmond, we were always taught to mark or gather the ball at every opportunity. 'Two hands!' Players who tapped the ball along the ground or over to a teammate were considered weak – 'Too cute!' – as though they weren't prepared to accept responsibility, or worse, weren't prepared to put their body on the line. But within the new Richmond system, we wanted the ball alive and flowing, moving at all costs, with tap-ons and risky forward handballs and screwed punts around the corner, because we had complete and utter faith that another Tiger would anticipate us. And that's the way it unfolded. I knew I could tap the ball down to Dustin, because I knew Dustin would be streaming towards me and that marking contest, and that he would be almost expecting the unexpected.

We took the lead later in the third quarter and never looked back. Although the last quarter was tough and tight, we edged away to win by nineteen points. The margin would have been greater if I'd kicked three goals instead of three behinds in the final term, but it didn't matter. We were into another grand final. We had been on a quest for redemption for 364 days now, and an opportunity to reclaim the chance we had lost was only a week away.

So many players were heroic in that win over Geelong. If there were any doubts about the impact Tom Lynch could have on the group when he was recruited, they were banished on this night. He kept us in the game during the first half, then exploded in the third quarter, finishing with five crucial goals. I was as rapt for him as I was for us. Tom had dealt with a string of injuries in his time on the Gold Coast, yet had always fronted up as a brutal competitor and fearsome leader. He needed time in his first season at Punt Road to hit top pace and now he was flying, throwing his body into packs, marking at the highest point, and punching post-high goals through the big sticks on the biggest stage, dominating the most important game of the season to date.

Another player who was unbelievably stoic was midfielder Jack Graham, who dislocated his shoulder during the first quarter. Jack spent some time off the ground getting treatment, then, despite knowing he most likely wouldn't be able to play in the Grand Final if we won, returned to the field and played like a man possessed. He laid bumps and tackles through the pain. He finished with more pressure points than any player on the ground, which is incredibly rare for a small forward, and rarer still for someone whose arm was barely attached to his body. He couldn't raise his elbow above his shoulder, yet threw himself into the fray with reckless abandon. His heroism that night will never be forgotten.

After the game, it was hard not to look at Jack and feel a strong sense of bittersweet melancholy. He had played a pivotal role in our win, yet there was no potential for a premiership medal in his future. There was recognition, however. Don't worry about that. Going into the preliminary final against Geelong, Jack Graham was sitting fourth in the voting for the Francis Bourke Award. But after that night, the leadership group unilaterally and unanimously decided that he would be made joint-winner with whoever topped the voting, such was the pivotal and inspirational nature of his preliminary-final performance. Jack shared the prize with his bad-luck badfellow, Alex Rance, neither of whom would take the field on Grand Final day.

We'd all expected to be playing Collingwood in the decider, so it was a shock when the Magpies suffered a four-point loss to Greater Western Sydney in their preliminary final. The Tigers versus Giants match-up would have contained a memorable storyline if our former teammate Brett Deledio had been fit. Sadly, Lids had retired the previous month, hounded to the finish line of a brilliant career by a chronic calf injury. For a player who had so rarely missed a game during his first dozen years in the AFL, his last few seasons would have been exasperating. At the end of 2015, Lids was sitting on 232 games, and was just twenty-eight. When he retired four years later, at the end of the 2019 season, he was still twenty-five games short of 300. The way he went out that year – breaking down in the Giants' final against the Western Bulldogs – was not befitting a player of his ilk. He was a Rising Star winner, a two-time All Australian, a two-time Richmond best-and-fairest winner, and his career ended in tears.

Lids leaving Richmond was also a true sliding-doors moment, insofar as no one knows what might have been. Both his and our worlds shifted in that time of flux. If he had stayed with the club, would we have enjoyed the success we did? Or, as he himself admits, might his body have broken down anyway? My cousin Nick talks about Lids as standing alongside him in the 'Misery Club' – his collective term for those players who got so close to the ultimate reward but were denied by luck or fate or hubris or happenstance. Nick calls himself the captain of the Misery Club, but there are others who might lay claim to that mantle: Gary Ablett Sr, Tony Lockett, Robert Harvey and Nathan Buckley come to mind.

Every year, selection stories dominate the media coverage of grand-final week, and in 2019, the story was all about who would replace Jack Graham. It basically came down to a battle between 2017 premiership player Kamdyn McIntosh, our

VFL team's form young midfielder Jack Ross, and mature-age recruit Marlion Pickett.

Marlion was on the cusp of becoming one of the greatest stories of the season. An Indigenous player from Western Australia who had spent time in jail during his tumultuous younger years, he arrived at Tigerland in the mid-season draft at the age of twenty-seven. Straight away, he showed his immense talent in the VFL, culminating in that VFL Grand Final victory over Williamstown, a week before our AFL decider. Marlion was best on ground, winning the Norm Goss Medal. Within our club and in the broader footy community, everyone was posing the same question: Could Marlion Pickett make his AFL debut in the Grand Final?

Early in the week, Damien Hardwick was keen to see what some of the experienced players thought about the selection dilemma. I ended up in a discussion with Dimma, Shane Edwards and Dustin Martin. 'I don't know who to pick,' said Dimma, to which Shane replied, 'Well, if it was round fourteen, who would you be picking?' Dimma broke into a grin – 'Marlion' – and Shane just looked at him and nodded. 'There you go.'

A day later, the players were in the Graeme Richmond Room, lying in darkness during a mindfulness exercise guided by Emma Murray. Tim Livingston, one of the key members of our football department, opened the door – 'Marlion, can you come out here?' He then sat him down with the coaches to deliver the news. In one of the greatest feel-good stories in the history of the game, Marlion Pickett would become the first player to make his debut in a VFL/AFL grand final since 1952.

The Pickett selection was another sliding-doors moment, of sorts. Back in May, one of my best mates, Richmond onballer and sometime 'ruckman' Shaun Grigg, retired after 214 games. 'I cannot help on the field this year,' he told us all, back on May 14, 'but this might be my gift in helping the club off the field, and realising someone else's dream, that they can come in and play.' Two weeks later, using the vacancy on the team list created by his leaving, we drafted Marlion. Grigga knew that pulling the pin early in the season would create that opportunity, whereas waiting until those long mid-winter months to step away would have been too late. He was the perfect combination of selfless and sensible.

Dimma used to say that Shaun was the smartest player at Richmond, and in light of those kinds of actions and gestures, it's easy to see why. Another case in point: Shaun wasn't remotely the best kick at the club, but there were few players I would rather lead to, owing solely to his football intelligence. You see, truly great kicks of the footy often know this about themselves – all their lives they've been passing perfectly, drilling darts and launching long bombs – and yet the art of kicking to a lead is all about anticipation and understanding. Shaun understood that weighting – and waiting – is everything. When you're a key forward, sprinting at top speed in one direction, and the ball is speared at you like a missile from the opposite direction, it doesn't always make for the easiest of grabs. Shaun never tried to kick the leather off the Sherrin, because there's no point in a sizzling drop punt if it's moving too fast to catch. He had this way of chipping the perfect little dink right out in front me, so I wouldn't even have to break stride.

There are guys who seem to have that intuitive chip in their brain, and I find myself connected to them. Shane Edwards was the same. There were times on the field where we had what felt like a telepathic relationship, completing sequences in play as though we were finishing each other's sentences. Of the young kids I played with late in my career, Liam Baker was on that level.

Shaun didn't get to play in the 2019 Grand Final, but he was there on the day, and in the minutes leading up to the match. He was invited into the rooms to present Marlion with his jumper. He pointed out that of the entire playing group that day, only thirteen were drafted the first time they tried. Others were selections in subsequent drafts, or pre-season drafts, or rookie drafts. They were people, he said, who had overcome adversity, and that seemed to be the theme for Richmond in 2019. 'I think that it's our year,' Grigga said, 'and I sort of look at Marlion, and his *life* has been that. For him to get where he is, taking it all in his stride, overcoming adversity.'

Damien Hardwick's theme in the lead-up to the match was about dedicating our game to someone. It's easy to do things for yourself, he said, but it's harder – and more meaningful – to do something for someone else. The inspiration for this theme came from when Dimma and our long-time strength and conditioning coach, Peter Burge, had walked the Kokoda Track when they were at Hawthorn together. Peter wanted to do something as a tribute to his father, who had died just a few years before Burge won a gold medal for long jump at the 1998 Commonwealth Games. And so, on day nine of the trek, before one last long climb, he put a five-kilogram rock in his backpack and carried it up the steepest of hills. Dimma noticed how driven Peter became to make it to the top once he'd dedicated his action to a higher purpose.

'Where he had struggled on climbs before, on this mountain he took off, like I hadn't seen,' Dimma said. 'You know why? Because he had dedicated it to someone else. So, every single one of you guys today is going to get a rock in your locker, and you're gonna dedicate this game not to yourself but to someone else, and that's gonna help us get the job done. Because if you do it for someone else, you'll work harder than you've ever worked before, and the love that you bring is going to be inside you all day.'

We walked back to our lockers and found the rocks, and were asked to write the name of someone we were playing for on one side, and the spark we would bring to the game on the other side. A lot of the boys, including Trent Cotchin, wrote Jack Graham's name on their rocks as well as the names of various family members. I wrote the name of my late grand-father, Ivan Eade, on my rock. He was my idol as a child, and I wanted to play well for him. Specifically, on one side I wrote: 'Grandad, I miss you. Poppy reminds me of you every day.' And on the other side? I wrote what I was planning to bring to the field: 'Run and jump.'

Just before we ran out, Trent Cotchin asked the property stewards to bring a guernsey for Jack Graham. Trent handed Jack the jumper, and asked him to put it on, to let him know that we were taking his spirit with us into the match. Then we ran up the race into gorgeous spring sunshine, and the noise when we broke through that banner made it seem as though there were twenty Richmond supporters for every Greater Western Sydney fan in the crowd.

We hit the Giants hard in the first few minutes. Trent set the scene with a massive tackle on ruckman Shane Mumford, then Shane Edwards flattened Jacob Hopper. We had the weight of the momentum, but we just couldn't score. It wasn't until the twenty-minute mark that Giants forward Jeremy Cameron kicked the first goal of the game, but we hit back with two late ones of our own, including one to Daniel Rioli on the quarter-time siren after some good work from Marlion Pickett on the wing. Early in the second quarter, the coaches sent Marlion into a centre bounce, demonstrating the confidence they had in his decision-making – and theirs for that matter. They weren't going to pick a bloke to make his debut in the Grand Final only to hide him away on a flank or in a pocket. They put him in the heat of the action, and a decision like that sends a confidence ripple through the group. If the coaches have that kind of faith in the interconnected parts of your team, then you do, too.

Marlion let no one down. At his first centre bounce he sharked the ball, did a blind turn around Giants midfielder Lachie Whitfield, then delivered a weighted pass to Jason Castagna – out in front, soft touch, with room to attack the ball in the air – just as Grigga would have done for me. Jason missed his shot, and in fact missed six shots that day – five behinds and one out on the full. He had the most metres gained on the field, and had he been straighter, could have won a Norm Smith Medal. A few minutes later, Marlion set up a goal for Dustin Martin and he was on his way to cult-hero status.

From there, we imposed ourselves on the game and I found myself in the thick of the play. I kicked three goals in the second quarter, while our defenders totally put the clamps on their opponents. Harry Himmelberg was quiet, Jeremy Cameron subdued. Jeremy Finlayson was shut out of the entire match by David Astbury, registering a solitary disposal for the afternoon. By half-time we led seven goals to one, and again this was where we called upon the lessons from those close elimination-final losses. In our defeats by the Blues and Kangaroos, we were well in front but played as if to save the game – to stop the contest in time – and it was our undoing. We knew we had to keep going. Keep pushing. Keep playing. And that we did.

We kicked five goals to one in the third quarter, opening a sixty-two-point lead by the final change. Marlion's afternoon got even better during the third term when he pushed forward and marked a kick from Dustin Martin inside 50. As Marlion's kick went straight through the middle, he pointed to the sky as a tribute to his brother-in-law, who'd died just a month earlier. I had tears in my eyes as I watched it all unfold. And for Dustin to go out of his way to kick the ball to Marlion – trying to give a friend a magical moment – was a tribute not just to his character but to our culture as a side. It made me so proud.

The last quarter was a dream. With time on our side and goals raining down, we were able to soak it all in, splashing around in the colour and movement of the day, savouring the whole spectacle. I remember catching the eye of my teammates, sharing knowing winks and appreciative little fist pumps. That feeling, when you know you've got it won, is impossible to beat, and the polar opposite of the mercy rule I longed for only a year earlier against the Pies. We kept pouring on the goals right until the end. In the last five minutes, Trent kicked a brilliant running goal, then Dustin bombed one from just inside 50 and, with thirty seconds left, Toby Nankervis snapped a kick into our forward line and I marked it on my chest. The Richmond supporters were already singing in the stands, and my shot, from just outside 50, was a bit of a hook but swung back late and sailed through for a goal. I raised my arms in delight. I had kicked five goals in a grand final.

As we prepared for the centre bounce – eighty-nine points in front – I yelled out to the sea of happy people on our bench – 'How long to go?' – but before any of them could answer, one of the field umpires, Matt Stevic, spoke up. 'Two seconds.' Dustin and I grinned at one another, then the siren sounded as soon as the ball was bounced, and we ran to embrace in the centre square, dragging one another to the turf in our delirium.

Dustin won his second Norm Smith Medal after finishing with twenty-two disposals and four goals. He was awarded the maximum three votes by each of the five judges. Marlion Pickett was third with four votes after ending the game with twenty-two disposals, eight inside-50s and a goal. Our defenders also deserved a huge amount of praise for the way we dominated the game, and Bachar Houli deservedly finished second in the Norm Smith Medal voting. We held the Giants to a score of only 3.7 (25), the lowest in their history, and the lowest in a grand final since 1960.

When I look back at 2019, I think it really was a year of redemption. There were so many stories of perseverance.

Jayden Short was a great example. Shorty had played a lot of crucial football for the team in 2017 but found himself out of the side on the day it mattered most. The 2019 premiership was just reward for his patience and effort. Liam Baker missed out on being drafted, and had arrived at the club as a rookie, having moved across from a tiny country town in Western Australia aiming to fulfil his dream of playing footy at the highest level. Now he was a vital member of a team that had just won the flag. Then there was Tom Lynch, who repaid the club's investment in him by holding the forward line together through most of the season, particularly those early weeks when half our list was limping. They say premierships aren't won in April, but they can be lost then. It can be simply too hard to climb the mountain if you don't register a few crucial wins in the dog days of autumn. Without Tom, I doubt we could have gone where we went that year.

In the weeks after we won the flag, I had so many great experiences, but one of the best was being part of Scott McLaughlin's entourage at the iconic Bathurst 1000 car race. I was introduced to Scott by Tim Hodges, who has been the head producer of *AFL 360* on Fox Footy for many years. I first got to know Hodgey when I started appearing in a Tuesday-night segment on *AFL 360*, and we've become good mates since then. Hodgey is a motorsport fanatic who'd done quite a bit of media stuff with Scott, including ghostwriting a book called *Road To Redemption* after Scott won the Supercars championship in 2018. Watching how Scott went about his preparation, particularly his mental prep before such a taxing race, was fascinating. Exactly as we had done at Richmond,

Scott was working with Emma Murray to get himself in the right headspace to perform at an elite level in the big moment. I had never been to Bathurst, but carrying my luck from one sport to another, on my first visit I had joined the winning team. I spent the night partying with Team Penske.

Scott and I struck up such a friendship that for a couple of years we co-hosted a podcast called *Balls & Bumpers*, which was produced by Hodgey. There was no pattern in terms of episode frequency. We might say at the end of an episode, 'We'll be back in two weeks,' and then we wouldn't get around to recording the next episode for two months. We talked shit and poked fun at each other, and both the motorsport fanatics and footy fans seemed to love it. The podcast came to an end after Scott moved to the USA to drive in the Indycar series.

When I think about getting to know Hodgey and the rest of the crew at Fox Footy, and the people and places that introduction has brought to me, I have to laugh a little. I hated the media so much in my early years in the game. At least I told myself I did. But slowly, with a glimpse behind the camera, and a quiet word in private to the identities behind the keyboard, I came to appreciate journalists for what they do. Take Mark Robinson, the *Herald Sun*'s chief footy writer. So many players would tell me how they hated him, and to be fair, I didn't like him early on either. But I've got to know him now. He's funny to be around. He's authentic. And he is who he is – a bogan who loves his footy and who's ridden his luck all the way to the top of his profession. Robbo will claim to know more about footy than anyone else, but in truth I'm not sure he knows much more than the average bloke in the street. What he does know, however, is how to connect with those punters. That's his skill.

Working in the media has given me a great appreciation of how the relationship between the clubs, the AFL and the media works. How reporters aren't some homogenous mob out to get players. How no one would know anything about the game and how the players wouldn't be paid well or watched by millions without coverage. How players and journalists are in a symbiotic relationship, reliant on one another to survive and thrive.

I suppose it was inevitable that I would find my way into that field. The media has given me a way to keep putting myself out there. Deep down I can admit that I've always craved attention. I was the class clown as a kid, from my first day at school all the way through to Year 12. I can't turn that off. I don't want to turn that off. I want to be the life of the party, I want to have fun, and I want people to have fun being around me. There's that family maxim again: Life is for living.

16

US AGAINST THEM

The year 2020 is now etched in people's minds as the moment the Covid-19 pandemic took hold of the world. In Australia, however, the turmoil started before we knew anything about an insidious virus hospitalising people in Wuhan, China. Bushfires torched vast swathes of our eastern states during what came to be known as the Black Summer, and the football community united to create a representative match to raise money to support the victims. Officially called the State of Origin for Bushfire Relief Match, it pitted Victoria against a team called the All-Stars.

I was lucky enough to get a call-up to play for the All-Stars – and it was a surreal experience, running around in the same team as Nat Fyfe, Lachie Neale, Harris Andrews and Tom Hawkins. My two-time Richmond premiership teammate Trent Cotchin was named captain of Victoria and ended with bragging rights, as the Vics won by forty-six points. True to form, Dustin Martin continued an imperious run as the best big-game player in Australia, winning the medal for best on ground. More than 51,000 people turned up to watch, and $2.5 million was raised for the bushfire relief appeal.

From there, we had to knuckle down and prepare for Richmond's tilt at winning three premierships in four seasons. Speaking personally, what was strange about that time wasn't just the constant news stories about the pandemic, but rather training without my great mate Alex Rance by my side. Rancey had dropped a bombshell before Christmas, announcing his early retirement. The football world was caught entirely off guard, no one more so than me. Having watched him strive so hard to return to the field – having spent all those hours in rehab with him throughout the previous season – I'd considered him the first magnet to hit the whiteboard for the opening-round side of the 2020 season. While I knew that Alex had been dealing with personal issues, I hadn't realised that he was considering quitting. And yet when he made his explanation clear – when he described to everyone how football was eating into quality time with his family and taking away his ability to deeply connect with his faith – his leaving made sense in the context of his world. Being an AFL player requires sacrifice and devotion, time and effort, sometimes at the expense of all other things. Alex no longer wanted to make that bargain with his faith or his life. I could respect that, but it was also still a struggle for me to come to grips with.

I love footy so much, and I know Alex does too, making it all the harder to put myself in his shoes. Both of us vocal, boisterous, competitive people, we each wanted to be seen and heard. We were the best of friends, but then we were asked – three times a week at training – to go out and compete like hell against each other on the track, and so for those periods we became the worst of enemies. We got angry, came to blows, at times full-on fist-fighting on the grass at Punt Road until separated by concerned teammates. We both led our own packs – the forwards and backs – and we made each other better. How could he leave all that behind? How could he walk away? In the weeks and months after he retired, I kept imagining him wandering back into the club. 'Sorry boys,' he would say to us. 'I mucked that up. I'm back!'

Alex Rance was a superstar. There is no question that he will be inducted into the Richmond Hall of Fame. He deserves to be inducted into the Australian Football Hall of Fame, too. Dustin Martin is a phenomenal player, an all-time great, and in 2017 had what Leigh Matthews described as the best season a player has ever produced. But in terms of individual impact on a season, I think Alex Rance's effort that same year – in which he was named skipper of the All-Australian side – stands above anything and everything else I saw during my career. Put simply, he's one of the greatest players in history.

I still communicate with Alex quite a bit, mainly through various WhatsApp groups, but I don't see him as much as I'd like to. He may have been right to depart. Footy is all-consuming, and when you stir in business and family and faith, there's scarcely any time left. Dimma would often implore us to savour our playing days – those shiftless moments spent shooting the shit together in the rooms, getting a rub down or strapping done; those idle hours when you're young and peaking, and everything seems possible. It's a good life if you learn to appreciate it – with the mates you make along the way. Dimma said as much in his final Jack Dyer Medal night speech: 'We don't play footy for the games we'll never quite remember, but for the teammates we'll never forget.'

I'll never forget my time with Alex. But as he began settling into his new life as a former AFL player, those of us still at Richmond were building towards something new. There was no sign of complacency in our camp. Despite the good times we'd enjoyed, we were desperate to climb to the top of the mountain again. If we'd been struggling for motivation, Geelong coach Chris Scott was doing his bit to ensure we were fired up, taking yet another veiled swipe at us. In the past three seasons we'd beaten Geelong in a qualifying final and a preliminary final, but just a week out from round one, Chris tried his hardest to convince the football world that we were overrated. He was asked about the era of the Tiger – perhaps even the so-called Dimmasty – and instead of duly acknowledging our ascendence, he spoke about 'deficiencies', allowing perhaps that we were 'a really good team' – but not much more than that ('with the greatest respect', of course).

'They're not Hawthorn in their multiple premierships in a row,' he said. 'I don't think they're Geelong or St Kilda or Collingwood through that 2009–2010 period. I think it's a lot more even than that.'

This was, of course, absolute nonsense. We had won two premierships in three years, but according to him we weren't as good as a St Kilda side that didn't win any. As always, we filed those comments away in our collective memory bank, ready to make a withdrawal and spend them later, perhaps in a final. Psychological warfare and a petty footy rivalry, however, turned out to be the least of our worries in the days approaching our traditional round-one match against Carlton.

By February 2020, authorities had confirmed the first cases of Covid-19 in Australia, and the World Health Organization was on the cusp of declaring a worldwide pandemic. Sporting events were being cancelled overseas and the media were talking about governments needing to introduce stay-at-home orders to stop the virus from spreading. A couple of days out from our round-one game, the AFL announced it was shortening the season to seventeen rounds, meaning each club would play the others once only. At the same time, they were reducing the length of each game. In hindsight, these changes were clever and proactive, made in the knowledge that when the viral wave reached its peak, all sport would likely need to be suspended. The AFL is desperately reliant on broadcast dollars, so the league bosses knew they couldn't afford to have no 2020 season. By scheduling a shorter season, they could still present a product, keeping the game running and the registers ticking.

There were more momentous announcements to come – so many more announcements, all season long – but the most significant one from a football perspective was that we would be playing our round-one match without any crowd in attendance. Gameday arrived and it was so strange rolling into the MCG and finding no one there. We jogged out onto the field for the start of the game, our theme song blaring through the PA system, with only players, coaches and trainers to hear the words. To listen to the song and hear no fans roaring that 'yellow and black!' crescendo was the most surreal part of all.

The silence was amusing for maybe the first ten minutes of the game. But by halfway through the first quarter we were looking at one another and shaking our heads: this was awful. We led by forty-six points at half-time before copping a bit of a fright early in the last quarter, eventually winning by twenty-four. It was a frustrating performance, and we ended up having the best part of three months to mull it over. Shortly after the final game of round one, the season was postponed until the end of May. Stay-at-home orders, or 'lockdowns' as they became known, had been declared in every Australian state.

With no football to play, and no club at which to train, players found new ways to exercise. I kept fit with my cousin Nick, who lived around the corner from me and had gotten into cycling. We would roll along the empty streets together (while socially distancing, of course). Once I'd decided that cycling was for me, I went immediately to the bike shop opposite the club, Total Rush, and picked up a pearl-white S-Works road bike with electronic gears and every possible bell and whistle. Google 'S-Works' and the first question that comes up is, 'Why are S-Works bikes so expensive?', and it's a fair question. The answer is quality and precision, tuning and alignment; the price tag for mine was $16,000. It's ridiculous, of course, but it also sums me up. I always want the best gear, the stuff people covet, the shiny new thing that will make me commit to my new hobby, state-of-the-art equipment to indulge my latest craze. It was always the same, no matter what I pursued. Whether as a child with a toy, or a man with a house, I've always lived with this constant appetite for the best. 'Bite off more than you can chew,' they say, 'and then chew like hell.'

When the footy season finally resumed in mid-June, most of the games were played without crowds. At first, we played in Melbourne despite the growing number of Covid-19 cases in Victoria. I struggled to find form in those early games, and my teammates were similarly lethargic. We drew with Collingwood in a scrappy, low-scoring and forgettable game, then lost to Hawthorn and St Kilda. Finally, in round five, we beat Melbourne at the MCG, but that was the last game we played in Victoria for the year. High case numbers meant the other states were preparing to shut their borders to people travelling from Victoria, and to keep the season alive, the AFL relocated all Victorian clubs to Queensland, where Covid-19 cases had remained low. The league soon announced that the Grand Final would be held at the Gabba, and during the rest of the season our games were to be played in either Queensland or South Australia (except for the Dreamtime game against Essendon – that would take place in the Northern Territory).

I'll never forget the feeling of guilt that gripped my body when I said goodbye to Carly and Poppy, and headed off to Queensland. I cried like a baby when I left them. Carly urged me to go, but still I felt as though I were leaving a single mother alone with fifteen-month-old Poppy – while fifteen weeks pregnant with our second child (whom we'd call Hazel). Carly was stoic, but the guilt weighed on me, nonetheless. As I settled into our accommodation on the Gold Coast, I could hear all these questions rattling around in my skull. 'Why am

I here? What am I actually doing? Did I just leave my young family to come north and play a game?'

We were told the hub would last only thirty-five days, but that timeframe was extended almost immediately, meaning my pregnant wife and my toddler daughter were left without me through the cold, lockdown Melbourne winter of 2020. We had just gutted our home for a renovation, moving into an apartment across the street, meaning once it was done, Carly was left to move us back in. She would pack boxes all day, then balance them on the pram and push them across the street, pop them in the front door, and start all over again. And when all of that was done, she was finally called to join us in Queensland, which meant packing up the house again, flying into a quarantine hub with the likes of Eddie McGuire and Gillon McLachlan. 'This has to be *The Truman Show*,' she told me once, 'because as a social experiment, it's too weird to contemplate.'

My parents had to go with Carly, too, because she was unwell, with high blood pressure and preeclampsia. It all began to feel a little terrifying and risky, but we were finally reunited. I'd left when she was fifteen weeks pregnant – now she was thirty-five weeks along. We went to see the doctors regularly at the hospital in Benowa, although when I say 'we' I mean 'she', because I wasn't allowed inside due to Covid restrictions. It was farcical at times, and frustrating.

Yet when I thought more deeply about the situation, I was also forced to consider what the club had given me over the course of my career. I also considered the young players, who hadn't been part of our 2017 and 2019 flags, and how they were striving for something of their own, and this was their window. I thought of the staff members with large families who they'd left behind to get on that plane and do their jobs in the tropics. I had obligations to all of them, too.

The last twelve rounds of the home-and-away season were hectic. We played matches on every day of the week as the AFL scrambled to complete its interrupted calendar. The aim was to finish the season by the end of October, one month later than usual. Our form had been patchy early, but we ended up winning ten of our last twelve home-and-away games while based in southeast Queensland. That success came down to mindset, to embracing the situation and finding ways to forge even stronger bonds between us.

Being in a hub environment was like being at the club twenty-four hours a day, seven days a week. At first the players felt like they were walking on eggshells, wondering if they could so much as enjoy a beer around Dimma. All it took was a few of the older players speaking up. 'I'd be having a beer if I was at home right now,' they reasoned, 'so I'm having a beer.' And that was that. It was a conscious effort to release the tension afflicting the younger boys, who felt beholden to the coaches and assistants and administrators. We created a fun yet professional environment, balancing work and play in a thoroughly unusual place and time.

When we arrived in Queensland, for instance, one of the first things we did was go to Bunnings and buy a flatpack fire pit and a bag of wood. After every game, without fail, there would be thirty blokes sitting around that fire pit sipping a wine or necking a beer. It became our gathering place. We passed a phone around and everyone added a song to a Spotify playlist. We talked absolute shit for hours on end, deep into the night. And it was the older guys – Dustin Martin, Tom Lynch, Nick Vlastuin, Toby Nankervis and me – who were usually the last to turn in.

After a couple of weeks at the resort, a few of the senior squad started a group called Wine Club – a smaller gathering, convened a few days after each game. The club was even supportive of that. Our high-performance manager – the drill sergeant of our physical preparation program – spoke to us about the need to maintain professionalism while inside the hub, but never at the expense of our humanity. We had to live, too. During our Wine Club sessions, Dustin Martin entertained us by going through his plans for a massive party if we won the premiership. He would joke with us about how he was going to get ARIA-nominated music producer FISHER and Gold Coast DJs the Stafford Brothers to do a show for us. He knew where the booth would be, and where the bar would be. He even had plans for the afterparty.

Various staff members joined us in the hub including our chief executive, Brendon Gale, who seemed to benefit – in a professional sense – from spending so much time close to the players. A corporate figure within the game – someone who was close to us but also at arm's length – he became more relaxed and personable. Less lawyerly. I know he missed his family, as did we all, but I think he enjoyed being close to the playing group. He was a player once, too, after all. Having a CEO like that is a massive boon for the list. People not only feed off success, but also off people in whom they can place belief and trust. We knew that he – and our iconic president Peggy O'Neal – could be counted on to set the standard. Under Brendon and Peggy, Richmond felt like a great place to be and an organisation to be admired, even envied.

The early part of the season – back down south in Victoria – had been so hard for the team, and it would have been easy to see that as the simple result of a lapse in form, a reaction to circumstance, or even a flag hangover, but in reality the more time we spent together in the hub, the more we realised how hard the pandemic had hit our group in those early rounds. It was tough for everyone, of course, and tough all over the world – I would never downplay that. But from a purely competitive point of view, we were a team that had lived in one another's pockets through 2017–19, and thrived. Our strength was our ability to feed off one another, so living and working in Melbourne – and abiding by Covid protocols that meant we trained alone, or in staggered groups of six at Punt Poad – was the antithesis of our strength. Connection was our advantage, so separation became our disadvantage. Heading north was a blessing. As difficult as hub life could be, it was the best thing for us. It gave us that necessary proximity to grow together again. And from then on, during those little form slumps we sometimes endured, Dusty or Dion would turn to me with a reminder: 'How good would a three-week hub be right now?'

We had so many good times while we were in Queensland, but not everything went right. Two of our less experienced players, Sydney Stack and Callum Coleman-Jones, had a drinking session at our resort, and then decided to head out on the town. They caught an Uber into the heart of the

Gold Coast nightclub area (a breach of hub rules in itself), then ended up in a drunken fight outside a kebab stand. If that wasn't bad enough, police were called and they were arrested. Sydney and Callum were ultimately banished from the hub and reportedly handed huge fines and suspensions. The club also found itself dealing with another public drama, when the media whipped itself into a lather over the way Nick Vlastuin and Jayden Short touched one of our most popular teammates, Mabior Chol, during the team song after a couple of our wins. It was jocular and immature, but innocent, yet Dimma was grilled by reporters about his players 'groping' each other. Our media manager, Jaimee Damon, did an amazing job handling each spot fire, but found herself constantly under the pump. And if the latest problem wasn't off-field then it was on-field. Tom Lynch, for instance, was hounded all season for the most trivial acts of aggression. Suddenly a narrative grew around Richmond, and it was no longer just about our exceptionalism, but about our hubris.

We were apparently arrogant and disrespectful. Nothing could have been further from the truth. There was an Amazon Prime documentary crew following us that season, and I wish we'd allowed them into some of our cultural meetings. It would have dispelled any myth of rampant arrogance. Guys would talk about how hurt they were, how much they were struggling, head in hands at times, sobbing and defeated. None of that was reflected with any balance, and so we developed a kind of siege mentality. It was us against them. And the constant attacks did nothing but galvanise the group. My opinion was that the best option for shutting stories down was to say nothing, share nothing, give them nothing. The media cycle is so short these days. One minute you're on the front page, the next minute all they care about is the back page. And you get onto the back page by getting to work and winning.

While the world closed in on us, we did exactly that. We played Geelong in round seventeen, and the Cats were flying. We lost ruckman Ivan Soldo to a season-ending knee injury during the game, then Tom Lynch went down with a hamstring strain, yet we still found a way to win. And with that we found so much belief. Before that match, we had spoken around the fire pit often about how we could win the flag – how we were *going* to win the flag – but that victory over the Cats confirmed it to our whole group. We knew we were good enough.

After thrashing the Crows at Adelaide Oval in the final round of the home-and-away season, we'd finished third on the ladder, meaning for the second year in a row we'd play the Brisbane Lions in a qualifying final at the Gabba. We made the mistake of travelling up from our hub on the Gold Coast to Brisbane on the day of the game. The Pacific Motorway is clogged with traffic at the best of times, and torrential rain meant the seventy-kilometre trip ended up taking us the best part of two hours. We arrived at the Gabba late, compromising our preparation for what was always going to be a fierce contest.

We started well enough but fell away through the middle part of the game and were unable to find the legs to get over the top of the Lions in the last quarter. The Lions went straight through to a home preliminary final, while we had to dust ourselves off and front up against St Kilda in a 'home' semi-final on the Gold Coast the following weekend. We were only average against the Saints, maybe a six out of ten if I'm being generous – letting them stay in the game until late in the last quarter – but experience and talent got us over the line.

Now we had to face Port Adelaide in a preliminary final at Adelaide Oval. Even though the Power had finished on top of the ladder and enjoyed a week off – a week in their own beds, at home, in their city – we knew we could get the job done and move into another grand final. We had every reason and right to feel exhausted, given we'd already done so much travelling and now had to fly to South Australia for the second time in a month, but we had become used to showing agility and flexibility. We had learned to adapt.

We always had memorable tussles with the Power in Adelaide, and this was no exception. It was a low-scoring slugfest in the rain, and we fell behind early in the last quarter, before Kane Lambert kicked two goals that won us the game. There were other heroic acts in the final stages when we had to run down the clock. Second efforts from Nank. Spoils and intercepts and attacking thrusts from Noah Balta. Clearances from Dustin Martin and Dion Prestia. Clean hands with a sodden, slippery ball from Bachar Houli. Tom Lynch's effort to put himself behind the ball and take a crucial mark as Port was mounting one last attack is something that was celebrated within the group. We held on to win by six points, and the euphoria in that moment was something else. We were all away from home, in our own little bubble together, and now we were into another grand final.

After the game, a police escort was assigned to help us get from the bus into the hotel. The Power crowd were there, snarling and roaring, held back by four white police horses. We were warned to stay in the hotel afterwards, too – anything we wanted had to be ordered. We sat around for a while, telling stories and reflecting on our previous premiership and the long journey the club had been on. We talked about all the great times we'd enjoyed so far, and then it was 4am, and we needed to be on a 6am flight back to the Gold Coast, to begin preparing for another grand final.

We expected to play the Brisbane Lions, given they had the advantage of a home preliminary final against Geelong, but the Cats had thrashed them, and suddenly we found ourselves preparing for a decider against our greatest modern rival. It was such an unusual grand-final week. There was no grand-final parade. The Queensland government had decided to allow a close-to-capacity crowd of more than 30,000 people to attend the game, but throughout the days leading up to that we had little contact with fans. Grand-final week in Melbourne smells of fresh-cut grass and sausages and face paint. It's a city that goes a little loopy over sport, and I missed that fervour.

Carly, who was heavily pregnant, and Poppy were already in Queensland by this stage, having spent two weeks in quarantine so they could be at the game if we made the decider. In the lead-up to the big match, it was announced that people would be able to travel quarantine-free between Queensland and Tasmania, so my dad and Carly's parents came up for the Grand Final as well. A lot of Richmond supporters who live in

Tasmania did the same. It was nice to have my loved ones so close again.

During the week, a few of us started chatting about whether we were going to Brisbane on the day of the game, like we had for the qualifying final against the Lions. None of us wanted to do that again. An off-the-cuff meeting occurred between my teammates Trent Cotchin and Dustin Martin, our footy boss Tim Livingston, Dimma and me. Dustin pushed hard on his belief that we needed to go up the day before, and after a little arm twisting, Dimma and Tim made it happen. (We later learned that Geelong's players and coaches, who were also based in the Gold Coast, chose to travel to Brisbane on the day of the game.)

We headed to Brisbane on the Friday afternoon, leaving our families to stay on the Gold Coast and then travel to the game on the Saturday. When we arrived at our usual accommodation in Brisbane, we discovered we'd been put up in the most amazing rooms. We were the only people staying in a huge group of serviced apartments, and so we felt as though we had our own little Tiger fiefdom. A few of us – Trent Cotchin, Dustin Martin, Tom Lynch and me – went out to a Thai restaurant and brought food back to Trent's room (virtually a presidential suite) and laughed about how lucky we were. What an adventure.

On gameday, we had time to kill before heading to the Gabba. After all, this was to be the first – and hopefully last – night grand final. The pandemic had given the AFL the perfect chance to trial a time slot that has long proven unpopular in fan surveys. They knew the ratings for a night grand final – beamed into a locked-down Melbourne – would be stratospheric, and therefore of benefit to the game itself, which had been hit hard by Covid. A few of us used our spare time during the afternoon to watch the Cox Plate. One of our great mates from the world of business – billboard magnate John O'Neill, a mad Richmond supporter – had a horse in the race. We cheered deliriously as that very horse, an Irish stayer named Sir Dragonet, crossed the line first. The distraction kept us from playing the game in our minds prior to the first bounce.

When we finally headed to the Gabba, the atmosphere had begun to build around the stadium. There were people wearing Richmond guernseys everywhere. It finally felt like finals, but it was still hard to believe that back in Melbourne people were barely allowed to leave their living rooms.

Early in our team meeting, Dimma mentioned Chris Scott's comments prior to the season. I sensed he might. The crux of the message? 'They don't rate us.' It was a reminder. We accessed that file we had kept on the club from Corio Bay, and we all fired up. We wanted to call out their arrogance with deeds, not words. Actions, not ideas. We wanted to show, not tell.

Running out onto the Gabba was brilliant, the roar from the Richmond supporters reminding me of a home game at the MCG. We started well, with Dion Prestia and Kamdyn McIntosh kicking the first two goals, but we lost star defender Nick Vlastuin to concussion in a chaotic passage of play that also saw Geelong's Gary Ablett hurt his shoulder after a heavy tackle from Trent Cotchin. The absence of Vlastuin meant we were without one of our best intercept players, leaving us unbalanced. The coaches tried to work out a new defensive method, but our contingencies kept falling short. We soon lost control of the contest and the Cats made us pay. Tom Hawkins kicked a goal eighteen minutes into the second quarter, and we found ourselves twenty-two points down, the game slipping steadily away.

But Dustin Martin stepped up, as he always did in the biggest of games, and kicked a goal just before half-time, narrowing the margin to fifteen points. He also showed leadership, pulling us together as a group before we left the field, reminding us we were in the game, in the fight, on the edge and ready to rumble. It's hard for people outside of the footy club to comprehend how well Dustin leads, and understandably so. Dustin is a private person who eschews the media, and the club respects that, offering very little in the way of insight into the example he sets for us. Inside that information void, the fans are left to surmise that he leads only by his actions with ball in hand – that he is what he does – but he has so much more to give. When we left the field, for instance, we could tell that the Geelong players were feeling cocksure and sensing a premiership. But Dustin's words kept us within a hunting mindset. He kept us angry. When we entered the rooms and Dimma presented the same front of aggression and belief as Dusty had, we all believed right along with them.

I kicked the first goal of the third quarter after my opponent, Lachie Henderson, had a free kick paid against him for holding. Just as we had in the 2019 preliminary final, we focused on putting the Cats under physical pressure. When we won the footy, we surged it forward as quickly as possible, and with Dustin, Jayden Short and Shane Edwards dominating, we slowly overwhelmed them. Dustin's second goal, late in the third quarter, put us in front and we didn't look back from there. He was unbelievable in the closing stages, too, kicking a pair of goals in the last quarter, including the last of the game – a ridiculous gather amongst three Cats, shrugging Patrick Dangerfield off his shoulder, before snapping square across his body from the boundary line. When the siren sounded, we had prevailed by thirty-one points, and were premiers for the third time in four years. We felt it all – the adulation and exhilaration, the exhaustion and the deliverance. In the strangest of seasons, one like no other before it, we had handled every bit of calamity and strife, proving every doubter wrong in the most emphatic fashion. Of the three premierships I won, this was the most satisfying, without question.

In a nice touch, global tennis star Ash Barty, a passionate Richmond supporter who'd won the French Open in 2019 and would later become an Australian legend by winning the 2021 Australian Open, presented the premiership cup to Trent and Dimma. It was the icing on the cake, and yet what capped off my entire 2020 journey was having Carly and Poppy come out onto the ground after the game, for the start of our celebrations and the lap of honour. If I were to make a list of the photos from my career that mean the most to me, the ones with my girls – Carly and Poppy – on the ground after the 2020 Grand Final would be hard to dislodge from the top.

Dustin Martin's heroics saw him become the first player ever to win three Norm Smith Medals. The party he'd been planning in his head for weeks became reality. We didn't have the Stafford Brothers, but FISHER found a way to be there, and we had a raucous and riotous time. When the time comes to look back at his career, I'll be in awe of what Duz achieved. I already am. He played his entire career his way, on his terms. Another remarkable thing about our 2020 premiership was the way it turned our beloved chief executive, Brendon Gale, into Nostradamus. All the way back in 2010, Brendon had released the ambitious 'Winning Together' blueprint, stating the club's intention over the following decade to win three premierships, establish a membership of more than 75,000, lead the AFL in average crowds and have no debt. Our victory over the Cats meant we had indeed won three flags during that decade. We also had more than 100,000 members. We had the highest home crowds in the league, as well. And we were debt free, too. Brendon had been widely mocked for his vision. Ten years later, he was the one left laughing.

Some good people left the club at the end of 2020, including assistant coach Justin Leppitsch. In Leppa's first few seasons back at the club he was the backline coach, and we butted heads often. Back then he coached like he played, in a tough and head-on manner, and we became combative often. But during his second stint at Richmond, after a failed senior stint at the Lions, a chastened Leppa realised you catch more bees with honey than vinegar. You need to work *with* people to get the best out of them, not just tell them what to do. In his last season at Richmond, he became the forwards coach, and we grew closer. He's a funny person, a great thinker, and a man who cares deeply. If he ever wants another opportunity as a senior coach, I'm sure he'll get one.

When I look back now, the whole 2020 season seems like a dream. It was a different world at a different time – a strange time but, for us as a club, a wonderful time. The players and staff from the clubs and the league who went to Queensland made a sacrifice for the sake of the sport, but we were also among the luckiest people in the country. Sometimes it's hard to fathom my good fortune, and the 2020 season is as good an example as any. We flew out of lockdown, away from the cold, into the sunshine, to live with our mates, and play the game we love, and sit by a fire pit, and win an historic flag, then celebrate with family and friends, all in the knowledge that the spectator sport we feed – the games people watch out of passion and compulsion and love – were a welcome distraction from illness and masks and confinement and death, in that crazy year when the world was turned on its head.

17

BE THE CHILD

Motivation isn't always easy to come by in footy. I found it in short supply before the 2021 season. My focus was on my home life, which now included a second daughter, Hazel, born in late December. Having spent so much time away in 2020, I relished every small moment at home with Carly and my girls.

As a group, we started to find some energy and enthusiasm on pre-season camp in Bright. Up in the Victorian high country, which was relatively free of Covid and Covid-related restrictions, the training tasks brought out the funny side of Damien Hardwick, too. Dimma loves mountain biking, for instance, and he thinks he's good at it, so one morning we rode to the top of a mountain – a winding 1000-metre climb with a rewarding view at the peak, called Clear Spot. The teams absolutely disintegrated on the way up. We had to drag every last man to the top, but the difficulty is the point of the exercise, as is the cooperation required to reach the summit, where the reward is that exquisite sense of achievement – and the panoramic group photo that follows. After that, the only issue was getting back down.

We had planned on taking a bus when Dimma roared at us – 'Boys, we rode up here, now we're going to ride down!' – then pedalled away like a maniac. He's our leader, so we followed, at which point it did occur to the high-performance staff that roughly $13 million worth of professional footballers were rolling down a rocky, treacherous slope of loose gravel at 60 km/h. It didn't seem to trouble Dustin Martin, who flew down, drifting at every turn, holding his leg out to the side and letting his soles scratch along the ground for balance, like a professional motocross rider. Others – all of us, really – followed suit. By this stage in the development of our side, Dimma was like a father to most of us, telling his usual terrible dad jokes, and expecting us to mock everything from his choice of clothing to his mood swings. We'd been on a long journey and become family. We willingly went wherever he led us.

The early weeks of the 2021 season were better than those of the previous season. We were allowed to have 50,000 fans at the MCG when we unfurled our premiership flag, for instance, prior to our traditional round-one game against Carlton. It was wonderful to play in front of the Tiger Army again. When we ran onto the field, it could have been a full house for all we knew. I perhaps didn't realise how much I'd missed the sound of a full-throated crowd, and at thirty-one years old, I was starting to realise how much I would miss it in the future. I kicked four goals as we defeated Carlton reasonably comfortably, then kicked another four when we knocked over

Hawthorn a week later. But that form was a kind of mirage. We were comprehensively run over by a young and enthusiastic Sydney Swans team in round three at the MCG, and that result was the true sign of things to come.

Still, where once I would have been wound up over winning and losing every week, spending time with my family had become less of a welcome distraction and more like the main game. That all-encompassing nature of AFL footy – the way it insinuates itself into every little bit of your life, into your diet and sleep and thoughts and plans – had begun to ebb ever so slightly. I started a new gameday routine, for instance, and it wasn't about mindfulness or stretching or visualisation techniques. It was taking Poppy to a local Brighton café, where I'd get a coffee and she'd get a cupcake. We'd talk and sing and sometimes dance. We'd bust a move together right in the middle of the café, because Poppy thought it was a good idea. And it was a good idea. It was the best idea.

As I found myself slipping into the warm glow of fatherhood, our form on the field ran hot and cold. We had been in that situation before, and perhaps because of that we held on to a little unfounded confidence that everything was going to be okay. Pull a rabbit out of a hat more than once, and you think you can always nail the same trick. You think you've got the answers, until you know you don't. We would throttle St Kilda by eighty-six points at Marvel Stadium, but sink to a dispiriting sixty-three-point loss to our new arch rival, Geelong, on a Friday night at the MCG. After ten rounds, our win–loss record was a Jekyll & Hyde 5 and 5, and we sat ninth on the table, in need of a 2019-style resurrection.

Instead we produced more unpredictability. A Covid outbreak would force us onto the road and to a victory against Adelaide in Sydney, followed by a dominant Dreamtime against Essendon in Perth, only to be flattened by a last-quarter capitulation to the West Coast Eagles, and a mortifying loss to St Kilda at the MCG in which we produced an embarrassing two goals for the entire game. A week later we were beaten by Gold Coast at Docklands, and from there we quietly slid down the ladder and out of the finals equation. Our season finished with a dreary draw against Hawthorn behind closed doors at the MCG. Dimma was grumpy in the closing stages of the season, while I was inhabiting the unhelpful mindset of *hoping* we would win, rather than *expecting* to win. Ultimately, I suspect all the work we had done over the previous four seasons finally caught up with us.

In a season of lowlights I was lucky to enjoy one personal high: playing my 300th AFL game. The lead-up to the match was humbling to say the least, although for someone who loves to be the centre of attention, it was a lot of fun, too – with mornings, afternoons and nights filled with well-wishes, congratulatory texts and posing for photos with legends like Kevin Bartlett and Francis Bourke, who at that stage were the only two men alive who'd played 300 or more games for the Tigers. When I had a quiet moment, I contemplated how this had been my dream, the one I mentioned to Mark 'Choco' Williams on my draft camp in 2006. That was now fifteen years ago. Time flies.

My milestone match against the Brisbane Lions was set for Friday night at the MCG, in front of family, friends and the Tiger Army. At least I thought it was set. On Thursday morning we received notice from the AFL: another Covid outbreak in Victoria had forced their hand, and the game would be relocated to Metricon Stadium on the Gold Coast. Three hours later we were on a plane bound for Queensland. We were told to grab some food before we boarded, so I ducked into the McDonald's at the Tullamarine terminal and grabbed a chicken wrap, figuring our nutritionist would understand. It was yet another whirlwind day, and in the hotel in Brisbane that night I found it difficult to sleep. Around 1am, I ordered meatballs from room service and sat on my bed eating them while watching the Tour de France. It was not the ideal preparation. On Friday afternoon, we piled onto a bus and headed south for the Gold Coast. The weather was fine but the traffic was atrocious. A crash on the freeway had caused a snarl so serious that the trip ended up taking two and a half hours, and the Lions were caught in the same jam. We were so late arriving at the ground that the start of the game had to be delayed by fifteen minutes. Still, rather than getting annoyed or upset, we used the time on the bus to bond. We pretended we were around the fire pit again and took turns telling stories and jokes. It put us in such a great mood, and that sense of fun and flow carried onto the field. My brother Charlie came up to watch that game, catching one of the last two flights out of Melbourne. He got stuck on the Gold Coast for eight weeks, a short holiday turning into a long one, but it started well and he wasn't complaining. We played with freedom and flair, rediscovering some of our very best footy – enough to upset finals-bound Brisbane.

281

I kicked six goals, too, and savoured every one of them. Yet one of the things I'm most proud of when I run my mind back through my career is how I had grown from a selfish player into a team player. But I should clarify the word 'selfish' here. It's often used in football to denigrate someone – to suggest that they're egocentric, caring only about what they want, and lacking any consideration for others. But that's not what it was in me. When I say I was 'selfish', I mean I was focused on the self – focused on what I thought was my singular importance to the side, which was my ability to take marks and kick goals. That was all I knew. I grew up as a striker in soccer and grew into a full-forward in footy. Scoring was what I did, so I did it as well as I could. But by the time I'd reached 300 goals, I'd learned – through introspection and examination, and with help from mentors and mates – that I could do more. I could bring other players with me. I could use my skills to tap the ball to advantage. I could use my focus to corral. I could use my voice to direct. I could use my vision to create. I could use my smarts to teach. My skill set didn't need to be so narrowly deployed. I guess I learned that I didn't always need to help my team by kicking goals – I could help my team by just helping out my teammates.

When the finals rolled around, I was jealous of the clubs that had made it, yet I was also relieved that our season was over. Another marathon pandemic lockdown was in full swing in Victoria, meaning all the finals would be played interstate, with the Grand Final to be held at Optus Stadium in Perth. Just the thought of travelling all over the nation adhering to Covid protocols made me tired. The Brownlow Medal count was also held in Perth, so for the first time in years I watched it at home on the couch, and I was quite happy with that arrangement. I had an early dinner with the kids, then sat in my favourite chair in front of the TV. I had a few cups of tea – Barry's English Breakfast, white with one – ate some cookies and had a bit of a chuckle, thoroughly enjoying my own company.

Midway through the count they awarded the mark and goal of the year – which was funny. The three finalists for mark of the year were my teammate Shai Bolton, Tim O'Brien from Hawthorn and me. Being a Western Australian, Shai was back home at that stage, and was invited to attend the count in person at Optus Stadium, while Tim and I were asked to put on tuxedos and then get a Zoom feed going from our respective homes, so we could all be on screen at once when the winner was announced. Shai was nominated for a reasonably spectacular leap and grab against Geelong, while I was nominated for a mark I took running back with the flight of the ball against Adelaide at Giants Stadium. That mark was probably the pinnacle courageous act of my career, and I think most serious footy watchers believed I should win the award. Instead, the accolade – and the $10,000 prize – went to Shai. I played up to the situation, acting bewildered and nonplussed, while Shai gave me a cheeky clip on stage. The host asked him if he had a message for me, and he did: 'Maybe next time, ay.'

On Grand Final day, it felt strange not to be part of it all. Instead, I just hung around at home, watching Melbourne execute an eerily familiar game plan, one based on fast-twitch ball-movement and a regimented but intuitive defensive system. The Demons used our playbook to great effect, rolling over the top of the Western Bulldogs in the third quarter to end their fifty-seven-year premiership drought. I was already in bed by the time the Dees got their hands on the cup.

Richmond was changing. The first big shift was Trent Cotchin's announcement that he was stepping down as captain. Trent forewarned me and the other leaders during a short catch-up after our season finished, dropping his bomb-shell out of nowhere – 'Oh boys, I'm just letting you know that I won't be captain next year' – before nicking off to go and help out his kids. I wasn't shocked, to be honest. It felt the right time for a change. My first thought was that having that little extra weight off his shoulders would be a good thing for him during the final stages of his career. I think he got a bit worn down by everyone watching him so closely in 2021, particularly when his form wasn't the same as usual. I think he was just exhausted, and he wasn't on his own. There's a reason we missed the finals.

His decision was also true to himself as a leader. Trent was always a good captain, but he became a great captain when he bared his soul a little more and stopped striving for the myth of perfection. Perfect player, perfect skipper, perfect son. He realised it was okay to have some flaws, and it improved his footy. Instead of seeking balance and style and stats, he chose the grunt – the hits that hurt, and the hunt. He was prepared to make mistakes, and that endeared him to everyone. And he found a way to connect, through care. He no longer butted heads with people who lived their lives differently, embracing them instead for who they were – Dustin Martin being the prime example.

When Dustin was very young, he and Trent were the anti-thesis of each other. But they each had something to offer, and those things eventually rubbed off and bound them together. Both are more well-rounded for that connection, Trent's smooth exterior taking on a few of Dusty's rough edges, and Dusty's guarded demeanour taking on some of Trent's open warmth. When you look from the outside at Dusty and Trent, it's easy to squint and doubt – 'I'm not sure this is real' – but the connection is genuine. The love is there.

The end of the 2021 season was the last for two defensive stalwarts of the club, too. Bachar Houli and David Astbury were both three-time premiership players, and colossal figures in our backline, and the season itself was punctuated by their retirements.

Bachar and I were both born in 1988 and both drafted in 2006. I think you tend to connect with players the same age as you, and that was the case for us. He has a dry personal-ity, and he's rightly portrayed as a model citizen, but he also has a wicked sense of humour. He was a constant puller of pranks, for instance. I remember there was this long thin box that was used to carry gear to interstate games – it looked like a container for a rocket launcher – and before a game in Perth one night, Bachar snuck off with it. Later he came running back into the changerooms with the box propped up on his shoulder like a bazooka. He had his shirt off and was yelling in Arabic. Half the team completely shat themselves, and Bachar couldn't stop laughing. One of his greatest contributions to the club was his famous annual barbecue, held at his place in Altona. All the players and coaches went along, and quite a few of us took our kids. It was an extraordinarily multicultural scene – an Islamic family hosting a heap of white and Indigenous people. You would try not to eat for two days beforehand, then gorge yourself on the feast that followed, then not eat for two days afterwards. (The 'two-day rule' was always in effect when Bachar was cooking.)

And as a player . . . damn, he could run. People think first of the fluid mechanics of his beautiful left-foot kick, but Bachar was a bona fide running machine, spending all game every game going flat out, up and down, across and back and across again. I think he would've liked to play one more season, but the salary-cap restrictions due to the pandemic meant it just wasn't possible for all the older boys to stay on the list. I suspect it even came down to him or me leaving. If I'd retired, Bachar could have stayed. But he retired and I played on.

Thankfully, Bachar remained around the club, running the Bachar Houli Academy. He could obviously do anything with his life from here – there are so many organisations that would love to have him on board – but I think he's too connected to footy to let it go now. The game runs through his veins and connects to his soul – at least maybe more than he thinks it does. I'm glad, too, because it means he'll stick around and keep sharing himself with that world.

David Astbury, meanwhile, was an unbelievably vital cog in our Richmond machine. I think a lot of people underestimate the role he played in our team. All the plaudits went to Alex Rance and Dylan Grimes – and they're superstars, sure, All Australians who could intercept all day or command like generals – but Dave was a gun. If we came up against Geelong, for instance, Dave would get the Tom Hawkins match-up every time, because he was our purest stopper – our most selfless key. I liken him to Shane Battier, a retired US basketball player who became a key member of the Miami Heat during their 2012–13 NBA championship teams. Battier was a high draft pick, who never quite became a superstar, but instead made himself into a kind of athletic epoxy, holding the group firmly together. Dave was like that, too.

My first memory of Dave was when he was still playing up forward, early in 2010. I remember a game against Melbourne, and we sat together listening to music – 'Brother', by Little Birdy – and developing a tight relationship over little moments like that. (He and Sam Lloyd emceed our wedding.) Then he went into our defence, and I remember being jealous of the partnership he had with those guys. He was tight with Dylan Grimes – another country boy with whom he could talk about birthing calves or farm fencing – and he was a perfect foil for Rancey. Rancey was so competitive and fanatical that he used to get hyper-aroused, but Dave could always bring him back to the right level. He had a powerful soft side to him, having been raised with three sisters in a small community.

Dave played only 150 games, having suffered so many injuries early in his career, but he made those games count. He began to find his footing in the group as a cultural leader, too, educating himself – and then others – on things like Black Lives Matter. Today, he's studying a Bachelor of Psychological Science at Swinburne University, and working with Emma

Murray's business, High Performance Mindfulness. Emma used to say he was the emotional-intelligence epicentre of the team, and I agree. He's going to make a big impact on society in his life after football.

It's hard not to begin sensing your football mortality in a season like that, in which you play your 300th game and your longtime skipper stands down, when a guy from your draft year like Bachar retires, and then a guy who's younger than you and was drafted later, like Dave, pulls the pin as well. You can't quite see the end, but it's definitely more front of mind than it was before. In those circumstances, you don't exactly look to secure your legacy, but maybe you peer a little into the future, and for me a part of that was working in the leadership space. It was in 2021 that this part of my future became a bit more realistic when Carly and I – and two mates – formed the Authentic Leaders Group. It felt like a natural segue for me – a progression of sorts.

I'd dipped my toe in those waters before, at the end of 2017, when I helped create a camp for the new first-year players. That was a random idea, based on a bushwalk I'd done as a fifteen-year-old student at St Virgil's. We'd been taken on the Overland Track – a place of temperate rainforest and glacial mountains and alpine plains. I thought it would be an ideal way for the draftees to integrate into the group, and, selfishly, it felt like the right time for me to explore how my style of leadership should look. I put together a plan – a very *brief* brief – and asked the club for some funding, enough to get us down there and buy us some camping gear. We went with a guide from the Tasmanian Walking Company, on a five-day trip from

Cradle Mountain to Lake St Clair. I brought senior figures with me – Kane Lambert, Toby Nankervis, Shane Edwards and Nick Vlastuin – and brought together the new kids on the block: Jack Higgins, Callum Coleman-Jones, Noah Balta, Patrick Naish, Ben Miller and Liam Baker.

It was the first time many of them had been camping. Jack Higgins carried on all night, at one point begging Toby Nankervis to help him because a possum kept scratching at his tent. Noah Balta ate so much food that on one night we simply had to stop him: 'Mate, you're not eating tonight,' we said. 'You've had all your rations.' We walked through snow and pouring rain. I remember pulling leeches from my face while we hiked, and stopping halfway through to help some strangers with hypothermia. I had persuaded the junior club physio, James Rance, to come with us on the trip, and at the end of each day he ended up giving everyone rubdowns. That must have looked odd to the other people staying with us in the public huts – for a group of guys to have their own masseur. But we laughed our way through the experience, and it felt like it drew the boys closer together and gave them some sense of who we are as a club. The camps have remained part of our annual practice, led now by Kamdyn McIntosh. It's nice to think we've stitched something new into the fabric of the organisation – our one little square on a giant cultural quilt.

In the short time we've been working in this space, our business has grown at pace. We do work with all kinds of corporate clients now, from shopping centres to media groups to building suppliers – everyone from Amazon and Afterpay to the billboard company QMS. Mostly they're looking for a circuit-breaker experience – a chance for staff to connect on a different level – and I've started to understand how what we do at Richmond is special. I never took that for granted, but I also probably didn't realise how different it was from other clubs and other jobs. You live only one journey, so you know only what you know, but one of our partners made it clear for me. 'There's something in this,' he said. 'I can't put my finger on it – it's intangible – but I can see how it [connection] can be created for a group.' Our first foray into it was actually helping run part of the Richmond pre-season camp in January 2022, again in Bright, including a competition in the style of *The Amazing Race*. It didn't all go smoothly, either. One group got completely lost. I blame Neil Balme for that – he was supposed to be standing at a checkpoint but didn't get there in time, and so Trent Cotchin's group missed the rail-trail turn-off and veered twenty-five kilometres off course. A police chopper was sent up to find them, to no avail. Once they ran out of water – the dry Weet-Bix challenge probably didn't help! – Cotch had to knock on the door of a stranger, who wouldn't let him in because of a recent string of burglaries. Eventually, a Carlton supporter grudgingly opened the door to his home, and Cotch called for help.

The group walked back into camp looking furious. 'Do we laugh at them,' I wondered, 'or is it too soon?'

Those sorts of moments are an adhesive, though, binding groups together. I remember a 2015 camp in Townsville, again with a kind of orienteering race built into the day, including abseiling down the cliff face at Castle Hill in the centre of the city. Alex Rance's group bent the rules, and Dimma gave them the biggest spray, sending them back to start all over again. Rancey's team came in stone motherless last, and by the time they were back, all the food had been packed away. I asked Rancey how he was, and he let me know: 'Don't fucking talk to me!' It only got worse for him that night. Half the side were sleeping in a communal hall at the local backpackers, and Ivan Maric and Shaun Hampson got the bright idea of sneaking in there and turning the heating system up to the maximum temperature. The guys stayed in there all night, sweltering, barely sleeping, assuming it was just the way things were in Far North Queensland.

And on the final day, we probably all almost died. Having been given lessons on how to paddle in a Polynesian canoe, we'd be making the eight-kilometre trip across the water from Magnetic Island to the mainland. No one listened properly, though, and so we didn't realise how to get in and out of the boats correctly, over the outriggers, and so we started capsizing and splashing and swimming in the sea, without realising it was a coastal feeding-and-breeding ground for tiger sharks.

That's what you do on camp, though – you behave like idiots, like kids, and that tethers you to one another, as if you've come up together in some way. The 2017 pre-season camp was famous for that. There was a challenge one day in a Gold Coast water park, with points awarded for various sections of this elaborate relay race. But there was also this blow-up shark, a plastic toy, and if you could capture it for your group, you would get enough points to win. It became the focus of every player there, until there were a few dozen guys fighting over it, climbing and clambering over one another, shrieking and screaming.

Dimma took a photo of that shark and put the photo up on the whiteboard in the changerooms before our round-one game against Carlton that year. We were about to go out and play in front of a full stadium, but he wanted us to remember those moments we spent recklessly knocking coaches off docks into the water. He wanted us to remember Alex Rance with two players in simultaneous headlocks. He wanted the team to remember me, faking a broken rib, just to try to sneak past the players guarding a goal. (Safe to say the club doctors weren't rapt with that one.) His final message for the night was written on the board next to the shark: 'BE THE CHILD – BE ALL IN'. Because when you're the child, you're always all in, and you have no fear. You ride a bike, you crash, and you go again. 'I saw that with that stupid shark,' Dimma said. 'It was you guys being kids, tackling and fighting and going mad. That's the attitude we're bringing tonight. It's fun. It's playing without fear. It's playing like you did with that shark.'

Part of my leadership journey is learning how little moments like that can have a big impact. For instance, many months later, just after the 2017 flag was won, and the speeches in the rooms were done, and the champagne had been sprayed all over the room, and Dustin Martin had sculled a shoey of beer out of his own footy boot, the boys all danced around the premiership cup, and from the back of the room, someone threw an object down on top of it. There on the silverware, deflated and thin, was the unmistakable shape of that silly shark we had fought over all those months ago in the Queensland sun, like we were kids.

18

BOURKE AND
BARTLETT

Once the pandemic restrictions started to lift in Victoria in late 2021, I couldn't wait to visit Tassie. I wanted to get out of Melbourne for a while and live a simple life back home – a short spell at a slower pace, in a familiar place. I wasn't close to breaking point or anything so serious as that, but I questioned whether I would have the energy to play footy at all in 2022 without a chance to recharge my batteries. Tassie always provides that charge. It's the circuit breaker – the place I can restore my spirit and soul. Some people renew themselves with a digital detox, or a regimen of fasting, or some kind of cleanse – using pills and powders and programs to reset their system. Generally, all I need is some time at home.

After a bit of back and forth, the club allowed me to head back to Tasmania for November and December, and I was grateful for the break. Clubs need to be uniform in their approach to the playing group, but there are also times when you need to make allowances for individual circumstances.

Consistency is overrated. In the off-season after 2016, for instance, Alex Rance badly needed an extended period away from the club, and they granted it, and he went around the world, satisfying his natural curiosity and returning energised and full of life. I needed something similar, but my version was less like wanderlust and more like a staycation. I needed to spend time with Carly and the girls, soaking up life without rushing. We quarantined for two weeks at a property in Bonnet Hill, then rented a place in Bellerive next door to Mum and Dad, and we lived for a time exploring our old haunts with new eyes.

I did my own training, too, pushing myself as I saw fit. There comes a point in your career when you can be trusted to do so, but the club had also put heat on the older boys to come back in great shape, given how hard it had been for some of us to get going in 2021. I found my own blend of exercise that would let my body heal and fitness build – and my vigour and vitality return – in time for the trip back to Melbourne in the middle of another summer.

Part of that was a charity ride I organised in December. Months earlier in July, builder and footy player Ryan Wiggins, twenty-six, survived an accident in which he suffered a near-fatal spinal cord injury, and I was asked to contribute to a video to raise his spirits. But I wanted to do something more, so I devised a plan to ride from one end of Tassie to the other, to raise $100,000 for his care. On December 19, I pushed off from the Gateway Hotel in Devonport, down through the rugged central plains of the state, finishing 9 hours and 18 minutes (and 303 kilometres) later in front of Parliament

House in Hobart. I had a support crew of family and friends, and riders join me for various stints – including champion Launceston cyclist Richie Porte – and was met by Premier Peter Gutwein. Only weeks earlier, six children had died in the Hillcrest Primary School tragedy, so I wore a badge in the shape of a wattle flower, the emblem of the school. Tasmanians were grieving, but also lending their support to one another. Local sponsors including National Pies, Fairbrothers Construction, Hartz Mineral Water, Tassal Salmon, Nubco and Blundstone all chipped in, bringing the total amount raised to $102,000. I don't know why I chose that moment or that cause to step up and help; it just felt like the right thing to do.

When I came back, the club felt different, as though a transition were underway. Bachar Houli and David Astbury had retired, so people assumed that Shane Edwards and I would be next. I think Shane knew it would be his last season, and I guessed that it would probably be mine, too. But I didn't want to shut the door either. After all, you're a long time retired.

On the eve of the season, Toby Nankervis and Dylan Grimes were announced as joint captains. When the players voted, we found it hard to split the pair, so we didn't bother. Adopting a joint captaincy was something different for the club, and it's always good to freshen your perspective from time to time. Our coaching staff got an injection of new blood, too, with the addition of former Carlton coach David Teague – a positive figure, adept at injecting enthusiasm into a group. Our beloved senior coach, Damien Hardwick, refreshed his own approach as well. He was heading into his fourteenth season at the helm, and a few of the older guys had given him some feedback – he needed to find some new stories to tell. There's only so many times you can inspire a group with the same tale of a particular mountain or boxer or NFL offensive line. The players wanted change, and Dimma took that on board.

With new leaders, new voices and new stories, along with a few tweaks to the game plan, we believed we were ready to charge up the ladder again, but we started the season slowly. We lost our opening-round game to Carlton for the first time in years, and I broke my thumb. I got home that night ready for ten days away from the club, which I had planned down to the last detail. I had organised for a group of the boys to fly to Tasmania to play golf at the famous Barnbougle Dunes, booking flights and accommodation and prizes for longest drive and nearest to the pin. Now I couldn't go. I tried everything. I remember standing in my backyard at 1am, hitting golf balls into the girls' trampoline netting, to test my own fitness. I felt as though I'd passed, but Dr Greg Hickey didn't agree. Instead, I swapped my golf trip for surgery.

I worked hard to get fit enough to be available for Maddie's Match against St Kilda in round three, sensing that it might be my last chance to play in the annual fixture. But when the teams were released on the Thursday evening, I wasn't named. The club said I hadn't been declared fit to play, but that was wrong. I was ready to go – I just didn't get a game. Too old? Too slow? I wasn't sure, but I sat frustrated in the stands at Marvel Stadium, my ego bruised, as we lost to the Saints by thirty-three points. We rebounded a week later to beat the Bulldogs by thirty-eight points, but that wasn't the start of anything. In what became a largely inconsistent season, the only consistency we displayed was an alarming ability to lose tight games.

There were so many close finishes in 2022, and so many results we would come to rue. We lost to Sydney by a goal after leading by thirty-three points. We lost an epic match to Geelong after clawing our way back into the contest and leading by seventeen points early in the final quarter. After leading the Suns by forty points, we lost by two, following an after-the-siren, set-shot goal by Noah Anderson. The following week, North Melbourne pulled off the upset of the season, stumbling past us by four points. And the week after that, we missed two late chances to edge in front of Fremantle and instead played out a draw. We'd developed a bad habit – and a bad reputation.

It's hard to explain how and why a run of close losses mounts, given that each game is separate from the rest. People assume that each loss is part of a trend, that there must be something in the collective DNA of the group that leads to a continuation of narrow defeats. Yet in the wash, you end up noticing how there is no wider trend; there are only small and seemingly random moments – an umpiring decision, a missed mark, a brain fade, an unlucky slip – that have outcome-determinative consequences. In the loss to the Suns, for instance, the media focused on missed goals by Jason Castagna, Jake Aarts and Maurice Rioli Jr, but what we talked about in match review was something altogether different: the need to take time off the clock – and our failure to do so. We'd led by twenty-eight points at three-quarter-time – if only we'd tried to take a minute away at the start of the quarter, then another minute a little later, then more precious seconds a little later still. Simple time management could have killed the Gold Coast comeback before it had begun. And in moments like that you begin to see how so many crucial match-winning practices are coachable and repeatable, and how they need to be addressed in pre-game meetings, perhaps more often than they are.

We do have game-scenario planning for close matches – a pair of play modes named Bourke and Bartlett. Bourke is the defensive play – for when you're protecting a lead – and it has so many elements to learn. We slot the wings behind the ball. We own the outside of the contest, to make sure the opposition can't get behind us. We allow them to outnumber us at the coalface with their spare man, too, knowing our spare will be further away, and we'll have them cornered on the spread, denying them an easy overlap. We keep the ball in tight through pack situations. And we dive on the ball, falling on it, not caring about the potential for a free kick against us. Why? Because even if a holding-the-ball free kick is paid, the turnover is slow, allowing time for the team to settle and structure up before the opposition kick is taken. Put all these pieces in place and you become hard to score against, because the principles are sound, and repeatable: *Fight like fuck, slow them down, force them wide, and force them long.*

Bartlett, by contrast, is the offensive play, which you use when you're behind. It's closer to our regular style of football, but with added urgency and zeal. We make sure only one player tackles at a time, for instance, so that we don't get too many players sucked into the contest, and no rolling mauls develop. At kick-ins and immediately afterwards, when everyone is expecting you to go long to the centre with a Hail Mary bomb, we go off the line at all costs, booting it to the open space of the wing perhaps, where we know we'll get a footrace, and perhaps a little opposition panic will set in. Above all else, we keep the ball moving.

Unfortunately, in 2022, we just didn't execute Bourke or Bartlett well enough, often enough, and then the pressure compounds and plays tricks on your mind. As a forward, you can watch the ball surge out of stoppage into an opponent's arms for a goal, and there's an element of total helplessness. When a tight game is slipping away, and all you can do is watch from the other end of the field, it feels like staring at an avalanche – horrifying and inevitable. And then when the game is over, those 'what ifs' begin multiplying in your head. As you lament the latest loss, you unconsciously calculate how you should have four more points right now, or eight more points, and how you should be a few places higher up on the league table, like you're playing some kind of dark reverse ladder predictor in your mind.

Sometimes, however, I wonder if such results are all but inevitable when you have so much player turnover. During our greatest seasons, we so often went into battle with a core group of sixteen, the lineup barely shifting from week to week, month to month. And those guys who ran out every week knew what they were doing, having learned all their lessons the hard way – together. But in 2022 it was different. After the draw against Fremantle, for example, I remember looking at the playing list and realising that a new generation was rapidly filtering through the side, and that the old guys were in a shrinking minority. While that's a great thing, new blood comes with risks attached, like the absence of institutional knowledge. They still have stuff to learn.

The development program is so important in that context, but with the AFL's soft cap spending reductions in place since the pandemic, it's been one of those areas that's been under-resourced. Sam Lonergan manages development, but his assistants have had no real constancy. Kane Lambert was helping out until he was required as a midfield coach. Steve Morris gets involved part-time and Ryan Ferguson comes in sporadically, but it's hard to share the syllabus when the teachers keep changing. And at any rate, there's nothing quite like a lesson learned the hard way. When the Giants beat us in 2017, with that Jeremy Cameron goal out the back, no one who played in that game ever forgot what we should have done to stop it, nor what they needed to do next time. Some lessons are taught in meetings, I guess, while others are tattooed on your brain by bad experiences during the game's harshest moments.

Despite it all, we finished seventh and played the sixth-placed Brisbane Lions in a knockout final at the Gabba. It was an incredible game of footy, but from a Richmond perspective, incredibly frustrating, too. Despite going in without Dylan Grimes, and despite losing Dion Prestia to a hamstring injury in the first half, we led by six points at half-time and by five at three-quarter-time. It felt as though we were in front the whole night, and just one goal away from breaking them, but we could never quite draw ourselves out to that twenty-point lead that would sap their spirit.

Every time we threatened to shake them, they kept pegging one back.

I kicked a couple of goals late, trying to will us over the line, but we couldn't make them go away. With only two minutes remaining in the last quarter, Tom Lynch had a chance to ice the game for us when he took a mark near the right behind post. He decided to go with a banana kick and the ball went close to the left-hand goal post, causing the goal umpire to call for a review. The 'soft call' from the umpire was a goal, but the review concluded the ball had gone over the top of the goal post and it was deemed to be a behind. I've watched this back more than a few times, and still can't believe they came up with that decision, given there was no conclusive camera shot taken from the top of the goal post. Still, it should never have come down to that. A player as good as Lynchy would usually put a shot like that straight through the middle.

That sinking feeling began to settle in again, and a minute later the Lions raced the ball forward. Zac Bailey took a mark about fifty metres from goal, and I ran down into the backline to help out. As Bailey's shot was landing in the goal square, four of us flew together trying to knock the ball through for a behind. Had we done that successfully, we would have won the game. Instead, the ball fell into the hands of Lions tall Joe Daniher, a key forward who'd stayed on the ground and received the ultimate gift. He dribbled through what would prove to be the winning goal. The final margin was two points.

The old changerooms at the Gabba are strange, like a rabbit warren, split by a pair of winding stairwells and broken up into three disparate areas, meaning you begin to find yourself physically separated from your teammates in this weird space while experiencing these weird emotions. You're baffled, first of all, because you had so much belief that you could win it, and would win it, and would challenge for the flag from outside the top four, and yet the brutal truth is that the season is over. You're sad, too, because you lost, but you try not to show it too much because there's a young guy next to you, Noah Cumberland, who's had a shocker of a night, and needs you to put your arms around him and let him know it's okay. You're sad, as well, because Shane Edwards is finishing up, but you don't want to mope around all maudlin and weepy and flat, because this is the last memory he'll have as a footballer.

Shane retired after playing 303 games and winning three premierships. It's funny to think back to our draft camp in 2006, when he thought I was a lunatic, and yet we developed such a great bond. He was such an intelligent footballer, but our connection was more than that. There were times on the field when our communication bordered on instinctual. When I saw him win the ball in the middle of the ground, I could read what he was about to do, and he could read where I would be. So many times, he delivered pinpoint passes to me inside 50 without any obvious signals being shared between us. He was brave and adventurous and talented. And he was my friend.

Another of my favourite teammates retired at the end of the 2022 season. Kane Lambert's chronic injuries meant he played only seven games that year, and wasn't able to feature in our final against the Lions. But when he was at his best, between 2017 and 2020, there were few more important players in our team and few better people at our club. Kane's journey as a mature-age recruit should serve as an inspiration for all the guys who don't get drafted in their teens. He didn't play his first AFL game until he was twenty-three, but by the end of his career he'd played 135 and won three flags. He won the Bunjil Award, for upholding the club's core values and best displaying what it is to be a Richmond person, three times, and the way he was revered within the playing group was no surprise either. He also won the Francis Bourke Award twice, in 2020 and 2022.

A few days after we lost to the Lions, all the players were scheduled for exit meetings with the heads of the football department. Whether I would play on in 2023 was unresolved at this point. In my heart, I felt like I wanted to go on for one more season, and I felt like the club still needed me, too. Key forwards are hard to find, and I believed I had plenty to offer both on the field and as a mentor for the younger players coming through the ranks. When I sat down for my exit meeting, I got great feedback, then Dimma spoke.

'What are you thinking for next year?' he asked.

'I want to play,' I replied, 'but if you say I'm not required, I'm more than happy to retire.'

They wanted me to stay, and I was thrilled. They'd just watched Geelong win the flag with a team made up largely of players aged over thirty, so perhaps old boys were in vogue. Or maybe they felt it was important to keep senior figures around the club as a way of letting the emerging players know that they would have to knock us out of the team to earn their Tiger stripes.

The end of a season is always strange, though, knowing you'll be off for a few months, away somewhere, and then you'll be back, but not *everyone* will be back. What other workplace is like that? Where at the end of the year a handful of your mates are shown the door, the rest of you go your separate ways for a holiday, and come back to find a new group of mates awaiting instruction and induction? It's a bizarre way to live and work, but after seventeen years in the system, it's all I know.

Our list manager Blair Hartley is the man who determines how the salary cap is carved up. To put it bluntly, he's the man who determines how much each player gets paid. Blair didn't have much money left to play with by the time I came to see him. If I wanted to play on, I knew I'd be playing for a small fraction of what I'd been earning at the peak of my career. In fact, I ended up on such a small guaranteed wage that I'd be eligible for match payments (extra money every time I played in the AFL) for the first time since I was nineteen. A deal like that was a dent to my pride, but one I was also more than happy to accept. I wasn't playing for money. I was playing to win another premiership.

I knew the club was targeting Greater Western Sydney midfielder Tim Taranto, so it felt as though there was a good chance we would be in contention for the premiership again. I remember having conversations with other senior players, and then with Blair, about making a push of that sort. People were talking about Jacob Hopper being available – I wondered if we could get him, too. Imagine a running midfielder to replace the engine of Kane Lambert, and a bull midfielder to shoulder the clearance load as Dusty settles into a role up forward. I had watched the Michael Jordan documentary *The Last Dance* and couldn't help imagining 2023 as a similar season for us, pushing our poker chips in on one last all-in bet – that chance to chase one final prize. *We can do this,* I thought. *We can go again. One more time.*

19

JUST LIKE THAT

It was over the Christmas break, as 2023 approached, that the idea of going back to Melbourne to play football got harder, embarking on yet another arduous pre-season when I could be staying in Tasmania. Why would I do that to my mind and body? The latter, especially, had earned a rest. Over a full career in footy, I can't count the various assaults on my person – the breaks and cuts and tears and splits and rips and ruptures – but I'll try listing them, top to bottom, head to toe. I've had three concussions, which seems a modest amount, though it's hard to measure the insidious impact of all the subconcussive hits you forget. Sometimes, the research suggests, it isn't the big blows that haunt you later so much as the smaller everyday knocks you barely give a thought to. CTE (chronic traumatic encephalopathy – the brain disease linked to repeated head trauma) researchers have a way of describing it for people, likening each blow to the head to a car driving over a pothole. A massive pothole might shake up your vehicle, even snap an axle. But it's rare. What's not rare is driving over one small pothole twice every single day, on your way to and from work, yet the wear and tear from that is ultimately just as devastating. I think I'll be okay, but I also understand the trepidation around this issue.

What else? Most recently, I needed eight staples in my forehead after my scalp was split open by an errant elbow against Sydney early in season 2023, during 'Gather Round' at the Adelaide Oval. I've also had a broken nose. Mabior Chol poked me so badly in the eye once that I needed stitches in my cornea. I've had three separate shoulder surgeries, including once from a partially ruptured AC joint, and another time from a labrum tear after subluxing the shoulder – stretching the joint beyond the range it was designed to accommodate.

I've broken five ribs, one time after landing on the wicket area in the centre of the Gabba. Ribs heal so slowly and painfully. I've fractured my wrist. I've broken a thumb and snapped a tendon in the hand at the base of my pointer finger. I've had nine finger operations – torn ligaments and split ligaments, breaks and fuses. I broke my fusion once after only a week, while painting a wall. I broke another one of my healing fractures by accidentally twisting it in a bedsheet. I had a titanium tip attached to one finger, and managed to break that off, too. That was in 2022. I remember playing with the wound for three weeks, wearing tape and a glove because the doctors were concerned the open cut would become infected. They were right to be worried. I went out after a game in Sydney, having a few drinks with club patron and heavyweight investor Mark Nelson at his Point Piper home, and it got infected and needed surgery – a screw inserted into the tip. I was supposed to be on antibiotics for three months.

I've had four hip surgeries, including procedures to get rid of floating debris. One time, I was messing around after training, decided to tackle Brendon Lade, and he fell on me as I rolled. He was a big boy when he was at full playing weight, so he was an even bigger boy as a coach. He came down directly on my side and micro-fractured the cartilage in my hip.

I had one minor knee operation, to shave an errant piece of bone from the inside of the joint. I missed twelve weeks with a posterior cruciate ligament injury, courtesy of a 2019 knee from Melbourne ruckman Max Gawn. It only happened because Toby Nankervis wasn't doing his job, leaving me in an aerial contest down the line against that monster. Nank did something similar early in 2023, leaving me alone on the island again, this time to cop the leap of Luke Jackson. (I quickly and sharply reminded Nank about the Gawn incident.)

I've had five ankle operations, usually for ligament retightening. One time, I was under the impression the surgery was going to be minor, but when I woke up, I found out the doctors had discovered some quite serious damage to a lateral ligament and had to reconstruct it to make sure my ankle would be structurally sound. I snapped my plantar fascia – a band of tissue that connects your heel to the base of the toes – in 2020, but played four days later in one of those short #HubLife turnarounds.

Throughout most of the 2023 season I battled a groin issue. I could hardly sit up. I never trained, except maybe twenty minutes of movement on a Thursday, during a light captain's run. I had to get jabbed with painkillers to play most weeks.

A groin problem is different for all players. Young midfielder Seth Campbell, for instance, had the same injury, but he didn't play for months because he was a first-year player and it wasn't worth risking his longevity by forcing the issue. But when you get near the end of your career, the equation looks different, and the odd injection to get an older guy onto the oval is just part of the devil's bargain you make. In a long career, you learn how to play knowing you'll never be 100 per cent fit.

All of which is a long way of saying that it hurts to play football. But you accept it all – all the training and matches, the running and the gym, the ice baths and recovery laps, the rubdowns and needles and the early mornings – because that's the deal. There's a certain masochism to it, too. You came up as a young player and saw the way a gladiator like Matthew Richardson absorbed the punishment and pushed through, and you suddenly knew what it took to reach his heights. There's also something mercenary about it, as though playing professional sport demands a blood contract – and the war wounds and surgery scars are your signatures. Sign here, initial here, and here. That's the deal.

My dad shared this philosophy with me once, back when I was very young: 'You always play better when you're sick.' It was probably a throwaway line, but I took it as gospel, and over time it became less of a general idea of his about life and football, and instead something specific to me. He seemed to think I thrived under duress. To this day, if I so much as sniffle in front of him, he'll tell anyone within earshot that I'm about to have a day out on the field. 'You watch,' he says. 'Jack's going to have a big one.'

Truth be told, the hardest thing about footy is the first run after half-time. You've had a nice break, a sip, a snack, a chat, and you wander up that race and jog out past the Auskick kids, and you trot out across the half-forward line to the flank, and then you turn to get going again, in a full team sprint from one corner of the centre square to the next. That one long stride down the wing, before you play another half of this hard, hard game – that's the toughest thing in football.

But once I was back at the club in January, I enjoyed the training. The presence of our two off-season recruits, Jacob Hopper and Tim Taranto, had created a real buzz around the club. I thought back to 2017 and the three players – Dion Prestia, Toby Nankervis and Josh Caddy – we recruited in the lead-up to that season, and how they changed everything. Jacob and Tim would bring so much as players themselves, but they would also allow us to extract so much more out of players already on our list. Dion Prestia, for example, would no longer have to carry so much of the load in the midfield, and Dustin Martin would be able to play a more flexible role that would keep the opposition guessing.

It was strange not having Shane Edwards around the club anymore – a change that meant I was now the oldest player at Tigerland. One of our rising Indigenous stars, Maurice Rioli Jr, took over Shane's No. 10 jumper. Given our lockers are arranged by number, Maurice took up residence near me and Trent Cotchin in the locker room – an area previously known as 'Old Man's Alley'. Footy clubs are funny like that. I was thirty-four, and clearly the oldest contributor to my workplace.

Dimma had some new coaching lieutenants in 2023. One of them was an old favourite, Ben Rutten, who came back to the club after losing his job as senior coach at Essendon. That ability to welcome people back into the fold at Richmond had become a real strength over the past decade, and it was pleasing to offer an opportunity to a coach thrown so coldly on the scrapheap by the Bombers. There's no doubt it would be awkward to take that step back from head coach to assistant, but the environment created by Dimma and Tim Livingstone made it easy. People make a lot of coaching 'family trees' – referring to the number of senior coaches spawned by a pivotal figure, like Mick Malthouse or Alastair Clarkson. Dimma was now in their company, with guys like Justin Leppitsch, Ben Rutten, Craig McRae and Adam Kingsley all appointed to top jobs after serving their apprenticeship under him at Punt Road.

Another addition to our coaching staff was Kane Lambert, who retired as a player at the end of 2022 but stayed on at the club as a development coach and to oversee the mindfulness program. Kane's appointment to the coaching staff was an example of a change in thinking at Richmond that had also been unfolding over the course of a few years. Early on in Dimma's stint as senior coach, there was a real hesitancy to appoint recently retired Richmond players to the coaching staff. This was partly because the club had not been successful, and partly because there was a belief that players needed to leave Richmond and go and experience the wider world of footy before being brought back when the time was right. This started changing when the club decided to give retired ruckman and cult hero Ivan Maric a development role, knowing his importance to Tigers culture. I was glad it continued under Kane.

In the couple of weeks leading up to our traditional round-one match against Carlton, I found myself pondering my career and wondering about the end. I knew that at various times throughout the year I would catch myself thinking about doing things for the last time. My last road trip. My last match against a tough opponent. My last game at the MCG. But I also pledged to myself that I would stay in the moment. I knew there was no guarantee I would be selected in the AFL team every week, and that meant contemplating running around in the VFL. I also knew that one bad injury could end it all in an instant, so there was no sense in looking ahead to what might come. All I needed to focus on was preparing as best I could, and making sure I came with the desire and intent to earn my place ahead of the young guys on the list who were thirsty for experience. I was excited by the prospect of the week-to-week battle.

Not everyone was, though. Truthfully, the first sign that Dimma was cooked came for me before the season had begun, back on pre-season camp in Apollo Bay, when we were mapping our year. In those early conversations, we started to focus more on the outcome than the process. The address from the coach and the messaging from the leaders was all oriented towards reaching the top four. Historically, you do need that high-placed finish to succeed, but our focus had never been on such things. It had always been about the journey. It had always been understood that our footy in round one would look nothing like our footy on grand final day – and that the season itself is the process of moulding and shaping the men and the method. Once you start looking at the cluster of clubs from bottom to top and putting your energy into finishing in that leading group, it requires you to win this game, and that game, and the next game, and you start focusing on things you can't control.

I'll put it another way. Dimma was always so keen on mountaineering metaphors, talking to us about the great climbs of the world – from Everest to K2 to the Shark's Tooth – but it was always about the individual steps it would require to reach the top. He'd never asked us to gaze up at the summit, to look for the peak, and yet that's exactly what he was doing now.

I had a conversation with Andrew McQualter about it. 'Mate, are we focusing on the outcome too much?' He wasn't sure. There's a weird tightrope you've got to walk between what you want – winning, being the best – and the daily, weekly, monthly effort required to make it happen.

Maybe the change in emphasis wasn't as glaring as I'm making out. Maybe the confirmation bias of Dimma eventually stepping down is what makes me remember it a certain way. Yet whether the new approach was consciously communicated or not, it slowly crept into everything, and when that happens, and you lose once or twice, your chance of rebounding diminishes, and everything turns to shit.

We played patchy football at first, and then we played poorly. Truly poorly. A loss to the Gold Coast at Marvel Stadium really hurt Dimma. He said to the group that he hadn't seen that kind of play from us before, or at least hadn't seen it in a long time.

'Shit, boys, maybe my message isn't getting through, because that's not us,' he said. 'I'm struggling for answers, though. I need help.'

I hadn't seen him like that. Ever. So bereft. That was a real show of vulnerability in front of the whole group. The CEO and members of the board were all there in those rooms with us, and he dropped his guard completely. He didn't blow up. He didn't apportion blame. He didn't rationalise. He didn't excuse. But I remember his final words clearly: 'I need help.'

When we lost to Essendon in the Dreamtime game – by a point at the death after squandering a bunch of simple chances to hold on to our lead – he wasn't so conciliatory. He was angry. Harsh words were used. Words he would probably walk back now, not that he has any need to. We understand the way the world works. For him it must have been a little like those moments when you have a go at your kids – you get so wound up and frustrated with them in the situation, and then you step back and realise you're wound up and frustrated about something else entirely. And you look at yourself later and think, 'That's me at my worst.'

Maybe that was the trigger for him to stop – to stop before anything got out of hand, before that kind of outburst became something he'd produce every other week. You have to respect that – that personal accountability, that self-awareness that you're miles from being the best version of yourself.

It was also as though he could see the passage of time. His senior players were now outnumbered by the next generation; those who hadn't won a flag outnumbered those who had. And he couldn't go back to those days of struggle. His 'Dimmasty' – not that he would ever call it that – was over. I think about that all the time, how we revisit our recent rich history too often, even through the imagery inside our club. The walls of the Graeme Richmond Room – our main meeting place – are wallpapered with floor-to-ceiling images from our flags in 2017, 2019 and 2020. Sure, it's wonderful to catch a glimpse and enjoy that fleeting feeling of glorious reminiscence, but half the guys in that meeting room who are looking up at those jubilant faces weren't at the club at the time of those successes, or worse, they were here but weren't out on the field with us.

Do they look at those same pictures I cherish and get envious? Do they look up and wonder how they can create something of their own – in that shadow? What does Jack Ross – who wasn't here for the 2017 flag, and didn't get to play in the 2019 or 2020 finals either – think and feel when he sits in that room? What do those pictures mean to Steely Green, who's been at the club for five minutes and, as of time of writing, hasn't played a senior game yet? Marking the past is a tricky business. How long do you keep it up? They say a year is a long time in footy. Well, 2017 is already six years ago.

Everything changed on a Sunday in June. I was sitting on a bench out the front of my house, enjoying a rare blast of winter sunshine, getting ready to play golf with Sam Banks and Rhyan Mansell, when Dimma texted me.

'Hey mate, are you around to catch up today?'

If your boss texts you that, and you're a senior player, and you played terribly on the weekend, you suspect you know what's coming next. I wrote back: 'I was half expecting this message. I'm not free today, but do you want to chat on the phone?'

He rang me immediately. 'It's not about you, mate, it's me,' he said. 'I've had enough. My time is up.'

What can you say in that moment? You're dumbfounded, so you say something dumb – 'Oh right, wow' – and then you can go two ways. You can probe and ask questions, or do what I did, and try to understand the decision, and every bit of thought he must have put into it before making it. You listen, too. Dimma rattled off thoses line he would recite to media later – 'I've cooked the sausages a thousand times; I can't think of another way to cook them; I think the group needs a new voice' – and you nod because you know he's right.

I'd always harboured this faint inkling that this might be his last year. At first it was from a purely romantic point of view – Trent and I were due to finish up, and so we would all end together, and one era would pass into another, just like that. Dimma had been at the club for thirteen years, been to the top of the mountain three times, coached more than 300 games, all this combined with everything else that had happened in his life in recent years, from divorce to his kids growing up. You let that all sink in for a second, and suddenly there was no surprise at all.

Then I had to go play golf, spending the day with Mansell and Banks, sitting on this huge story, unable to tell the junior guys about it. We played the south course at my club, Peninsula–Kingswood, and I played well, or well enough to beat them anyway. I spoke to Dustin, and Trent. Both understood – we all did. I spoke with Tim Livingstone and Blair Hartley and Brendon Gale, and we talked about who should take over as senior coach in the interim. It was unanimous that

Andrew 'Mini' McQualter would be the man. Mini has many strong suits, but relationships are his strongest. He had also been at the club the longest and was more deeply connected to the playing group than anyone else.

On Monday the news still hadn't gotten out, and an all-hands meeting was dropped into the calendar for 10am the next day – a 'must attend'. I think many people assumed that Brendon Gale, 'The Chief', might be leaving the club for a mooted role with the AFL, steering the establishment of the new Tasmanian team. But no one really knew, except those who did.

The hours ticked by, and I was at home having a massage when I saw that Nathan Broad was appearing on Fox Footy's *On the Couch*. Within thirty seconds of that, the news broke. I texted Blair – 'Please tell me Broady knows' – and thankfully he did. It turns out he was doing an extra weights session that day, and the Chief had grabbed him on the way out of the club and filled him in. Fox Footy wouldn't have put him on the spot and asked him impromptu about breaking news anyway. My friend at *AFL 360*, Tim Hodges, was adamant about that. 'No way, mate,' he told me. 'We couldn't do that to a young fella who had come in to help us out after losing a game of footy.' After the ad break, people began to text and call, and I just lay on my back, looking up at my phone screen, pinging and blinking with dozens upon dozens of alerts.

We had an leaders meeting at 8.45am. I'm not usually in that group, but it was expanded to include me and Trent and a host of senior players, not just Dylan Grimes and Toby Nankervis but Tom Lynch, Liam Baker, Jayden Short, Marlion Pickett, Nick Vlastuin, Jacob Hopper and Nathan Broad. Our leadership and culture consultant, Shane McCurry, was on a trip to the USA, so we had to drill down into what we wanted to do without him. Are we going to go out and train? What does today look like? The one thing that shone through was how Dimma had always had our backs, and so on his way out, we were going to have his. We were all going to attend the presser. We would talk to any reporter who had a question, and we would say the right things. We were determined to make a clear and conscious effort to stand by our coach.

Dimma met us all first, at 9.45am. His main message was simple and sweet: 'Thank you, boys.' He spoke about sacrifice. He spoke about how he still believed in the group – with unshakeable faith in us as players and people – but he also didn't believe he was the man to take us forward anymore. If I were a bookmaker, I would have had him odds on to bawl throughout the entire speech, but he held himself together well. He did the same in the press conference later, which was muted but celebratory. Despite the mournful public outpouring over his decision, somewhere along the way I reflected that he was saying goodbye, but also see you later. He was leaving, not dying. I could still ring him. We could still have a coffee. He just wouldn't be out on the oval with us when we trained later that morning. And if I knocked on his office door, as I so often had, he wouldn't be there anymore. It was someone else's office now.

After that, excitement was the natural reaction. We were entering the unknown, with zero expectations, and no pressure – we had been given a free swing at the rest of the season. In the coming days when anyone broached the topic with me, I had my talking point set: 'It was the best thing that could happen,' I said, 'for all parties.' It gave Dimma clean air to go and do something else and recharge his batteries and live a normal life for six months (until the itch to coach returned). And it gave our young group a chance not just to experience something different, but to create something of their own, with no entanglement to the past.

Mini got up and spoke that day, too. There's always a bit of uneasiness going into the unknown unless you have someone like him at the helm. Mini settled everyone, immediately. 'We're not going to change too much,' he said. 'We're not going to attack everything from another angle.' He said we already have a plan in place that works – and we just need to hone a few things, adjust a few dials, and tweak the settings. And that's what we did. In the coming days he distilled that message further, giving us a sense of direction and a reminder of who we are, and what we want to do. 'We want to be a forward-half team,' he said, 'and we want to be top six in forward-half pressure, and forward-50 pressure', which we quickly became. Despite missing four of our best players, we should have beaten league leader Port Adelaide, and lost by only ten points. Then we got a sizeable monkey off our backs, winning three tight contests in a row against the Giants, Dockers and Saints. The emphasis was taken away from the end of the year, and instead we started setting two-week goals, and three-week goals. We began reducing everything to basics again, teaching the kids and reminding the elderly. 'We want to be the best at pressure, so how do we get there?' Mini asked. 'What do we do?'

Mini must have seemed like a fresh chance for a lot of the younger guys – an opportunity to be seen differently – while for the older guys, he gave us a reason to re-engage as leaders, to shoulder some of the responsibility for directing the side and to keep the focus on the important things. Things like acknowledging Trent Cotchin playing his 300th game, chairing him off afterwards, taking photos and soaking in those moments. As winter took hold, I started to savour each open training session, each visit to a familiar stadium, and each interstate trip. At the start of the year, I wanted nothing more than to get another premiership, but now I wondered . . . Maybe I've got all I need already.

On a rainy Thursday night at the MCG, I wore long sleeves. Dimma had enacted a blanket ban on long-sleeved guernseys during his time in charge, but the moment he was gone I put in an order with Puma. It arrived in time for a chilly, wet match at the home of football. We won a tight, tough contest against the Sydney Swans, and then sat back to enjoy the victory. One of the things I'll miss most in retirement is the first ten minutes in the changerooms after you've had a win. You play footy for many reasons, but for me those times were the most special. When it came to winning premierships, the minutes and hours after the game was won were a fairytale. Partly it's the bittersweet feeling when you're banged up and bruised and bitten by the cold, but blessed with a sense of fulfilment. We call it 'the winners' ache'.

You sit down in the changerooms almost at random, on those white plastic chairs, and you're utterly cooked but in that moment you want for nothing – your cup is full. You reminisce about what went well minutes earlier, out there, upstairs. 'How 'bout that little kick you hit me up with in the second quarter?' and 'How great was he?' On this night, I talked about debutant Sam Banks ('How good was Banksy saving that goal?') and emerging tall Tylar Young ('How great was he, shutting down Buddy Franklin?')

We talked about how, after Toby Nankervis had smashed into Jake Lloyd, Swans defender Nick Blakey came charging in to remonstrate with whoever was on the scene, maybe not realising that would mean squaring up against Marlion Pickett. The look on Blakey's face when he arrived – 'Oh, shit, picked the wrong fight here' – was priceless.

It's always such a great environment, filled with friends, and with family, too – immediate family in my case. Carly brought our son, Tommy, to his first-ever game, and I held him in my arms while being interviewed on camera. Just four months old, he was born on March 7. I remember my nerves that day. As a professional athlete, you become so accustomed to going into hospital yourself that when you're not the one going in for a procedure – when the shoe is on someone else's foot – you're more scared than you need to be. We drove in early in the morning, and I was a ball of nervous energy, just knowing our family was changing – growing from four into five – while not knowing whether we were having a boy or a girl. Toy trucks or tiaras, you don't care either way – you just take an interest in what your kids are interested in. You just want to be there for them and support them in what they love, and you want to pass on what you've learned. Tommy's middle name is Ivan, after my grandfather on my mother's side, the writer, the one who penned that book with the perfect title, *Life's Little Pieces of Magic*. What's a newborn if not a little piece of magic?

It meant an enormous feat of juggling having a newborn in 2023 – on top of a child and a toddler – going into a final football season. Carly had to pick up a lot of the load, but the club was fantastic with us, too. I've been lucky to be afforded so many luxuries. You get to skip certain meetings or commitments, from ducking out of training for obstetrician visits to going home early for the school pickup.

Most of 2023 I would get to work at 8.29am on the dot, after dropping my kids at daycare, even though the first meeting would start at 8.30am – and no one batted an eyelid. So many new dads and mums are part of the decision-making tree at Richmond. Andrew McQualter, the assistant coach given the opportunity of a lifetime to trial as our senior coach, jumped into that role only a few weeks after his third daughter was born. The hierarchy within the football department and club executive was acutely aware of his workload, but still confident in his capacity to meet it because within Tigerland now there's always a shoulder to lean on, always someone ready to offer understanding and advice, and to make allowances.

When I arrived at the club, there was less of a focus on wellbeing. There was a circle of care of sorts, but it's since been expanded to include players' families – wives and children and parents. In a nutshell, the club wants to make sure that everything is all right – for everyone. It's an all-in mentality that entails investing in every young person who arrives at Punt Road.

As my career started to wind down, I felt all the wistful cliches guys talk about in their retirement speeches. My career lasted seventeen years, such a long journey. But in those final weeks it was staggering how fresh everything seemed. I began to realise that I was stopping weekly, daily even, to smell the roses.

In team sport, for instance, it can be on the nose to express any pride in what you've done. You're not supposed to bask in your achievements – it's as if that's tantamount to gloating. For years, I toed that party line. But now I wish I could have been more honest about the pride I felt in what I'd achieved, because there's nothing wrong with that. We all say, 'You don't play for individual awards', but you do play to be the best version of yourself, and if a trophy helps confirm that, offering proof of how hard you've pushed, then that's worthy of celebration.

The biggest lessons I learned in my time were all about people. The game has changed so much, and thankfully, instead of embracing the simplistic old-school notion of training ever harder to get better results (*You only get out what you put in*), we now also invest in culture and people, in making football a fun, tolerant and rewarding sphere in which to work.

I also noticed how, in my senior years, we began to savour diversity in clubland, too, completely blowing up the idea of cramming people into the same cookie-cutter mould. I think of the different blokes who sat alongside one another in our meetings: Liam Baker, a farm boy from a remote wheatbelt town, next to Bigoa Nyuon, the son of a Sudanese military commander, next to Jayden Short, a ratbag from the northern suburbs of Melbourne, next to Dustin Martin, the son of a bikie, next to Kamdyn McIntosh, the son of a fly-in fly-out miner.

That's what clubs do, of course: they pluck kids from all over the country, from different backgrounds. That was driven home for me one day when it was Daniel Rioli's turn to choose the Jungle Beat songs to play in the stadium before a home game. One of his selections was 'My Island Home' by the Warumpi Band. I knew that song well. I grew up thinking that it was about Tasmania. It was in one of our tourism ads. Daniel grew up thinking it was about his home in the Tiwi Islands. In fact, it's about Green Island off Cairns, but the point remains: two completely different Australians, from completely different backgrounds, from opposite ends of the country, having a connection through the same song, the same club, the same game. Footy doesn't discriminate. People do, sadly, but the game never does. Another great revelation for me was mindfulness/meditation/visualisation – all those things that might once have seemed left of centre to a younger version of me. I see now how they can help you as an athlete. And they'll be a part of my future, too.

Something I know I can do to keep scratching the competitive itch is to continue working in the leadership space with Authentic Leaders Group. There's something special about taking a group away for a circuit-breaker workshop weekend. We've been to Uluru to camp on a camel farm under the rock, to Bright to glamp in the hills of Wandiligong, to the southeastern tip of Tasmania to walk the Three Capes Track – always knowing that the best classroom is outside, and the best teacher is experience. You train and prepare for those events, and you have to be switched on, and you have to get out of your comfort zone – just like gameday.

There'll always be an element of sadness associated with giving up footy and moving on to what's next. Football is one of the great loves of my life. You end up being institutionalised by it. But now, hopefully through a role in the media, I'll get to look at the game through a different lens. I'll go to more footy and see more of other teams. It's easy to become tribalistic about Richmond. I'll never fully let go of that, but now I'll get to see what others do well, and learn to acknowledge success in other colours and sashes and stripes.

I'm looking forward to going home a bit more, too, taking my kids to Tassie and letting them explore what I explored as a kid. I'd love for them to feel connected to the place, to value what I valued about it. They were born on the mainland, but they'll be pseudo-Tasmanians.

The most daunting thing is the absence of daily structure. My life has been so regimented for so long. Even the off season has a certain rhythm. I guess my best move will be to breathe in some fresh air, sharpen my sense of curiosity, and get busy building a new life around new interests, new habits and new people.

I won't have the certainty of my daily drive into the Richmond Football Club anymore. I'll still have a full calendar and a busy itinerary, but I'll no longer be drawn inexorably each morning along New Street, veering left onto Brighton Road, before swinging right onto Punt Road. For seventeen years that was my destination, and every time I got high on that hill in South Yarra it was like the lyrics of a Paul Kelly song were playing, with the Yarra River and the clock on the silo and the MCG below, and my office right there in the middle. What a way to start the day.

EPILOGUE

On the last day of my career, I wake up and do nothing differently. The same food, the same smiles, the same conversations.

This feels different though, like the morning of a final. I'm mindful of the time, for instance – watching the clock and counting down. Family and friends are in town, too, and they arrive at 11am so we can all leave at 11.10am sharp in a three-car convoy led by me and Carly and Poppy and Hazel and Tommy crowded into my orange Mitsubishi Triton. The kids are excited because they're going to Tigerland. I know I'll miss taking them there whenever I please; that sinks in as we pull up at Punt Road.

My walk to the MCG is filmed for television. People are picnicking in Yarra Park, having a beer in front of the Jack Dyer statue, and yelling idle thanks my way. I'm pushing the girls in the pram, Carly is carrying Tommy behind us, and sportscaster Mark Howard is asking me questions while the camera rolls, but I'm only vaguely aware of what I'm saying as the stadium comes into view.

We walk the last stretch as a family, under the hulking sculpture near Gate 6, and along Brunton Avenue. It feels real now. I've been stopping to smell the roses all season long – now I smell the garbage in the loading bay of the ground.

Deep down, at the start of the year, I knew this would be my last. I had conversations about it, too, but you wait for little moments to nudge you over the edge and confirm the truth. You don't want to speak too early, too soon, because you can't say it and then take it back. You can't walk into Punt Road the next day and say, 'I've changed my mind, let's go again', so you wait for all the 'what ifs' and 'maybes' to fade.

My grandfather, Ivan Eade, wrote a book of stories called *Life's Little Pieces of Magic*, and one of those stories is about me, talking to him, the night before the first day of high school. I had packed my bags three times over, tried on my new shoes again and again, and attempted to memorise the school rules. Grandad remembered me calling him about the big transition I was about to make, and he wrote about how I seemed to him in that moment:

> *He seemed immensely calm about the whole new adventure, but underneath I sensed the agitation of uncertainty. There is always a slight doubt of the unknown. It is funny how the size of a fish grows smaller with the passage from a small pond to a larger one. How history repeats itself.*

How indeed.

When did I really decide to retire? Probably after our

comeback win over Hawthorn. I had played on James Sicily, who had played well. I had opportunities to kick goals, but I didn't really fire. I sat next to our list manager, Blair Hartley, and murmured, 'I think I'm done. I think this is it for me.'

But even then, I couldn't formally acknowledge it. That only came later, talking with Trent Cotchin in Tasmania while doing a sportsman's night in Latrobe, outside Devonport. There was something about the smell of the mud from the oval where Darrel Baldock had played – it made me nostalgic. Maybe I was tired of being asked about retirement and responding with a Cheshire grin and a lie.

I walk on the MCG turf before the game, drinking it in, chatting with Dustin Martin. 'How weird is this?' we say. 'We're never going to be here like this together again.'

I walk into the rooms and need a moment alone to compose myself, so I sit in the empty drug testers' room to absorb the moment and soak it all in.

I go into our line meeting and coaches meeting, and the messages are tailored to me and Trent – encouraging everyone to celebrate our journey by playing tough, hard, Richmond footy. It's weird when you sense you're about to take part in your very own memorial match.

I'm sitting in my usual spot – the back left corner of the briefing room – and Kane Lambert rises to speak about Trent: how amazing he's been off the field, what he's taught us all about ourselves, about being imperfect and being okay with that. Then Tom Lynch stands up to speak about me: how much I care, how accepting I am of people, and how I helped to make them better.

I go into the player dressing rooms and there is my jumper, neatly pressed and laid in my locker, number eight facing up. We put on our guernseys together – players only, a tradition started by our former captain, Chris Newman – but it's all a blur because all I can think of is running through the banner with my kids, which we've never done before.

I walk up the race with Trent and Dustin, and it feels as emotional for Duz as it does for us. He's a very sentimental and spiritual person, big on revelling in those moments. They're important for him, too. Six rounds into the season, without really knowing Trent and I were going to retire, it was Duz who decided: 'Every week, we're going to run out together, and when we sing the song, let's always stand together.'

After our last walk up into the mouth of the MCG, I meet Carly and the kids on the turf at the top of the race, and I'm already crying.

The game whizzes by. Duz finds me with the ball, and he finds Trent, too. My first shot on goal will take everything I have, and I absolutely whiff it – a hideous miskick off the instep. Later I kick a goal in the square. I take a hanger. I have a few shots in the last quarter, too, and a few laughs, and Duz gives me some advice: 'Oi! Just snap it!'

I don't just snap it, but it doesn't matter either. Deep down it's irrelevant whether I kick five or none. I get to the end, the siren sounds, and Dustin is there, Trent isn't far away, and that's all that matters.

There are interviews, and photo opportunities, and a guard of honour with our families and friends, but mostly one long walk around the boundary line. After the 2017 Grand Final, the AFL's media manager, Patrick Keane, said, 'don't rush – you never know when you'll get this opportunity again,' and that advice is ringing in my ears right now. I know I'll never get this opportunity again.

I shake hands and take photos, and this full circle lap feels as though it's going in slow motion. I'm carrying my kids, and I'm in incredible pain. In the last forty seconds of play, I ran completely afoul of forward 50 structure, sprinting through the stoppage, which is 100 per cent not my role. I got the ball and got absolutely annihilated by ruckman Tristan Xerri, fracturing a rib and straining my AC joint. (When they name the teams the following week I'm out of the side as 'managed' or 'retired', but I'm actually injured, so technically I should get a match payment, or at least that's what I'll tell the club!) I wince while holding the girls and tell Carly I think I've broken a collarbone.

I hug so many people, and wave to so many strangers who call out my name. It sounds stupid, but I think the fans knew what they had to do. More than 59,000 people turned up for a dead rubber, and they stay for all this – it feels like they're part of a pilgrimage. There are sixteen-year-old Richmond supporters thanking me; they weren't even born when I was drafted to the Tigers.

My favourite moment – the one I can't help but tear up over – is in the goal square at the Punt Road end. Poppy was so nervous about today, even about running through the banner. She practised it at home, charging through the curtains between the double doors from the lounge room onto the patio. Now she's got a chance to kick a goal, back toward the cheer squad, who cheer her on, encouraging her to have a roost. She takes the longest run up ever, sinks her little boot into it, and it falls over the line. The crowd is a wave of rapture and applause. The last shot for goal on the MCG from a Riewoldt (for a long time, at least) is a straight one. Poppy will talk about this goal every day for the week that follows.

People come up to me all the time, after I've interacted with their son or daughter – signing an autograph or taking a selfie or simply saying hello – and they're always so grateful, always saying 'You made my kid's year.' I get that. The Tiger Army just made my kid's year.

Downstairs, we sing the song, and the club has supplied Cascade Draughts from Tassie especially for me. Trent talks to the group. I talk to the group. There's so much fanfare that I'm almost embarrassed by it now. We didn't cure cancer.

When it's time to celebrate, we head back to the club, where an afterparty of more than 300 people will spill out of the building, which is lit up, raucous, and filled with love. But we have to get there first.

My first ever footy memory is sitting on the shoulders of my dad as we walked up the hill from the Clarence clubrooms to our house on Bellerive Bluff.

As this long, beautiful day ends, it's now me and Poppy walking back along Brunton Avenue, past the stinky garbage loading bay, under the giant metal sculpture near Gate 6, and up the hill to Punt Road, with a security guard ten metres in front of us.

I've done this walk hundreds of times: by myself, with my teammates, with my coaches, with my club. And now, as dusk falls, I hold hands with my daughter, and we talk about her goal, and running through the banner, and singing the theme song in the rooms, and we enjoy this walk together – the first time for her, and the last time for me.

ACKNOWLEDGEMENTS

To my family – football, although a team game, can be a selfish piece of work, always investing in yourself for the betterment of the club. Thank you to my parents for not only the sacrifices they made from my early days, but for the passion and wonder they instilled in me to chase my dreams, explore my curiosities and to never give up. To my own family, who have made climbing this mountain so much easier and more thrilling, thank you for always being by my side. To Poppy, Hazel and Tommy – thank you for reminding me that life is for living. I look forward to seeing life through the wonder of your eyes. You are, by far, the best things to have happened to me.

To my teammates – much like your family, you really don't get to choose your teammates. The wins and the losses, the ups and downs, the experiences we have had together will last a lifetime. Thank you for the ride and for being the best of mates on this adventure.

To the Tiger Army – I was adopted into a yellow-and-black army that passionately went out to battle with me on the field every week. I may not have met all of you, but I will share a connection to you all for the rest of my life.

Now that the time has come to retire from this game, one of my first loves, I feel neither hesitancy nor sadness, but gratefulness for what it has given me: the connections, the shared experiences, the support of friends and family, and the magic that comes from the human experience. It is with pride, and a great thrill, that I close my AFL-playing chapter for new adventures – to experience more of life's little pieces of magic.

ABOUT THE AUTHOR

Jack Riewoldt is a celebrated AFL player. The Richmond Tigers forward is a triple-premiership player, triple-Coleman Medallist, was selected three times for the All-Australian Team, and twice won Richmond's Best and Fairest, among other awards. In his home state of Tasmania, he's a Football Hall of Famer. A revered leader and loved by Tigers fans, the veteran played 16 seasons with Richmond, kicked 787 goals (ranking him third in club history), and sits second behind Kevin Bartlett for most games played for Richmond: 347. Jack lives with his wife Carly and their three children in Melbourne.